Untethered Success

Handbook for Entrepreneurs and the Self-Employed

C.S. Thomas, CPA

D1637396

ISBN: 0-578-43574-8
ISBN-13: 978-0-578-43574-9

CONTENTS

ACKNOWLEDGMENTS

A special thanks to my present, past, and future clients. Your questions and reliance upon my advice has pushed me to be a better accountant and keeps my career challenging and rewarding. I very much appreciate the opportunity to be of service.

Christopher S. Thomas, CPA

INTRODUCTION

I f you are hoping to find yet another book with flowery, nostalgic, or idealistic recipes for achieving the American Dream, you can stop reading now. Entrepreneurialism isn't a get-rich-quick scheme. Many end up making less money and working more hours than if they simply had a regular job that paid wages, which isn't always an option. Some become entrepreneurs before they even realize it. I've worked with successful and not so successful entrepreneurs. Sometimes the difference comes from understanding. Some have a solid starting point for knowledge and skills, and for others it's like trying to figure out quantum physics. They don't teach much entrepreneurism in school. The amount of noise we are inundated with in just trying to get to the right answer is astounding. Sure, you can hire a lawyer or accountant to figure things out for you, and even with a solid level of understanding, having professionals take care of certain aspects may make sense since your time is valuable. But you should have the choice and the ability to make informed decisions with a base of knowledge as it pertains to entrepreneurialism. That is what this book is all about.

Small business ownership and self-employed individuals make up a considerable portion of the economy. Self-employment represents over 10% of the American workforce, and the gig economy is expected to top 40% by 2020, so entrepreneurial economic participation is here to stay. Regardless if by choice or necessity, one can increase the odds of being in the winning category and not just another statistic of fear that keeps droves from even thinking of trying. It's about time solid resources are made available for those who are self-employed or who are considering self-employment or engaging in a small business venture.

This book isn't for accountants; it's for the layperson, the independent contractor, the self-employed virtual assistant (business analyst, carpenter, etc.), the small business owner, the entrepreneur. As such, there won't be any talk of complex international shell corporations, captive insurance companies, or other aspects that are typically only applicable in unique situations for the super wealthy.

Don't "Just Do It"

There are so many people that surround us who are incapable of telling us no (in Minnesota, we call it being Minnesota Nice). So, when you ask them if starting a business or going into self-employment is a good idea, many answer with, "Of course, yes, you should do it." But that may not be good advice for everyone. If you have a decent job with benefits, it can be a rude awakening to discover how much it costs to replace what you have from your employer, and as the saying goes, "A bird in the hand is worth two in the bush." The point is that a decent job can be far superior than several unsuccessful ventures.

You probably have a reasonable approximation of your monthly household budget. When considering going into a self-employed situation, don't forget to consider costs that you may not see your employer paying for. This includes costs like the employer portion of health insurance, retirement contributions, life and disability insurance, employment taxes, and business operating expenses, to name a few.

Employees are expensive, and many companies would prefer the flexibility and variability of having contractors rather than employees. It may sound great. You get to be your own boss, make your own hours, and the earning potential appears to be more than what you were making as an employee. So it's a win-win, right? Not necessarily. Say, for example, that you have a wage of $60,000 per year in addition to benefits like health insurance (especially if you have family coverage), retirement contributions, and other fringe benefits. To equal this total compensation package, a contractor would likely need to generate (after expenses) over $80,000. Sometimes it isn't a choice, as in, the offer is as a contract worker or nothing at all, which certainly makes the decision a lot easier. But nonetheless, understanding the economic reality will greatly help in understanding your value.

There are critical components and decisions that everyone who will be a small business owner or self-employed individual should be aware of. In my experience, far too many people start asking the right questions and seeking the appropriate advice until after the pain of not making the right decision sets in. This means, as an accountant, I'd usually start seeing new business owners around tax time when someone says, "Oh man, that's right, I started a small business last year and I don't know what that means for taxes and what I should be doing." And this is when I'd get questions on how they can save on taxes. First tip: The best time to save on taxes is before you have to file a tax return and certainly before you spend a bunch of money on an SUV because you heard that you can write it off.

Cash is King

Where did all the money go? Sometimes I wonder that myself. Many self-employed individuals are new to the painful experience of how our complex tax system works. Unfortunately, making money in self-employment is very taxing (pun intended). Though we've all heard about the wonderful benefits and special considerations that are only available to the self-employed, at the end of the day (year), taxes will need to get paid. Though we can get some benefit for a home office or vehicle mileage, we will still need to eat, pay the mortgage, and have money for all sorts of things. It is impossible to encapsulate one's personal life entirely into deductible expenses for business, though I have seen people try really hard to do so. As such, there will be taxable income, which is the money we rely on for our personal lives. Taxes for the self-employed can be much more than what we are used to as employees and certainly taxed more than investment income, which can be very frustrating and seem punitive. With self-employment taxes along with federal and state income taxes, one's tax rate on their self-employment earnings typically starts out at around 30% and is quite a bit more depending on one's circumstances. There isn't anyone withholding the taxes for us, so it is up to our own self-control to not spend the money so that when it is time to pay the piper, it's there and not spent on that Caribbean cruise.

Taxes get the most attention, and rightfully so as they make up a significant obligation for the self-employed. But unless one is basically an employee who just so happens to be receiving a 1099 MISC instead of a W-2, there will also typically be expenses, such as office expenses, rent, utilities, subcontractors of your own, and so on that require cash. Managing cash flow can be difficult enough to do on the personal side. When you are a small business, it is doubly challenging as you need to eat, and your business needs to eat, so keeping enough money available to feed the beast can be difficult. The added difficulty comes in with the fact that the "beast" typically needs to get fed before the business receives cash for the products or services you are providing, which can result in running out of cash, especially since so many start up a business without an understanding or appreciation for time and capital.

Knowledge is Dangerous, Understanding is Power

The main focus of this book is to provide an understanding of the various aspects of entrepreneurialism, from the bare essentials of self-employment to the point when one closes up shop. Memorization of various facts and figures at a point in time may temporarily provide knowledge but that is dangerous. We can come to rely upon knowledge that can be dated, inconsistent or incorrectly applied to different conditions. Far better to develop an understanding based on principles and universal concepts that can be applied to just about any situation. No, I don't expect you to finish the book and decide to go be an accountant like me. But ideally, you'll be more informed and aware of the variables that entrepreneurs and self-employed individuals encounter, allowing you to make more informed decisions. I can't promise to make you rich; aside from winning the lottery or some other windfall, wealth accumulation occurs over many years and is the result of making many intelligent decisions. That's what it's all about; providing the framework of intelligent decision making as it pertains to entrepreneurialism.

Every business is different and unique just like every person is different from one another. Two people who do the same job at the same company are not identical, and their household budgets wouldn't be the same either. Similarly, two businesses in the same industry and geography will have very different circumstances. Yet, even though businesses and circumstances are unique, a set of universal principles based on economic reality forms the foundation for intelligent business decision making. Different tools and resources are abundant and sometimes create a confusing and contrasting amount of noise. Cutting through the noise and determining the baseline impact of decisions is a critical skill in being successful; otherwise, we might as well be guessing. Guessing is just as good as gambling—sometimes you get lucky, sometimes you are able to make educated guesses and improve your odds, but wouldn't it be better to take the guessing part out and execute on certainties? That is what knowledge provides. And yes, as cliché as it is, it is powerful.

ESSENTIALS

For those new to self-employment, there are many important considerations that should be taken into account. Unfortunately, from my experience, many newly self-employed don't adequately protect themselves or do much in terms of preparedness prior to entering into a self-employment situation. There is no employer to provide you with fringe benefits and insurance coverages—it is all on you. No, you don't need to have every possible option under the sun, but at a minimum you should have the bare essentials to mitigate risk and understand the basic aspects that come with being your own boss.

Health Insurance

No one likes the idea of being injured. But what is worse than being injured is being injured with huge medical bills, which is why you would ideally have health insurance. If you are lucky and have a spouse with decent coverage from their job, then you can avoid the painful process of buying health insurance. If you haven't begun your self-employment and will need to buy health insurance for the first time, I strongly urge you to look up the price of coverage needed because it is no joke. The cost for coverage can be expensive and may impact one's decision to enter into self-employment in the first place. For those who have to get their own coverage, the marketplace is where you'd turn (health insurance marketplaces or exchanges for obtaining coverage).

Many states have their own health insurance marketplace, and for the states that don't, the federal government has one set up for them www.healthcare.gov. The reason you'd go through the exchanges instead of going directly to a carrier like Blue Cross is that the carriers don't always tell you that by not going through the exchange, it limits some of your potential benefits. You may not make that much money your first couple years in self-employment, and so even if you normally wouldn't qualify for certain benefits, you may for a couple years.

The biggest benefit as it pertains to health insurance is the premium tax credit. The premium tax credit can be worth thousands of dollars a year. The income limit to qualify for the credit is up to 400% of the federal poverty guidelines. This means that a household of four could potentially qualify for the credit with a household income slightly higher than $100,000. The exchanges would typically provide you with access to "Navigators" that help you select the right policy for you and apply for certain benefits like the Advanced Premium Tax Credit, which is as it sounds, an advance of the premium tax credit used to reduce out of pocket costs for insurance premiums. The government, in a sense, lends you money by paying a portion of your premiums for you because there is the expectation that you are getting a tax credit. Be warned though, many have fallen into a trap where a temporary setback in income qualified them for the advanced premium tax credit only to have to pay it all back when they did the tax return, which calculates the amount of credit and reconciles with how much of the advanced credit you have received already. Err on the conservative side so you don't have to pay too much of the advanced premium tax credit back.

Life and Long-Term Disability

Medical bills are not the only potential disaster to guard against. Loss of income can wipe out whatever savings you've managed to build up in no time if disability strikes, and it can happen to anyone. Long-term disability is insurance the provides for an annuity payment in the event of disability, incapacity, or inability to work after a certain period of time replacing a portion of the income one is no longer able to earn. The policies for long-term disability can vary; some start to pay out after three months of disability, some at six months, some have a cap or end to their payouts, and some are perpetual, so evaluate carefully. You could also get short-term disability, but those policies can be expensive. If you are able to keep a few months of cash in reserve for emergencies, long-term disability should be sufficient. If you are part of an industry or profession, they may have partnerships with carriers that offer policies that are more reasonably priced and provide better coverage than going it alone, so check with your state or national society or association for options.

Life insurance isn't for you per se but for your loved ones by providing a payout if you happen to no longer be alive. You should have life insurance, even if you are unmarried. While the coverage amount can vary, at the very least, make sure you are not leaving behind liabilities for others to tend to. If you are the breadwinner of your household, you'd need more than if you are single with no dependents. There are options for Group Variable Term Life or other wordy titles. Generally, some of the wordier titles refer to policies that have both the death benefit and allow the accumulation of a certificate value which can be an additional way to save money on autopilot. The contributions are not tax deductible, but drawing the principal portion back out isn't a taxable event either. The money can grow tax deferred, you'd pay tax on the gains in the certificate fund beyond your contributions, and you can borrow against the certificate value as well in most cases.

In certain aspects, like for leases on commercial space and borrowing or securing long term financing, the landlord or lender may require you to have life insurance and assign a certain portion of the potential proceeds to them as a mitigation of risk.

> The last thing you'd want your spouse or kids to have to deal with if you die is selling your business. If there are lease obligations, long-term debt, or other liabilities, it's a real kick in the teeth when lenders and landlords claw out portions of a death benefit to get their cut. Plus, if unprepared, it can be like a fire

sale—each day there could be client losses, and without a structured transition plan, the estate would only get pennies on the dollar for the value of the business you were building.

Whether building a practice (professional service firm, medical/dental provider, etc.), a traditional small business, or other operation in which there is a going concern value (as in, you could sell your book of business or client list, etc.), an additional insurance to consider would be practice continuation agreements or contingent buy/sell agreements. These establish that in the event of death or incapacitation, the business would be sold for x-multiple of x-factor (usually sales or billable revenue over the previous 12-month period) to a particular person or business. The agreements and procedures you enter into help ensure a better transition and higher value for the business (and for your family) in that case.

General Liability and Commercial Umbrella Coverage

These policies provide a safety net of coverage for the "just in case" situations. The premiums can vary based on risk, but are typically not very expensive to get. In certain cases, like with leases and unsecured debt, such policies may be required. As they are not very expensive, having coverage is a good idea. You may go your entire career without ever filing a claim, but there is that chance that someone slips on some ice outside your office or gets electrocuted from your coffee maker, so having the coverage is what will protect the business and the wealth you are trying to accumulate over your lifetime.

Credit

Do you need to have good credit? No, of course not, anyone can start a business or enter into self-employment regardless of credit. However, life is much easier with decent credit. After you set up your entity and want to open a bank account, the bank is more accommodating when you have decent credit. Furthermore, certain advantages become available. A big benefit is the lower cost to accessing capital. If you need a loan, line of credit, or even a credit card, the terms are better.

A business credit card is a great tool. It can help with cash flow, build credit, and in the case of a rewards card, provide you with points that you can use later on for various purposes. Though there is some grey area with rewards points on business cards, redeeming personal card points isn't considered taxable income and is more like a discount on personal spending. With a business credit card, the transactions that were used to generate the points were generally tax deductions. My opinion would be that redeeming those points would be income, but it's one of those areas with little enforcement from the government and limited reporting from credit card companies.

> If your credit is poor, regardless of your status as an entrepreneur or self-employed individual, it is wise to take steps to improve your credit. When I'm meeting with a client who has poor credit, many times they don't really know what their score is or what is on their report. This is the first step in the process of reclaiming your financial reputation. Get your credit report and score, and then address the items that are negatively impacting your credit like loans in default, etc.

Unemployment

Wait, what? I thought we were talking about self-employment. We are, and a potential consideration for those going from employed to self-employed is the unemployment compensation that may be available. The laws and regulations can vary with respect to eligibility, especially as it pertains to self-employment, but if you are able to "legally" collect while starting out, it can provide a crucial subsidy to help propel you into self-sufficiency in your self-employment. I am not advocating for anyone to cheat, lie, commit fraud, or try to get fired just to collect it. All I am saying is that if you are eligible for unemployment, it would be wise to look into and see what it takes to maintain your eligibility to collect it.

Budgeting and Cash Flow

Cash, and the ability to access it, is essential. The business cycle, taxes, compliance, and other obligations are not always so clear cut or on a consistent monthly cycle like many of us have with respect to our personal finances. As an employee, most can expect to receive a paycheck on a regular basis. However, when you are self-employed, you may have to invoice and wait a couple weeks (or months) to get paid. Then there is the risk of bad debts, or slow payers. A bad debt is when you complete the service as agreed and invoice your customer, but they decide to not pay you. It can be very frustrating to say the least. A small business owner doesn't have all the time in the world to go to small claims court or hire an attorney to collect an outstanding invoice of $325.

Most small businesses don't start out making a ton of money, or even making money at all. This is why having cash saved up and reasonable credit in order to have access to cash is critical. Just because it may take a year or so to build up a business or practice that can sustain your lifestyle will not mean you get to put your mortgage on hold. If you have a business plan or other analysis that can give you a reasonable approximation of revenue and growth, you can calculate what your cash flow deficit might be, and then you are better able to manage through it to the breakeven point without sacrificing your vision.

Far too many small business owners struggle with separating business and personal finances. If you want to accumulate wealth and save on taxes, the best thing to do is treat your business or consultancy as a business and separate the two. Put yourself on a scheduled salary or draw that doesn't sap the business's ability to make moves later on. Many unsuccessful business owners are out there buying everything with their business account: going to the movies, buying a single cup of coffee every day, paying for their kid's music lessons, etc. What typically happens is when it is time to pay taxes, make additional contributions to retirement accounts, put a down payment on a better space for the business, refinance equipment, etc., the cash isn't there anymore. Then I get the question of "where did the cash go?" If you view the business accounts as an extension of your personal finances, it is all too easy for your personal lifestyle to "creep" and consume what would otherwise be wealth accumulation. Do not use your business as just an ATM.

> Protect yourself from yourself. I treat my business bank and credit accounts as if they are my parent's accounts. No, I didn't inherit my practice, I built it from scratch just like most entrepreneurs do. I pretend because it adds a level of control to the cash. If I had to ask my dad to buy a sandwich for myself or purchase a higher-end vehicle, he might say, "Is there a client or prospect you are meeting with for lunch?" or "How does the fancy car you want add value to the business?" and so on. Even though these conversations are not happening for real, going through the exercise in your head provides a bit more conscience effort into spending. Getting that sandwich is like taking $50 out of your kid's college fund. Is it worth that? Many things aren't clearly aligned to a cost/benefit analysis, and if you had to justify everything, then nothing would happen. We can't be second-guessing getting decent business cards, or having a website with good search traffic, etc. I am mainly referring to that grey area of personal/business expenditures in which it may potentially be a tax deduction, but does that alone make it an investment for the business or even your household's long-term wealth accumulation goals?

I am a big advocate of living within your means. I have seen many times when a small business owner's income increased, so too did their lifestyle, and when that occurs the entrepreneur is not accumulating wealth. Income and business expenses for the self-employed can fluctuate considerably, but if one is diligent about staying on track with a personal budget it becomes much easier to accumulate wealth in good times and weather the storm in bad times. Warren Buffett was asked what is the secret to accumulating wealth, and his response was perfect. He said, "It's simple, spend less than you make."

Creating a personal budget doesn't have to be super complex. It can be with a spreadsheet, on a legal pad, using a program from an online platform like youneedabudget.com, mint.com, personalcapital.com, or others, many of which are free (ad supported). You sync your accounts and the program can provide you with an analysis to see where and how much you are spending. Alternatively, you can look at a few months of bank and credit account statements. This is a good exercise in this digital age as it is far too easy to have recurring and automated charges that go unchecked, and we can spend money on things that are no longer providing value to us. It would be a good time to cancel or adjust services to better align the cost and value to you.

But Chris, what does my personal budget have to do with the business or self-employment I am getting into? Everything. You need to know how much income you need in order to determine if the business is viable for you or if you need to adjust your personal finances in order to make it work. Winging it is not advisable, and starting out by tightening the business belt or pinching pennies can hamstring growth opportunities. It's better to be prepared so that you don't have to make cuts when it comes to marketing, branding, office supplies, software, or other business expenses that can add a lot of value towards your goals.

After you have an idea of what kind of take home pay you need from your business each month, you can then work backwards to determine the top line numbers. Rather than getting too complex and using pivot tables or other algorithms, I prefer to use calculations that can be done on the back of an envelope (which I've literally done before). Let's suppose you need to bring home about $5,000 a month in your new business, and we'll assume a 30% overall tax rate, for simplicity, to get to a pre-tax earnings figure:

$5,000 / (1 - .30)
$5,000 / .70 = $7,143

We'd also want to add to that items that are new expenditures. Using a 30% tax rate instead of a more conservative 35% allows us to add the cost of health insurance or other items that may have some additional benefit without needing to change the tax rate or be too optimistic and under account for taxes. Family health insurance might be around $1,000 per month. Long term disability should be $50 or so, similarly life insurance is typically $50 or less depending on coverage. Adding it all up:

$7,143 + $1,000 + $50 + $50 = $8,243

So even without making retirement contributions, the business needs to net $8,243 each month to provide you with the $5,000 per month in take home pay free of liabilities. Keep in mind that is the net income for the business. Now you'll need to get an idea of what your business needs are (rent, marketing, insurance, etc.), which can vary considerably. A similar approach of working backwards from the bottom up will give you what you need to generate in income. Simply add your business costs to your net income number to get your gross income needs.

Continuing with the previous scenario, suppose your venture will have rent of $600 per month, marketing budget of $400 per month, office supplies and software of $300 per month, and various other items totaling another $300 per month. Additionally, maybe you'd like to do $500 per month in retirement contributions so you don't fall too far behind:

$8,243 + $600 + $400 + $300 + $300 + $500 = $10,343

After taking into consideration the business and personal budgetary needs, the business would need to bring in about $10,343 per month in order for you to take home $5,000 without accumulating liabilities along the way. You can also divide that number by what your average bill rate or product price is to be to see how many billable hours or units sold per month you'd need. Even for those in sales that earn on commission like real estate agents, if you have an idea of the average transaction value, you could easily determine the number of closings to get to your target. A similar process could also apply for determining how many prospects you'd need if you have an idea of what your conversion rate is. That is where marketing and lead generation activity comes in. It's just envelope math, not too scary.

Capacity

Consider your capacity. Time tends to be the resource in greatest scarcity. If you determine that the business needs to have gross revenue of at least $125,000 and you are a solo consultancy that bills on an hourly basis, what will be your bill rate? That was a trick question. Your bill rate should be determined by market forces, of course. Just because you need x per hour, doesn't mean the market will pay that much. So, say the going rate is $65 per hour, would that be enough to generate $125,000 per year? The answer would depend. If you are engaged by a single contract that gives you 40 hours a week and you take three or less weeks' worth of vacation/sick/holiday time off, then yes. If you are serving multiple clients and will have to solicit, engage, bill, collect and do all the other stuff that goes with being in business, then probably not. The reason is your practical capacity for billable time is not going to be 2,080 hours per year (40 hours per week times 52 weeks in a year equals 2,080 hours), it might be closer to 1,400 hours a year, and if you are doing that, you'll likely be working 60 hours a week to make that work. So, if $65 is the going rate and 1,400 is your practical capacity, it would provide you with the potential for $91,000 of revenue. In that case, if your needs are $125,000, the answer would be no—$65 per hour is not enough—and you'd need to make adjustments (to your lifestyle, business proposition, etc.).

Moonlighting

Moonlight… as in, work some self-employment gigs on the side. Maybe do a little Uber, be a part-time real estate agent, or do just a few specific projects here or there. There's nothing wrong with having some side action (economic action, that is). I've seen many struggle with trying to turn a side (hobby) business into a self-sufficient business. The reason is that we only have so much time in a day/week/year, and if you are working 2,080 hours per year for an employer, that doesn't leave a lot of time on the side to build a business that can replace your wages. For many, it is just too risky to take a leap and hope there will be that branch to grab onto, but by not taking the leap, it is very difficult to build the business up to that point. What further stresses these kinds of situations is that the side business often isn't generating the kind of revenue and cash flow to justify certain business expenditures like software, an accountant or having an entity structure that can add value beyond the increased compliance costs. My advice would be to treat a side business as a side business. When you are ready to take the leap, then do the math and take a chance on yourself.

Practice Makes Perfect

Understanding costs is essential for sustainable and self-sufficient self-employment. One doesn't have to be a math whiz to add and subtract big ticket assumptions that come with being your own boss. If the math doesn't add up on paper, it can be really difficult to make reality do so. Besides paper and pen or spreadsheets, there are also some good tools for business planning. I am a fan of liveplan.com which may be a bit more than a self-employed person needs, but it can help quickly extrapolate and incorporate multiple scenarios into projections to give you a good idea of revenue, cash flow, and profitability.

ENTITY

An entity is a construct by which business (or potentially a nonprofit operation) is conducted. An entity is set up and creates a unique identity and legal separation from its owners. This means the entity (like an LLC or corporation) would have its own bank account, engage in business, have title to assets, be the primary debtor on loans and notes, etc. and the entrepreneur would own the entity and conduct business on behalf of the entity as an employee, principle, partner, proprietor, etc.

Sometimes the lines can get fuzzy—where does the individual end and the business begin and vice versa? Big businesses have had many years and enormous amounts of resources at their disposal to ensure that the enterprise controls its own assets and requires employees to meet certain requirements in their duties. These duties include tasks like filing expense reports for expenditures that were not paid directly by the business. A small business may only have the owner who isn't likely to be filling out expense reports every time they use their Discover Card for business. Having an entity doesn't mean it has to be complex or create headaches in order to provide the protection and potential benefits. Though the lines can be fuzzy, economic reality would continue to be the primary foundation for clarity. Just because the owner used their personal card does not mean it is a lost transaction, though it would be a lot easier to keep track without the commingling.

Selection of an entity seems like a really big deal, and in some cases it is. Your circumstances will determine what the best choice is. Not everyone needs an entity. If you are moonlighting, or just doing some side work for Uber or as a real estate agent and have no plans to be involved in complex business structures, then adding an entity may not make sense.

Having an entity makes it so much easier to separate your business from your personal life. You can then have bank and credit card accounts in the entity's name. It provides some liability protection and allows for the potential to raise capital or take on partners if needed. Additionally, if you want to be an S corporation or anything other than a sole proprietorship for tax purposes, then you'd need to have an entity set up.

Not all states are the same when it comes to forming an entity. The fees for original filing (creating the entity) vary and the annual renewal of the entity too can come with a more than annoying fee. Some states don't charge anything to renew the entity, which makes the decision much easier since you don't really need to pay much beyond the original filing fee in order to set it up.

Generally, you'd want to set up your entity in the state that you will be operating in. Just because you read somewhere or heard it on the ninth hole at the golf course that getting a Delaware or Nevada LLC exempts you from state taxes doesn't mean it's true. That just means you may have to also file in the state you are operating in, still pay taxes, and pay for additional filing fees and compliance costs. Nexus, which for tax purposes is generally referring to a state's right to tax certain economic activity, determines which state taxes what, not where your entity is set up.

It can be complex when one considers all the online commerce and Amazon businesses out there. Certain goods and services may be sold in states other than your home state without incurring the requirement to file an income tax return or file with the secretary of state for that state; though you may still be on the hook for sales tax, even if you can be exempt from that state's income tax requirements.

Many jurisdictions allow for reporting and remitting sales tax without needing to set up an entity in that state, but you'd want to verify what your taxing obligations are in various jurisdictions and leverage software to automate as much as possible.

> Generally, if you need to set up an entity that isn't a plain vanilla, single-owner entity, you should probably consult with an attorney to better understand the differences and make sure all the documentation (articles, bylaws, operating agreement, etc.) are in order. Especially when there is going to be more than one owner as some states have a pro rata–per capita voting, control, and distribution as their "cookie cutter" framework (as in one person one vote regardless of actual ownership interest, same with how profit distributions would be handled when using the boilerplate template). I've seen it where the 60% owner ended up getting fired and sidelined from his own company by the minority partners because it was two against one, even though he owned well over 50% of the company.

Sometimes when I ask a prospect, "Have you elected S corporation status?" they reply with, "Oh, no we are an LLC." This tells me they probably don't understand the difference between a legal entity and how that entity is taxed. The LLC, which is a separate legal entity, is most often a disregarded entity for tax purposes, meaning that activity flows through it, but the taxes are determined at the owner's level (which could be another entity like a corporation). Just because something is the default doesn't mean that is what it has to be. When you set up an entity, you are creating a legal entity, and the default tax status for that entity can vary. The default tax status is how the government will expect you to calculate, report, and remit your taxes unless you make an election to be treated differently. When you establish an employer identification number (EIN) with the IRS, they generally let you know what your default is. Here is a short list of the default tax status:

Entity	Default Tax Return
LLC with only one Owner	1040 (Sched. C, E, F)
LLC with two or more owners	1065 Partnership Return
LP, LLP, LLLP, GP, etc. (partnerships)	1065 Partnership Return
Corporation	1120 Corporate Return

The LLC (Limited Liability Company) is a very popular form of entity to set up for many reasons. One of the big advantages is its flexibility. For tax purposes, the LLC can be a sole proprietorship, a partnership, a corporation, or an S corporation, so it can be just about anything for taxes. It provides liability protection while still allowing its member managers to participate in the business. Whereas a general partnership or limited partnership (GP/LP/LLP) would have general partners with unlimited liability exposure and limited partners with limited liability who would also be limited in their participation. There is a Limited Liability Limited Partnership (LLLP) with similar protections and functions as a LLC, but again, if you are setting up such entities, you should consult with an attorney.

Corporate Veil and Limited Liability

Limited liability can be an important characteristic, but what does that mean? Just because one has an LLC doesn't mean that's all it takes to be protected. Especially if there is negligence or maleficence, an entity may not offer much insulation. Certainly, limited partners and non-officer shareholders are entitled to the limitation of liability, being limited to the value they have in the shares of the corporation or equity in a partnership, which could potentially be lost, but not to exceed that. What determines they truly are not officers or managers? Passive investors with limited liability would typically NOT:

- Manage the business or be involved with the day-to-day decision-making process;
- Have signature authority over the bank accounts;
- Engage in the solicitation and binding of contracts on behalf of entity; or
- Authorize the disbursement of funds, sign tax returns, or execute other authoritative functions.

Most self-employed and small business owners can't really say they don't manage their own entities. That doesn't mean they are exempt from limited liability protection, but one has to maintain and protect the corporate veil in order to ensure the liability protection cannot extend beyond the entity. As an example, if the entity has large vendor accounts that it is unable to pay and shuts down due to its inability to continue as a going concern, the vendors could seek to have the officers/owners of the entity personally liable and could succeed if it is determined that the business has not maintained the entity in satisfactory ways. Those satisfactory ways include:

- Maintaining a separation of your business and personal life; don't commingle funds—use the business account for business purposes, and personal accounts for personal purposes;
- Performing and documenting corporate meetings with minutes, records, resolutions, voting, officer appointment, etc.; and
- Using your company name in the business operations; invoices, statements, letterhead, etc. If you are going to have a "doing business as" (D/B/A), then register that name as an assumed name or other legal status of the entity, otherwise include the "LLC or Inc." as appropriate.

Even though not all entity types (like the LLC) have the same requirements for annual meetings and corporate governance procedures like the corporation, it would be wise to incorporate into the operation. It could coincide with the review of the entity's annual tax return and annual renewal of the entity for simplicity. Don't have shareholders, partners, or other members of your entity? I guess that means you'll be winning the election to the board of directors. But in all seriousness, even though it's just you, documenting your review and continuance of the entity's structure and governance helps to establish and maintain your bona fide existence as an entity that is separate and legal, and should ideally provide the liability protection intended.

Single Member LLC

When you want an entity as a sole owner of a business and don't plans for being corporation or other complex structure, an LLC is the way to go. It provides the liability protection, allows you to establish banking and credit accounts in the business's name, helps you separate the business from your personal life, and still allows you to elect to be taxed as an eligible entity later on, especially through the "check the box" regulations where a simple form or election on a tax return changes your status as a taxable entity without having to change your legal entity.

The single member LLC, being so simple and easy to set up and operate, can allow one to easily slip with respect to the protection of the corporate veil and governance since there isn't a board of directors, annual meeting requirements, or other headaches. One would still want to be proactive and keep things separate and maintain its legitimacy as an entity that is separate and distinct from its owner.

C Corporations

The C corporation (or other eligible entity that elects to be taxed as a C corporation) is taxed on the net income of the corporation. When you get dividends from the corporation, it would be reported on a 1099DIV form and gets taxed a second time on your personal tax return, hence the double taxation concept. Other than dividends, to get money from the corporation, it would generally be in the form of wages or management fees and be reported on a W-2 or 1099MISC form. Though wages and management fees would be a deduction for the corporation, it would be taxable on your personal taxes and likely be subjected to employment taxes as well. As such, it is generally not the first choice of entity structure for most small businesses.

Sometimes you may need to set up a C corporation, like if you wanted to use your retirement funds to capitalize the business. Basically, you'd be setting up two entities—the C corporation that is the operating business, and a 401k plan that allows the discretion to make the investment into the C Corporation, but don't try this at home, if you plan to employ such a structure you'd want to utilize a company that can do it for you as errors can be very costly.

C corporations can have all sorts of flexibility with respect to different classes of shares or shareholders and allow for certain fringe benefits (like certain insurances or cafeteria plan options), but do the math first and make sure it makes economic sense. Generally, I advocate for economic reality. Make decisions that are in the best interest of your business and household, regardless of taxes as a default; don't make decisions or enter into transactions that could potentially save a couple dollars on taxes if and when the planets align to smile upon you. Make money first, then we'll talk about how to keep it. Taxes aren't keeping most people from accumulating wealth—people are keeping themselves from accumulating wealth. That being said, if you have specific requirements that justify the C corporation structure, then set one up. But as a general rule, a pass-through entity would be the more logical choice.

Partnerships

Partnerships and LLCs taxed as partnerships are a good option. They offer the pass-through avoidance of double taxation, the legal limited liability protection, and are considerably flexible. Their flexibility is what makes partnership tax matters the most complex. A partnership can have special allocations of income and expense items, disproportionate capital accounts and profit participation, guaranteed payments, variances between inside and outside basis (don't even ask, just know it's a mess), and more.

> You may have heard the old adage, "How do you turn your best friend into your worst enemy? Go into business together." It is so true. No matter how good intentioned people are, the handshake and can-do attitude only gets you so far. Sometimes it may seem like an ideal arrangement—Partner A is looking for a place to park some capital, and Partner B is trying to deploy a concept but needs capital, so let's form AB Ltd., a match made in heaven. For a short while… until B doesn't like sharing profits with A when B did all the work and A doesn't like that B

spends money in wasteful ways and isn't as good at selling as he promised and so on. Even when there is a seemingly logical division of labor and an equal profit and capital participation, what may seem logical on day one isn't necessarily that logical on day 286 when B is out playing golf because he closed on enough new clients for the month while Partner A is bogged down in the office onboarding and scheduling workflow for the new commitments that B made on behalf of AB Ltd. All I am saying is get it in writing first and foremost, spell out who does what, who determines what, what kind of expectations and contingencies should be incorporated into a vision, etc.

We can profess a level of egalitarianism all day long, but when it comes to business, it is a war, and armies at war need commanders not committees. Like in the movie *Highlander*, there can only be one. So I'd advocate for deciding who that one is and what the limitation to that is, and then make sure that everyone is okay with that before writing checks. Not that collective, collaborative, and coordinated effort shouldn't be done in concerted manners, which is the main reason you form a partnership—to aggregate resources (financial, human capital, property, etc.) to make greater economic success than going it alone. Just that like any business or operation, things can get bogged down in groupthink or passive-aggressivity if it's unclear, and you end up needing permission to buy paper clips.

Partnerships can be partners in other partnerships (as in a tiered structure), own C corporation shares, engage in operating businesses, and engage in passive activity. Besides the considerable flexibility that the partnership offers, there is the added benefit of basis. Basis for tax purposes determines how much of a business's losses are allowable as deductions in the current year. How basis (and the allowability of losses) is determined differs between entity types. For a partnership, in general, basis would include not only the capital account (partner contributions, less draws taken, plus or minus the cumulative net income/loss of the entity) but also the proportionate share of the partnership's loans and liabilities for the most part. This can be a big factor if a business operation is leveraged (as in, has a reasonable amount of debt that it relies upon) and would, at least on paper or for tax purposes, show a loss that the owners would like to use to reduce their personal income tax. Certain businesses may generate positive cash flow but report negative net income, which can come from non-cash deductions like depreciation, so a business can potentially provide both cash to the owners and not increase taxes; though there will come a time to restore the capital accounts when the partnership is to dissolve.

S Corporation

The S corporation is not a legal entity but a tax election to take a corporation, LLC, or other eligible entity and have it taxed as an S corporation. We'll cover taxes later on, but the basics of an S corporation include the following:

- Pass-through entity, avoids the double taxation
- Limited to 100 shareholders (married couples count as one shareholder)
- US citizens or resident aliens cannot be owned by foreign nonresidents
- Shareholders cannot be corporations or partnerships, must be individuals (and certain trusts occasionally)
- Must pay reasonable compensation to officer owner
- Profits (after deducting officer pay) avoid employment taxes, though are still subject to income taxes

The last point is the biggest reason to set up an S corporation. Self-employment taxes can be very punishing so the ability to structure your income to limit your exposure to those taxes has been a strategy used for decades.

With the new tax reform, which allows for the Qualified Business Income Deduction providing a reduction of taxable income attributed from pass-through businesses, the 20% deduction would not include the S corporation owner's wages. As such, a sole proprietor would have a larger QBID than an S corporation with the exact same income/loss; the sole proprietor would have higher (self) employment taxes. Even so, there is still the potential for tax savings with the S corporation election, but it may also depend on other factors (like your marginal income tax rate).

Debt and other liabilities can create basis issues. Basis in an S corporation is calculated differently than a partnership. When the entity gets a loan or has other liabilities, the shareholders do not get additional basis; as such, there can easily be situations in which an S corporation ends the year with negative equity (total value of liabilities is greater than the total value of assets, especially after accounting for depreciation). When this occurs, it would result in shareholders having to suspend the losses (not being able to deduct on personal return) and/or could potentially create additional taxable income if there were distributions in excess of basis. I have seen many S corporations that create loans to shareholders (as in, reclassifying distributions as a loan) in order to create additional assets and restore basis to avoid the taxable income and allow recognition of losses. Having loans to shareholders is not against the law, but one would want to make sure it is above board by drafting a note with a specified rate of interest and other applicable terms, which can help protect the transactions in the event of an audit. This method is not a guarantee fail-safe, but it's certainly better to try than just having to pay whatever bill the auditor wants to give you if they decide the transactions lack economic reality.

If you want to elect S corporation status, you can use Form 2553, available at the IRS's website. Just complete the form (mainly just page one and two), fax it over to them (fax number is in the instructions for the form), and you are an S corp. The rule is two and a half months after setting up the entity to make the election. There is relief for late filing of the election, especially if you haven't filed any tax return yet, but life is much easier to make the decision and file the appropriate elections within the specified timeframe and avoid having to file it late under special revenue procedures. If you have been an LLC filing taxes as a sole proprietorship for one or more years and want to make the switch to an S corporation, the timeline is two and a half months after the close of the fiscal year (generally March 15th for calendar year end fiscal closing) to apply for that year.

B Corporation

The B corporation is a newer addition to the construct of entities. It is a for-profit corporation, which can be a C corporation or an S corporation. The main function is the addition of a public benefit (i.e., 10% of proceeds will go towards climate change efforts), which become engrained within the corporation's charter or legal organizational mission. That way, officer's that divert profits towards such a mission on behalf of the stakeholders who may not be in concert with the wishes of some of the shareholders would have legal protection against injunctions or other recourse shareholders would typically have in a corporation absent the "B."

Does it matter? For many small businesses, having the "B" corporation status is little more than a marketing tool. And this could just as easily be accomplished by simply stating in your branding that you contribute to charity or some other message without having the requirements of being a B corporation. As most small businesses are closely held with one or possibly two people that control the business, the discretion to be a good corporate citizen doesn't require having a B corp status. If the entity is sold, future owners may revert it back to a non-B corp, so there wouldn't be that much permanency to a B Corp without current and future owners that support it. Occasionally, there may be specific customers that insist on doing business with a certified B corporation, and in such cases, the evaluation of becoming a B corporation would change, but for the most part, it isn't necessary.

D.I.Y.

Besides going through an attorney to set up an entity, you can set one up yourself if you are so inclined. Generally, each state's secretary of state office would handle entity filings and renewals. Some states have a sort of one-stop shop for convenience where you could register for sales permits or tax types alongside the entity filing. Other states keep these processes separate. Generally, if you have a social security number and are a resident of the state in which you are registering the entity, there shouldn't be too many roadblocks, but sometimes it can be a bit confusing to navigate to the right place. Most, if not all, allow for registration online resulting in the ability to have an entity set up, with a tax id number and a bank account, all in an afternoon.

To get your employer ID number (EIN) from the IRS, you'd go to www.irs.gov and they have right on the homepage a section titled "Employer ID Number (EIN)," which allows you to navigate to and apply for an EIN online. Again, if you have a valid social security number, there usually aren't too many issues. Some caution on the EIN setup—this is where the IRS defaults your tax types, so if you set up an LLC and indicate that you have more than one owner, the IRS will expect a 1065 tax return unless you elect S corporation status. Similarly, it will ask if you expect to have employees, and if you answer yes, it will expect you to file quarterly payroll tax returns and annual federal unemployment tax returns; generally, if you are not sure if or when you'll have employees, the answer would be no to this question. You can always start filing employment tax returns when you set up payroll if applicable.

With your articles of organization that you should have been able to print from the secretary of state's office online and the EIN that, again, you would have been able to print, you can stop at your bank of choice and set up business bank and/or credit card accounts. Then, you are all set to do business as an entity.

Office of the Minnesota Secretary of State
Certificate of Organization

I, Steve Simon, Secretary of State of Minnesota, do certify that: The following business entity has duly complied with the relevant provisions of Minnesota Statutes listed below, and is formed or authorized to do business in Minnesota on and after this date with all the powers, rights and privileges, and subject to the limitations, duties and restrictions, set forth in that chapter.

The business entity is now legally registered under the laws of Minnesota.

Name: ENTREPRENEUR, LLC

File Number: 1234567891011

Minnesota Statutes, Chapter: 322C

This certificate has been issued on: 11/27/2018

Steve Simon
Secretary of State
State of Minnesota

Sample of what a certificate of organization would look like when you do it yourself, the certificate shown here is from Minnesota and is the first of a three page document.

IRS DEPARTMENT OF THE TREASURY
INTERNAL REVENUE SERVICE
CINCINNATI OH 45999-0023

Date of this notice: 11-27-2018

Employer Identification Number:
99-1234567

Form: SS-4

Number of this notice: CP 575 G

ENTREPRENEUR, LLC
CHRISTOPHER S. THOMAS SOLE MBR
123 MAIN STREET
SAINT PAUL, MN 55101

For assistance you may call us at:
1-800-829-4933

IF YOU WRITE, ATTACH THE
STUB AT THE END OF THIS NOTICE.

WE ASSIGNED YOU AN EMPLOYER IDENTIFICATION NUMBER

Thank you for applying for an Employer Identification Number (EIN). We assigned you
EIN 83-2641120. This EIN will identify you, your business accounts, tax returns, and
documents, even if you have no employees. Please keep this notice in your permanent
records.

When filing tax documents, payments, and related correspondence, it is very important
that you use your EIN and complete name and address exactly as shown above. Any variation
may cause a delay in processing, result in incorrect information in your account, or even
cause you to be assigned more than one EIN. If the information is not correct as shown
above, please make the correction using the attached tear off stub and return it to us.

A limited liability company (LLC) may file Form 8832, *Entity Classification Election*,
and elect to be classified as an association taxable as a corporation. If the LLC is
eligible to be treated as a corporation that meets certain tests and it will be electing S
corporation status, it must timely file Form 2553, *Election by a Small Business
Corporation*. The LLC will be treated as a corporation as of the effective date of the S
corporation election and does not need to file Form 8832.

To obtain tax forms and publications, including those referenced in this notice,
visit our Web site at www.irs.gov. If you do not have access to the Internet, call
1-800-829-3676 (TTY/TDD 1-800-829-4059) or visit your local IRS office.

IMPORTANT REMINDERS:

* Keep a copy of this notice in your permanent records. **This notice is issued only
  one time and the IRS will not be able to generate a duplicate copy for you.** You
  may give a copy of this document to anyone asking for proof of your EIN.

* Use this EIN and your name exactly as they appear at the top of this notice on all
  your federal tax forms.

* Refer to this EIN on your tax-related correspondence and documents.

If you have questions about your EIN, you can call us at the phone number or write to
us at the address shown at the top of this notice. If you write, please tear off the stub
at the bottom of this notice and send it along with your letter. If you do not need to
write us, do not complete and return the stub.

Your name control associated with this EIN is LABO. You will need to provide this
information, along with your EIN, if you file your returns electronically.

Thank you for your cooperation.

Here is what the EIN document would look like when you go
through the IRS and obtain one online. The combination of this
document and the certificate of organization are typically all that
would be needed to setup a bank account along with other functions.

TECHNOLOGY

Technology is your friend. Software is what allows you as a small business owner or self-employed individual to leverage automation, enhance your quality control, increase efficiencies, improve your customer engagement, and so much more. You may not need much for software, especially if you are self-employed for a single contract or are doing everything through a platform like Uber or Airbnb that can provide much of the information and perform most of the functions necessary. However, for those of us who have to market, solicit, engage, bill, collect, or do other aspects of business, software is essential.

> I like to think of software as a toddler; if you try to force your kid eat caviar or salads, it'll be frustrating. If you learn to eat mac and cheese, then you and your kid will be fat and happy. What I mean is, many try to get software to perform everything under the sun and end up being disappointed because the software isn't doing everything, but when you redefine your workflow around the capabilities and limitations of the tools and software you plan to use in your business, then it will work much better. Lower your expectations, increase your outcomes.

If you are in a particular industry or profession, there is likely some industry-specific software out there. Franchisors will often have proprietary software that you must use. This would be the first place to look and evaluate, as selecting other software first could mean that you end up with multiple solutions to the same problem. Industry-specific software would be like a solon management suite that does your CRM (customer relationship management), scheduling, invoicing, workflow, etc. Sometimes the sticker price for fancy suites can be alarming at first, but if you consider how many hours it can save you every month, then it becomes a bit more agreeable.

For the most part, software gives us back time. Sure, we can have spreadsheets, manually email customers and confirm appointments, invoice them and hope they pay, nag them when they don't, write checks and affix a stamp to an envelope to pay a bill, etc. We sure could do all of that, and in the beginning, maybe that makes sense, but many of those manual processes reduce your capacity to deliver products and services, which costs you money. Making the investment in efficiency from the get-go is far better than to do things the old-fashioned way in order to save a few hundred dollars a month. Remember, you're building the foundation for the business you envision, not the business you have currently.

Eventually, as you grow and wish to achieve some scale, it is way more work and frustration to convert legacy processes to a modern workflow than to be using more efficient processes (albeit a bit more expensive) from the start. If a few hundred dollars a month is a deal breaker, then I would advise you save up a bit more before starting out so that you can incorporate software into your plan.

If you find the industry software isn't to your liking or is limited, that is when you should look for other options. It helps to define your workflow, which ideally would be structured around your value chain. Your value chain is made of the components of service that add to the perceived value; your workflow consists of the tasks necessary to deliver a product or service. Comparing your value chain to your workflow can help identify and eliminate steps in the process (i.e., does a client need a paper copy of an invoice or are they fine with an emailed invoice, etc.). After streamlining your workflow, you can identify opportunities for automation, which is the process of having the robot do certain tasks for you. For instance, if you have a contract with a fixed recurring monthly fee, rather than billing your client every month, waiting for them to write a check, and then going to the bank and depositing the check, automating it would be to have them sign an authorization to have an ACH or credit card charge each month, and syncing with your accounting software to match the invoices and payments that you are no longer manually creating and reconciling.

Some of these automation opportunities tie back to your capacity. Reducing or eliminating 10-20 minutes of wasted time per month per client may not be that big of a deal if you have just a couple clients, but if you plan to have 40+ clients, those gains in efficiency add up to more clients and more profit. Moreover, it serves as a potential and critical competitive advantage, especially if your competition is wasting time, or has unnecessary overhead costs. Being nimbler and understanding your costs to deliver a product or service allow you to win more bids without lowering the amount of profit you'd like to take home. It is a win-win—the client/customer can access higher quality services at lower prices, and the service provider can serve more clients with less per client value but the same or greater profit overall. With few projects or clients, it may initially be a bit challenging as software is generally more of a fixed cost that can create something of a hurdle. But again, we are working towards the business we want to have, and you have to "plan the work and work the plan," as the saying goes.

In the Cloud

The Cloud means that programs and files are accessed through the internet and are physically located in a multitude of places like data centers, one wouldn't have to use their dedicated machine to access information or applications necessary in getting work done. The old-world duopoly was Mac or PC, which was the hardware that determined what operating system applications and file formats were in. The enterprise world has typically used PC (Microsoft Windows) based operating systems and applications for decades but due to more applications being available on iOS (MAC) along with the proliferation of cloud-based applications one is less likely to be limited by being a Mac Person.

There are different interpretations for what the cloud is and what it means to integrate or sync with other software. To me, if a software is truly a cloud-based, it should be operated from a browser, and more than one; I should be able to access from any device anywhere in the world and not have to "remote" into a server somewhere to log into a local instance of a non-cloud software. Anything that requires Windows, or only works on a specific browser like Internet Explorer, is excluded from my list. The device isn't the important or critical factor anymore. If your business is operated using cloud software, even the most devastating disaster isn't as devastating since you could just go buy a Chromebook and be back and operational within a few hours. That is what it should mean by being "in the cloud."

When you are committed to a cloud-based operating environment for your business, don't want to deal with servers or managed service providers, and want a seamless and beautiful relationship between your office products and the other applications in use for your business, then Google "just gets it." They have made considerable strides in the small enterprise cloud operating ecosystem. Google Chrome is a solid browser with many built-in features that tie to your Google account, combined with the GSSO (Google Single Sign On) and it's a solid foundation for a cloud-based business. The Chromebooks and Chrome-Boxes extend this ecosystem with enterprise-grade workstations that have dual monitor support and can be easily provisioned to the enterprise's fleet of hardware without needing IT support staff to do it. Additionally, there are many add-on applications that layer on top of the Google environment (email, storage, contacts, etc.) that can provide the capabilities to take an everyday application like Google Drive and have it be HIPPA compliant, as well as plugins to Gmail for email encryption and so on. The big thing with Google is providing enterprise-grade capabilities without the enterprise burden of an IT staff or managed service contract needed to support it.

I decided to use Google Drive as my document storage, and using the native programs within Google Drive works a lot better with fewer hiccups; though you can "open in Excel" from Google Drive, it is not the same as working with a G-sheet. Plus, data belongs in databases. It is far too easy with a powerful tool like Excel to extract data out of its source to manipulate, configure, analyze, and do all sorts of cool stuff to, and now you have a separate dataset from the source that you'd need to manually update and configure.

In the everyday deliverable and recurring service tasks, I strive for as much streamlined and standardized workflow as possible. Not to sound like I prefer robots, but every point of human interaction between data and deliverability of service is a point of potential quality control concern and bottleneck that can create inefficiencies and service failure. My perspective is derived from my operating environment. Each business and self-employment situation will be different, so one's decision on the toolset and fleet of integrated software will depend on what their needs are.

The Office Suite

Office suites generally comprise of office products that are bundled into a sort of fleet of interconnected applications that include email, calendar, basic contact management, spreadsheet program, writing and composition, and cloud storage among others. Microsoft is still the dominant player with respect to their office suite; Outlook (email) has approximately 400 million users. Microsoft's applications like Word and Excel remain the most powerful office suite tools on the block with the greatest amount of functionality and capabilities, the greatest number of fonts, formulas, customization, and other features that are far and above the competition. But it's not always about the features within an application.

I used to use Outlook and the Microsoft Office Suite as a mainstay; they're fantastic products. I may have a bit of bias, but I am a Google Business user myself. It was a bit getting used to their G-docs and G-sheets programs as opposed to the more powerful Microsoft Word and Excel, but Google's prowess comes from the integrated and collaborative capabilities and not as much in the core functionality. Powerful applications for local manipulation of data like Excel can be a great tool for adding value or doing additional analysis beyond what is allowable from database outputs natively, which can be a good and bad thing. Good since you can have better, more accurate, and relevant information for you and/or your clients, and bad in the fact that being outside of the main database it creates additional touchpoints and workflow requirements that can reduce efficiency and create quality control risk. Though it should also be noted the Microsoft's Power BI which can be utilized separate from its main core of office suite products, has some really nice features and are constantly improving real time live synchronization with actual databases, so it's possible to get additional analysis and better information output without creating additional datasets.

Some of the decision when choosing an office suite is a continuation of the Mac versus PC conversation, where the main choices are the Microsoft Suite, which can also work in a Mac world, the Native Mac applications (Mail, iCloud, Numbers, etc.), or Google (Gmail, G-Drive, Google Calendar, etc.). As business is ever on the move, having strong mobile capabilities may be a must. Additionally, being able to easily collaborate with colleges and clients as well is an important consideration. All of the suites will have the ability to send calendar invites and to collaborate in screen-to-screen meetings. I prefer Google's suite as the programs pair well with the Google Maps app (which is generally considered far better than other mapping applications), and their Hangouts application (which doesn't require any installation on the end-user side) makes it frictionless to collaborate and engage in business on the go. Plus, their calendar invites automatically create private hangouts sessions so customers, prospects, coworkers, etc. can just click the link in the calendar event to jump into a screen–to-screen session.

Have you ever had a "no show," where you have an appointment set up and they simply don't show up? I don't know why, maybe they don't value your time, maybe they are super busy, maybe they forgot or don't use a calendar, but for whatever reason, it happens. To help tamp down on it, there are appointment apps that integrate with your calendar. I use calendly.com, and there are others out there that can send the reminders. Calendly had a nice simple and modern-feeling user experience that I liked, and it sends the reminder automatically so I don't have to call or message the other contact. When you don't have a support staff, automating the support functions are essential so you can focus more time on higher value tasks. These applications often create that static page for accessing your calendar, and if you're not careful, prospects and network affiliates will get it and consume your time without your permission. I generally have it available to my clients only and still manually set up appointments for prospects that have been qualified (screened to see if they are a good fit as a potential client of the firm).

Project Management

This is the heartbeat of the business. Surprisingly, most entrepreneurs don't use a project management software or have any written procedures or checklists for that matter. For some, that works just fine; they know what they need to do, when and for whom, so adding software may seem like a duplication of effort that doesn't add value for them.

With respect to industry-specific software, this is usually the bread and butter of what their software does, and for good reason. Software designed specifically for a particular industry is built around the workflow of that industry to alleviate the pain points that many in that industry experience. For instance, a construction or general contractor software would encompass bidding/prospecting, contact management, work orders, change orders, purchase orders, UCC liens and lien waivers, billing and collections, work delegation/staff assignment, project scheduling, and more. Such software can be expensive but can end up replacing a half dozen other software programs and processes in addition to saving countless hours along the way.

For those who are not in love with the options out there for their industry, or in an area that does not have specific software, there are still good options. As a general-purpose workflow and project management tool, I am a fan of Asana. It was built and designed by some of the people that were core to Facebook's development. It is simple to use, easy to collaborate, clean, and is relatively inexpensive. You can create recurring tasks, have different teams, projects, tasks, attachments, etc. It can be a bit too freestyle for some, so if you have rigid recurring tasks, need routing functionality (where a task or project gets assigned to another person for review or authorization upon completion of a lower task), or greater control and more structure to your workflow, it may not be the best option for you. In any case, evaluate a couple different applications like Trello, Basecamp, and others.

Your project management tool should be your go-to place. If you've never used one before, it may take a bit of getting used to—creating tasks and projects even for simple or silly little items might seem pointless, but if you are committed to getting rid of the post-it-note system or that legal pad with all the chicken scratch on it, forming good habits is what it takes. The project management software can typically be synced with other programs like your document management and communication tools. Additionally, it can serve as a collaboration hub encompassing task-oriented conversations with other team members, so if you have specific project specifications, or an RFP or other procedural documents, those too can be built into the project, task, subtask, and other checklists and deliverability status of the systems. This eliminates the endless email chains with several people being cc'd on the conversation who have little to do with it.

Additionally, if you are solo or don't have an outside sales or dedicated pipeline management team that is working on bringing in new clients for you, and you are in the market for new clients, project management software can also work as your CRM tool. You may want to evaluate what your sales and pipeline workflow is to determine if this tool will be able to double up. I've tried to use CRM tools but was frustrated having two or three different locations for workflow. I just want one board that tells me what I need to do and when, not three. For smaller enterprises, it can be more than just a tool for core operational functionality, even basic items like "get more toner for the copier machine" can be a task that gets assigned and completed.

If you have a reasonable customer support aspect to your business, there are some nice starter versions of Zendesk and other customer support software that integrate with email to create tickets, have a centralized communication with customers, and more that would be worth looking into. But again, evaluate your workflow—maybe your sales and customer support team can use one and your production staff uses another. Find tools that your workflow can be configured to without also having to have the spreadsheet or whiteboard to augment it.

Time and Billing

If you bill by the hour, you need to track your time. Even in professional services where you do value billing (or fixed fee) engagements, you may want to track time in order to provide a billing realization along with other analysis. Billing realization is the difference between your desired bill rate and billable time deployed versus what you actually collected for a project. For example, you budgeted for a 20-hour project at $150 per hour and engage on a fixed fee of $3,000. If it takes you 25 hours to complete the project, your realization rate is only $120 per hour ($3,000/25) and not $150 as you wanted. A good time and billing software would be able to show you a report that might look like:

Gross Billings	$3,750.00 (25*$150)
Net Write Downs	($750.00)
Net Realized Billings	$3,000.00

Reports like that, especially over time, with multiple staff, project types, etc., can show you which clients and projects are the best for your practice, which ones you need to evaluate, which project managers are responsible for the most write ups or write downs to create incentives for partners or staff to be more efficient, and so on. Maybe there was a learning curve that created some inefficiencies initially, but the project type and projected budgets are adequate going forward. Or maybe there is more staff supervision needed, quality control was lacking, or you were charging too much for certain projects, etc. Some software suites incorporate project management, document management, time and billing, and more.

For a straightforward time-based project billing, stand-alone applications like Harvest (www.getharvest.com) can be a great tool. There are continuously new applications being developed along with improvements to current software out there that strive to make the process as un-intrusive as possible. Like having a sync between your client list and calendar, so you could just put items into your calendar and it would automatically fill out your timecard, associate billable and non-billable time, and prompt to populate invoices and reports without having to use another tool, just the calendar. Most accounting software has the ability to track and bill time and expenses, so evaluate what you need from such a software to ensure you're not simply adding tools that don't also add value.

CRM and Pipeline Management

Whatever happened to the good ole days of the Yellow Pages, or when you could literally hang a shingle and get customers? Well, I don't remember those days either. Since the evolution of the internet, and search theory became the mainstay, people don't gravitate towards the old way of finding products and services. The entire sales process or pipeline management has become a comprehensive process that isn't just about getting to a yes or executing a transaction. Many people don't like the idea of "selling," but we all have to sell ourselves to a certain extent. Even if you are an employee, you have to get an employer to hire you, and some of the same fundamentals as to why an employer would choose you as an employee apply for why a prospect would choose you as a good fit to provide services or choose your product for their needs. Branding, SEO (search engine optimization), web development, PPC (pay-per-click advertising), and other aspects would get far beyond the scope of the conversation. For now, we are to assume you know what you sell, what your target market is, and how to get their attention and generate leads. If not, you may want to consider getting some outside help to get things going with a well-optimized website, PPC search, and social media campaign, along with branding and other avenues in order to get the phone ringing.

Great, now the phone is ringing, How do you keep track of prospects, and/or manage relationships? After all, if you are in the business of providing services, the relationship is paramount to your economic success. There are many different tools like Salesforce, Freshdesk, Nimble, and others. Many have a focus on the eventual transaction or sale. I found this frustrating since the focus of many service-based businesses is on the long-term relationship where there is no one transaction but rather a continuum of service delivery and fee collection. As such, the "target" or value from long-term relationships should be built around more of an engagement model that can track things like service delivery and communication, along with client's interaction to ascribe value to aspects other than just the "sale." Plus, if you are solo, using a stand-alone CRM or pipeline management software ends up creating a completely new workflow tool, so you'd have tasks, projects, and due dates here and there and everywhere, and now you're getting saturated with notifications and reminders.

Technology, in general, can be something of a balancing act between what currently is, what will soon be, and what you are able to use on the ground in the real world. Software is generally not static; one product may be limited today but will be outstanding tomorrow, or there could be a totally new player that you weren't aware of, so periodically evaluate your inventory of software solutions. But today is today, and we have to, as former secretary of defense Donald Rumsfeld put it, "go to war with the army you have, not the army you want." If we wait for the most pristine and perfect AI and software stack to deliver services with the most optimized and technologically leveraged capabilities, we'll always be waiting, we have to put our (metaphorical) tanks in the street and take the fight to the enemy regardless, constantly improving along the way. So, balance your immediate needs while keeping an eye out for upcoming developments and budget and schedule rollouts and process improvements along the way.

If you have an employee or outside sales rep that you can lean on, having a good CRM tool can be profound. It is how you can define objectives, improve the sales process, centralize and track communication, and incentivize the right behavior and interactions that you want your brand to have with the public. Oh, and of course the big one, generate leads and convert those leads into clients and customers for the business, along with taking current customers and clients and adding additional touchpoints, upselling opportunities, remarketing, and engage referral programs and incentives to get the machine churning out productivity. If you have the capacity for it, then it can be a good value to invest in, but like many things, you get out of it what you put into it. If you treat your sales as a necessary evil or a dirty diaper that you don't want to touch and just dump it on someone else, it may not work out so well. You, as a proprietor, are the greatest selling point of your business or practice.

Communication

Communication can encompass a pretty wide swath of different mediums, tools, and purposes. The mainstay for many large organizations is the email, which is also the primary communication method between customer and enterprise across the board. However, there is a continuous growing amount of interaction points, collaboration, and ways to connect, like through social media, text messaging, instant messaging through one of various apps, and of course, there is the old-fashioned phone call.

Telephony – Telephony operations would typically encompass text messaging functionality as well as voice. Many entrepreneurs just use their cell phone. You may have, want, or need a landline phone; however, there are many options where you wouldn't need to be bound to the physical landline. Grasshopper, Google Voice, and some others establish a phone number that gets routed to your cell phone. This allows you to have a public facing number without the additional hardware or software commitments and still protect your personal privacy. It is nice to be able to use your cell for business without giving out your cell phone number, and you can change the settings so that when you are off duty, you don't get calls or texts, the way it should be. It also allows you to be fully mobile and not miss a call or text when you are "on duty."

> Protect your privacy. In this day and age of instant access and immediate resolution, clients and customers can come to expect instantaneous access to you. If they have your personal cell phone number, they will use it, and then you'll be getting text messages at 10:30 at night and so on.

There are a number of other telephony operations depending on what you are looking for. If you have a customer support "ticketing" service model, then the software or platforms that form the hub of such operations typically either have native telephony functionality or preferred deep integrations, which allows for a call from a particular contact to get automatically routed to the owner of the project or ticket so that the customer can "skip the line" in a sense. Everyone just calls, texts, or emails the one centralized communication point and there is no need to go through the process of finding your case, or validating your identity—we know it's you and Chris will respond very shortly with deeper knowledge of your situation and ideally higher quality service for the customer.

I use Dialpad for my call and texting functionality. It doesn't forward the call to your phone; it is an application of its own, but works great in a browser or on your cell phone, and has the ability to allow you to have a desk phone if you don't want to always use your webcam mic or a headset. Call routing and other rules allow you to have an office line as well as a direct line; if the office line doesn't get picked up, it goes to the next person. Another option is to not answer the phone. Especially if you are a one-person shop, getting calls can be very disruptive to your concentration and work. So, you could have all calls go right to voicemail with a nice message, and then just call people back.

Email and Messaging – For email, you probably have decided on Outlook, Gmail, or another application that might be part of the office suite of your choice. Of big concern is privacy and security. Encrypting email communication can be a big challenge.

Fortunately, there are applications like Virtru that provide end-to-end encryption for Google and Microsoft email platforms. What is really nice is that the way it works doesn't require some complex, convoluted process to establish the key (or secure handshake to set up the channel of communication) on the client's side, so it is relatively easy to use for clients as well. Plus, the price point is pretty affordable; there's no sense making it easy on bad guys when you can take some preventative control measures.

Messaging apps can be great tools. I love Slack along with their "screen hero" which enables an instantaneous collaborative and interactive screen-sharing environment where multiple parties can interact with the same screen instead of the usual one presenter and everyone else is just watchers. So, if you have staff that are located all over the place and need to quickly provide some guidance or direction, you can rapidly jump in and see what they are seeing, simultaneously interact with the screen, and have a much deeper interaction between users. Google Chat is catching up and has totally redesigned the user experience to provide a richer and more complex environment for messaging. There are increasingly more integrated solutions where one could use a Slack or Google chat and have conversations tagged to workflow components so that people don't have to have eight different conversation streams going on.

External messaging applications can be a bit more complex as the end user, your customer, may not have Slack or whatever preferred application you'd like to use to connect with them on. Fortunately, there are tools that enable consolidation and centralization of communication mediums, whereby you may be using your preferred messaging app, and on the customer side they are sending and receiving SMS (text) messages. Being able to channel communication from customers and prospects is important because we only have so much time and if all communication has to go through the owner it becomes difficult to grow and scale since we can only manage so many conversations in a day.

Other Communication Mediums – External, or client-facing, apps are progressing along nicely. There are various places in which the client can interact with the service provider. It could be in a platform in which services or products are solicited and secured (like Amazon, Airbnb, or another lead generation marketplace), through social media like Facebook Messenger, common tools like Google Chat or Hangouts, Apple's Facetime, or others. It can be daunting to imagine the inundation from all the various ways in which clients and prospects can connect. The bigger challenge is more to limit or channelize the conversation within the context of the engagement, proposal, or products and services that you are to provide. This is what some applications do, such as Intercom or Hootsuite. Granted, there is still some focus on either the lead generation or the targeted ticket resolution perspective to some of these apps and they don't necessarily integrate with the rest of the software fleet you are building, but they can do a lot to centralize communication and branding. The big takeaway is to determine via what channels you'll be connecting with your audience, which would logically coincide with your workflow, sales pipeline, and other more objective alignment with what it is you do, and then have those channels be typical of your customers so there aren't pain points in order to just connect with you. Though it may not be frictionless, having as few barriers to client adoption as possible is essential.

Accounting firms and other organizations were sold on the "portal" concept for the better part of a decade. The tax and accounting software providers would cram it onto the accountants and they in turn would spend an inordinate amount of time trying to get clients to use it and would fail. Clients wouldn't adapt to the portal; it was basically just a document sharing apparatus that often didn't actually retain documents, so clients would have to log into this secure place to manually download and extract information only to put it somewhere else. They'd forget their password and have to call to get it reset—it was an awful way to try and not print a tax return. Fortunately, companies like Apple, Microsoft, Google, Dropbox, and others have advanced their products to eliminate the problem without requiring such a painful process to solve. The moral of the story is that technology can be great, but don't get ahead of yourself—just because there is a bullet train doesn't mean the tracks are there to ride it. Balance the capabilities, limitations, desired outcomes, and other aspects along with the vision and planning for tomorrow's environment; things take time, enjoy the ride and get comfortable with change.

POS and Inventory

If you are in the business of selling products, you may need a POS (point of sale) and inventory management system. Not necessarily though. If you only sell on a marketplace like Amazon and use their FBA (Fulfilled by Amazon), many aspects can be handled through the third party (Amazon, in this case). But, if you will have inventory (either on hand or through a contracted warehouse location) and make sales in a store or online, you'll need to know how much you have, when to order, and so on. This is what these systems are designed to do.

They can get quite robust with respect to their capabilities, such as automatic reordering, freight minimization optimization, comparative pricing analysis, and more. They don't always sync beautifully with your accounting software, but that is okay because when you are in the retail industry, it is more important to have the right tool for your products, sales, and inventory than to just have something that syncs with your accounting suite. The software that communicates to your vendors and can connect the multiple steps in the process would be of the highest preference. So, when you sell something via dropship, the system should be able to send the purchase order with the dropship location, track the shipping info for the customer, and close out the transaction once delivered. The system should provide you with the reporting and analytics you might need to see what your gross margin is or what your inventory valuation is, conduct an inventory at the year end, and so on.

Sales tax can be such a pain. It sounds simple enough: you sell something, then you collect sales tax. But with over 30,000 separate taxing jurisdictions, it is an awful experience to say the least. So, ideally, a good POS system will have the ability to, at a minimum, integrate with a sales tax automation software like Avalara, or be able to report and remit the sales tax for you. Some may just provide you with reports and then you would have to go to the various agencies for various states, set up tax ID numbers and other aspects, register for tax types and filing frequencies, and so on all manually. It is a nightmare. If you sell (sales) taxable products, and especially if you are selling through the internet across state lines, sales tax should be a high priority to leverage software.

You can track inventory and sales tax through the accounting software packages, but if you are tracking more than 20 products or items and deploying your taxable products and services into multiple jurisdictions, then it is not likely to be a good fit and will create a lot of frustrations trying to get the little donkey to pull a large wagon load.

Security

Security has been a focus for technology companies for decades. With the cloud, stand-alone security software is less critical considering enhanced browser security is built into the internet experience, dual factor authentication capabilities, biometric and enhanced security protocols, and applications themselves making it their priority that the end user isn't as stranded in the Wild West as much anymore. We've, in a sense, circled the wagons by storing data in highly secure cloud databases like with Google, Apple, Microsoft, and others. Sure, some of these trillion-dollar companies could get hacked, but it's not like there is even a master key anymore. Data in these databases are fragmented, encrypted, decentralized, and partitioned where even if Google were hacked, they couldn't access any individual user's data. The weak point is still with the user.

> Data belongs in databases. Those databases are typically in the cloud behind juggernaut security systems operated by Apple, Google, Microsoft, and others, and access is provided through whitelisted access you provide that can have dual factor, biometric enhancement, and other security measures to enhance security.

Being proactive about security and protecting your identity and data in your possession is very important. Different people have different setups, and we've likely all heard the same speeches about how to not use P@ssword as your password anymore. I don't store data on any of my computers; nothing is stored locally. The email server is not local. In fact, I don't have a server at all. Everything is in secure cloud databases that is only accessible through whitelisted users using strong passwords with dual factor authentication and only on trusted browsers like Chrome or Firefox. I use a password management software which provides extremely strong passwords for just about everything you need. So if someone or some robot was trying to access my data, they would not only need my login credentials, but also my phone which is biometrically tied to my fingerprint and is generally always in my possession. No, it is not impossible, but extremely unlikely.

> I get really excited when I see a client using password management software. Some are built right into the browser like with Chrome, so when you login to your Gmail account, it also syncs your "remember login credentials" information for all the logins that you've had it remember for you. Password management software may seem like an additional or unnecessary step (plus, I think some are afraid of losing their login to the password management software), but it is an incredibly valuable part of being secure in today's environment that is full of hackers and thieves. The software is typically pretty inexpensive considering what it does, and once you get used to using it, it's not much of a pain at all. Many can integrate with your phone and traditional browser experience, so it becomes very seamless to use while making it much more difficult for the bad guys.

It doesn't hurt to have security software. There are free ones like Malwarebytes, as well as paid subscription providers like Kaspersky, Norton, and MacAfee. But don't think that just because you have an anti-virus software you can be careless. It is far better to have a secure posture in this digital age.

Accounting

Much like other aspects of software, accounting software has many options to choose from. There are free versions as well, though some of the free ones don't have the kind of full featured robust capabilities of the more mainstream options but can suffice for the relatively simple needs of some entrepreneurs. Of the paid versions, the main choices are Xero and QuickBooks Online (QBO) which account for the vast majority of all small business accounting utilization. Yes, there are others like Zoho Books, and if you have a specific justification, then certainly it makes sense. Zoho is a platform like Google with a whole suite of various apps and customizable stackable software that allows you to have deep integrations between your Zoho CRM, Zoho Subscriptions, and others. I generally find Zoho to be a bit too unstructured and DIY for my liking, but there is some potential to keep an eye on this. Freshbooks is another paid accounting package which offers a bit more on-the-go mobile invoicing, hourly billing capabilities, and user experience for the self-employed but is lacking when you get into things like reconciling your bank account, generating an estimate, budgeting, class tracking, or other capabilities. You may prefer one of the many other options out there, which is fine, of course, but for the purposes of this context, going forward will be geared more towards the assumption that one is either a QBO or Xero subscriber.

Both QBO and Xero are full featured sets of small business accounting software. Xero is a newer addition to the space and does have some catching up to do, but it is very aggressively adding features to earn their status as number two and potentially number one someday. Both have a slew of auxiliary products and make acquisitions to deeper integrate other aspects to their core product like document retention, workflow, time and billing, and others. Both have an apps marketplace and developer network to encourage and liberate the process of data integration and sync between various systems, which makes your accounting software a default hub for all financial data. For companies that don't have thousands of products, services, customers, and vendors, it is often the hub for almost all pertinent data on just about everything.

As a core database, much of the potential automation and headache reductions are built with the data in your accounting package. So, for bill pay, payroll, subcontractor payments, invoicing and payments, etc., it all is built from the database at hand.

Some do express some resistance or reluctance to sign on for these software suites when they see the price, which can vary, but for a standard license without many additional bells and whistles is generally $35-50 per month, more if you have payroll, bill pay, or other modules added on. Both do have a partner program working with accountants like me which creates the potential to receive discounts and other benefits from partnering with a partner of their software.

Engagement or Contract Management

Engagement or contract management software is a solution set I am surprised took so long to gain traction. This aspect would be a mainstay for some of the all-encompassing industry specific software suites out there as well as standalone tool sets. What it does is standardize the engagement and money movement piece. For instance, if you bill on a fixed fee engagement with a recurring monthly schedule, the software would collect signatures for the contract or engagement that gets consent for the work to be performed as well as banking/credit card info to automatically collect payment per the schedule outlined in the engagement proposal. Many allow for the bill upon completion, so even when not on a fixed or recurring schedule, with the approval and banking info up front, you'll get to collect as soon as you bill—no more receivables or collections needed.

If you work with more than 10 clients or projects a month, this can be a game changer. No more manually invoicing or processing payments, no more trying to match and reconcile 50 different transactions to specific clients. The software does the annoying work and sends the info to your accounting software so that when the bank gets the deposit, it lines up nicely with the batch of data from your engagement software.

As an engagement management software would encompass engaging service providers to provide services, many of these software platforms form the building blocks for your workflow and service delivery requirements. I use an engagement management software which outlines what services I am to perform, the start dates, and other data, and in turn, my delivery of services is directly tied to the scope of work outlined in the engagement. This can be a big deal, especially if you are in a profession in which people kick tires or try to steal your time. By restricting access to you and the deployment of your time, you can have greater assurance that the time you are putting into the marketplace is being valued and you will more likely be compensated for that, automatically in many cases.

ACCOUNTING

A ccounting is the foundation to understanding your business. It is the process of aggregating and compiling financial data into usable information like financial statements, budgeting and forecasting, tax returns, etc. I know many people don't get as excited about it as I do, but that doesn't mean it has to be such a daunting chore.

I am not going to drag you through 20 pages of Accounting 101. We'll cover the elements of accounting and its related impact as a more useful and practical guide. The goal is to have more money coming in than going out. Accounting doesn't help you make more money by itself but will let you know when you do and how much; and that information can lead to better decision making and better financial results down the road. There are two main methods for accounting: cash basis and accrual basis.

Cash Basis – For the most part, cash in is income and cash out is an expense. Many small businesses use this method for its simplicity.

Accrual Basis – Income is recorded when earned and expenses are recorded when incurred, even if you haven't received the cash from a customer or paid out cash to a vendor.

Cash-in and Cash-out

Depending on your size, you may have chosen to not have an accounting program, and that may be a reasonable choice, especially if you have less than 100 transactions in a year, only one bank account, don't need to invoice customers, create estimates or do other business actions—meaning, your business is very simple. Without an accounting software, you may only do a full-blown bookkeeping once a year in preparation for taxes.

To approximate net income for an interim period for a very simple business operation with just one bank account, log into your online banking, search by date range from the beginning of the year, take total cash inflows minus total cash outflows and add back any of your draws. As an example, say you've got $60,000 of cash inflows, $40,000 of cash outflows, and took $25,000 of personal draws (out of the $40,000 cash outflows). Your net income would be:

$60,000 - $40,000 + $25,000 = $45,000

With that, you would be able to estimate what your tax liability is and how much to pay in estimates. Not too bad, right? Sure, it doesn't account for vehicle mileage, home office, or other potential deductions, but it gets you to shotgun range.

Spreadsheet

For the year end, when you'd like to actually do the full bookkeeping, you can use Excel, Google Sheets, or another spreadsheet program, and export the transactions for the year to a csv file, which might look a little something like this:

A	B	C
2/21/18	-299	Debit Software
2/21/18	-125.05	Staples
2/20/18	-6500	xfer to x4687
2/20/18	-7.87	Trx Fee
2/20/18	400	Deposit
2/16/18	-17.65	Trx Fee
2/16/18	-850	xfer to x4687
2/16/18	8,030.25	Deposit

To get the data from a simple list of transactions into a more meaningful report that can be used for tax returns and other needs, you'd categorize the transactions and total it up. In the spreadsheet table with the transactions, using categories based on a logical function like sales, auto expense, advertising, etc., you would go down the list of transactions, and in the empty column next to each transaction, assign a category. Then, make the list of categories in yet another separate column, and, finally, using a formula to total up each category, the result should be a simple receipt and disbursement summary that can be used to prepare taxes.

			Enter Categories	Categories w/o Duplicates	Formula
A	B	C	D	E	F
2/21/18	-299	Debit Software	Computer	Sales	8430.25
2/21/18	-125.05	Staples	Office	Computer	-299
2/20/18	-6500	xfer to x4687	Draw	Office	-125.05
2/20/18	-7.87	Trx Fee	Bank	Draw	-7350
2/20/18	400	Deposit	Sales	Bank	-25.52
2/16/18	-17.65	Trx Fee	Bank		
2/16/18	-850	xfer to x4687	Draw		
2/16/18	8,030.25	Deposit	Sales		
TOTAL	630.68				630.68

As a double check, the column totals should match, which means there is a zero difference between them, and zero is an accountant's favorite number. With more than one account, you can still use a spreadsheet and do the same exercise for each account. Then, create a grand total for all the accounts, being careful with transfers between the accounts.

Using Software

The preferred method is to use an accounting software like QuickBooks Online, Xero, or others. Many of these software suites are built with DIY (Do-It-Yourself) in mind and often have lower tiered packages for the self-employed so it isn't a massive cash outlay or recurring commitment to have a top-notch accounting system in place. Though it can easily get out of balance, a little understanding of how the systems work should help keep it clean. The software with a paid subscription like QuickBooks Online and Xero have a very comprehensive suite of learning tools with videos and lessons, as well as community forums where users ask questions and get answers. When you have a question about how to do something, you can usually find the answer with a simple Google search like, "How to apply a payment for more than one invoice in QBO." The first result is a YouTube video that explains exactly the answer to your question in under two minutes. I mention that because many of my clients lean on me for some of these questions, and I am happy to be the resource they have come to expect. But there are a good number of instances where it isn't on the top of my head and I'd be doing searches to get the answers. The answers are not locked away in secret accounting club vaults (you may not have an accountant to lean on either); it's all public and accessible. You just need to know a little bit of search theory in order to frame your question or specify the information you are looking for in order for the oracle (Google) to give you what you want.

In Sync – A critical component of these platforms is centered around the sync with your bank and credit accounts. Most will have the same bank and credit account availability. Generally, if your bank is available to sync with QuickBooks online, it would also be available on Xero and others. Basically, it downloads transactions to the platform from the various financial institutions. The amount of information can vary based on the bank or credit union. For the most part, the larger and more prominent financial institutions convey more information that gets downloaded as the description, but there should usually be enough information to decipher what the transaction was for regardless, especially if you were the one who swiped the card at a particular vendor or pushed a PayPal transaction through.

Every business is different, and every vendor that sells products and services to those businesses may be for different purposes. As such, it's on you (or me for many of my clients) to tell the system what the various transactions were for or how they should be reflected in the books (coding the transactions), which is what most think of as "bookkeeping." The robots are getting smarter, making better suggestions and matching recommendations to make the process of keeping the books as simple and fast as possible. What used to take several hours a month just a few years ago is closer to 30 minutes or less for many small businesses (if you know what you are doing, that is).

For the cash basis business that doesn't send out invoices within the system, it's relatively painless. Most deposits would be considered sales and outgoing transactions would likely be an expense. Small enterprises and self-employed businesses will typically have a good amount of owner transfers or will write checks to themselves. Generally, owner transactions would be associated with an equity account with a name like owner draw, distribution, or perhaps a catchall like owner's equity, etc. Owner draws are not an expense or deduction for the business, which is why such transactions should be associated with an equity account and not an expense account. There could also be legitimate loans to and from the entity of course, not to mention potential payroll or other transaction types; it's up to you (or someone like me) to apply judgement and discretion to determine what the economic reality behind transactions are and account for them accordingly.

The initial setup of an accounting system is an area of error-prone consequence. The systems are designed to get you shooting from the hip as fast as possible and will plug accounts to artificially make it balance which may be confusing later on. For example, if you are getting things set up in the middle of the year but have been in business all year, the sync may not automatically go back to the beginning of the year. It may just go back 90 or less days in some cases, but these accounts typically have balances in them. So to make it balance, the system will put the beginning balance as something along the lines of "opening balance equity" and move you along. The account can balance and you can reconcile the account, but now there is the potential that one excluded a lot of information in the beginning of the year that is not in the books. They do this because they want you to engage with the system and not spend a lot of time in the sales process explaining the arduous process of getting things set up correctly.

To set up correctly, you'd want to ideally encompass all transactions of the bank or credit card account. That may not be practical if the company has been in business for many years and/or switching between software. In such a case, encompassing the current year's transactions and establishing the beginning balances that correspond with the previous year's ending balances would be the preferred method. That way, at least the current year's financial information and later on, the tax returns can be correct.

With respect to the simple cash basis business, keeping the books is a manageable task, so long as it was set up correctly and bookkeeping is done on a regular basis. As all transactions that are in the books come from the bank sync, when you complete the process of coding the transactions, the balance in the books (QuickBooks, etc.) and the actual account balance in your bank account should be the same, which for the most part means you probably did it right.

Equipment Purchases – Many small businesses keep their books in line with their tax return and would use the IRS's allowable deductions for equipment, which for most part would be $2,500 per item or invoice. So if you bought a vehicle or equipment for over that amount, you would want to account for it correctly so the tax return is prepared correctly as well. This means an equipment purchase would be categorized as equipment or some other asset account and not as an expense. You still get to deduct the cost but may have to deduct it over more than one year through what's called depreciation.

Beyond the Basics

Just because you intend to send invoices to your clients or perform other functions within the accounting software doesn't mean you are complex or that the process will be arduous to maintain. Nonetheless, knowledge going beyond basic functionality of these tools can help you understand the overall impact so when you create a transaction, you'll know what that will mean in the bigger picture. Not to mention, using software can add a lot of value by saving you time, creating a more professional and polished process for invoicing and collecting payments from your customers, and much more.

Before moving right into actions within this system, let's review the basic set of financial statements. Generally, the two basic financial statements are the P&L (profit and loss, also income statement, revenue and expense statement, etc.) and the balance sheet (statement of financial condition, assets liabilities and equity, etc.). The P&L is a summary over a period of time showing the revenues, expenses, and net profit or loss for the business. The balance sheet shows the assets, liabilities, and net equity for an entity at a point in time. Generally, the two statements would be presented together: a P&L for 2017 (January through December) would be shown with the December 31, 2017 balance sheet.

Entrepreneur, LLC

PROFIT AND LOSS
January - April, 2018

	TOTAL
Income	$92,281.40
Cost of Goods Sold	$14,990.91
GROSS PROFIT	$77,290.49
Expenses	
Advertising and Promotion	658.98
Bank Charges	268.00
Computer & Internet	42.83
Insurance - General	2,140.00
Interest Expense	553.91
Laundry & Uniforms	1,881.66
Legal & Accounting	2,005.00
Meals and Entertainment	378.06
Office Supplies Expense	122.19
Operating Supplies	51.60
Payroll Expenses	
Taxes	1,898.60
Wages	20,609.35
Total Payroll Expenses	22,507.95
Payroll Service	219.74
Permits and Licenses	724.21
Professional Development	7,550.18
Rent	8,015.00
Telephone	710.56
Utilities	387.97
Vehicle Expense	1,737.73
Total Expenses	$49,955.57
NET OPERATING INCOME	$27,334.92
Other Income	$0.04
Other Expenses	$420.80
NET OTHER INCOME	$ -420.76
NET INCOME	$26,914.16

Entrepreneur, LLC

BALANCE SHEET

As of April 30, 2018

	TOTAL
ASSETS	
Current Assets	
Bank Accounts	
Cash in Checking	18,323.78
Savings Account	494.07
Total Bank Accounts	**$18,817.85**
Accounts Receivable	
Accounts Receivable	20,225.40
Total Accounts Receivable	**$20,225.40**
Other Current Assets	
Inventory	2,500.00
Total Other Current Assets	**$2,500.00**
Total Current Assets	**$41,543.25**
Fixed Assets	
Fixed Assets	22,248.25
Less Accumulated Depreciation	-22,248.25
Total Fixed Assets	**$0.00**
TOTAL ASSETS	**$41,543.25**
LIABILITIES AND EQUITY	
Liabilities	
Current Liabilities	
Credit Cards	
Credit Card Payable	3,257.42
Line of Credit	8,379.54
Total Credit Cards	**$11,636.96**
Other Current Liabilities	
Payroll Liabilities	322.00
Total Other Current Liabilities	**$322.00**
Total Current Liabilities	**$11,958.96**
Long-Term Liabilities	
Notes Payable	5,397.52
Total Long-Term Liabilities	**$5,397.52**
Total Liabilities	**$17,356.48**
Equity	
Capital Stock	100.00
Retained Earnings	19,795.61
Shareholder Distributions	-22,623.00
Net Income	26,914.16
Total Equity	**$24,186.77**
TOTAL LIABILITIES AND EQUITY	**$41,543.25**

Notice the "Net Income" from the Profit and Loss statement ties to the "Net Income" in the equity section of the balance sheet. That's how we know we are looking at the correct pair of financial statements. The retained earnings is typically a default account from the programs that represents prior period net income/loss; that prior period is typically the previous year. So if you are looking at a month instead of the year to date, the net income numbers may not match. That doesn't mean the information is wrong, it just means that the balance sheet's representation of the net income figure covers different periods than the profit and loss.

Another important statement which isn't shown here is the statement of cash flows, which covers a period of time and provides a reconciliation between the change in cash and the net profit/loss for the business over that period. I generally like to show the statement of cash flows as it helps explain questions clients will ask like, "What happened to all the cash? It says I made X, but my bank account went down." The statement of cash flows starts with net income and goes through items like changes in accounts receivables (what customers owe you), changes in liabilities, equipment purchases, and the big-ticket item being owner draws resulting in what the overall change in cash from one period to the next is.

Every line on the financial statements (other than the subtotals and totals lines) represents an account, which could also be grouped. There could be parent accounts with sub-accounts, etc., but we'll keep it simple for the time being. An **account** in accounting is anything that a transaction can get associated with, including bank accounts, liability accounts, expense accounts, equity accounts, revenue accounts, etc., all of them. The **chart of accounts**, which you may not see very often, is a listing of all of these accounts.

Double entry accounting is a concept that is a half millennium old. You may have heard of debits and credits—this is where that comes from. All debits must equal credits. The double entry part forces every transaction to impact two accounts. Interacting with an accounting software, you may not see it happening, but it is. When you code a deposit transaction to sales, in the background, it is debiting the checking account and crediting the sales account, and so on.

Within the software, which again could be QuickBooks, Xero, or others, their functionality is more or less universal in how they impact your books (and later on tax returns). See the image on the next page for a summary of the basic actions one can typically execute within their bookkeeping system and what impact that has on the financial statements.

Sales and Accounts Receivable

Invoice – An invoice is a document sent to a customer/client for products or services rendered. In accrual accounting, the date the invoice is generated is the date that revenue is earned; when the invoice is paid is when a cash basis business would recognize it as revenue. An invoice can sometimes can be confused with a bill since when you "bill" your customer, you are sending them an invoice which to them is a bill. It would increase your sales and also increase your accounts receivables (money your customers owe you). The major software suites would generally incorporate a merchant account functionality that enables the ability for customers to "click and pay," so when you email a customer an invoice, they can pay it electronically, which would automatically get recorded in the books and match up with the deposit when it hits the bank account.

Receive Payment – If only all of our clients or customers would click and pay us electronically, life would be so much easier. This step or action is necessary when you receive a check, or cash or some other non-automated medium for payment. The action associates a payment to an open invoice and would thus update your accounts receivables balance. If you don't use your accounting software to keep track of your accounts receivables or to send invoices, then this action would not be necessary; for the most part, you'd just consider most deposits as sales for simplicity.

Action	Impact					
	Cash Basis			Accrual Basis		
	P&L	Balance Sheet		P&L	Balance Sheet	
Create Invoice	N/A	N/A		Increase Revenue	Increase AR & Net Income	
Receive Payment for Invoice	Increase Revenue	Increase Cash & Net Income		N/A	Increase Cash, Decrease AR	
Create Estimate or Quote	N/A	N/A		N/A	N/A	
Sales Receipt, or recieve payment for services not previously invoiced	Increase Revenue	Increase Cash & Net Income		Increase Revenue	Increase Cash & Net Income	
Credit Memo	N/A	N/A		Reduces Revenue	Decrease AR & Net Income	
Issue Refund to Customer	Reduces Revenue	Reduces Cash & Net Income		N/A	Decrease Cash & Increase AR	
Create a Check or Expense	Increase Expenses	Decrease Cash & Net Income		Increase Expenses	Decrease Cash & Net Income	
Enter or Create Bill	N/A	N/A		Increase Expenses	Increase AP & Decrease Net Income	
Create Purchase Order	N/A	N/A		N/A	N/A	
Vendor Credit	N/A	N/A		Reduces Expenses	Decrease AP & Increase Net Income	
Receive Refund from Vendor	Decrease Expense	Increase Cash & Net Income		N/A	Increase Cash & AP	

Sometimes less is more. For instance, if you are using a franchise software or industry specific software that does your project management, CRM, and your invoicing and payment processing, you wouldn't necessarily need the duplication of having customers, invoices, and other items living in both data sets. Though some software integrates with your accounting system (and is nice if it works correctly), it can also create additional problems where things are not matching up as nicely as you might think. Square is a good example where it could be pouring in hundreds of transactions a day and if there is something off or not matching up, it can be a nightmare to try and fix. Some prefer to avoid that by using the accounting system as their general ledger and would use the other software as their main hub to operate the business and interact with their clients, track their receivables balances, etc.

Undeposited funds – When you "receive a payment" from a customer, the undeposited funds could be the default account where it goes in your accounting system. Xero doesn't actually use this account. For simplicity and as an appropriate function for most small operations in which the owner is receiving payments and making deposits, the default can typically be set to the bank account in which you'll deposit the funds to (which is what Xero does). Generally, the undeposited funds account is used for deposits in transit, but if that transit period is basically the time it takes you to go to the ATM, it might make more sense to not use it. The typical issue is that a small business owner will record payments and it shows up in the undeposited funds account, then later on they go through the bank sync section and maybe it doesn't match up with a particular transaction in undeposited funds and gets called income again, which double counts the transaction. Or perhaps the amount received from a customer differs from the invoice amount, so the transaction doesn't match up, which would get caught in the bank reconciliation except transactions that go to undeposited funds are not in the bank register; plus, not all small business owners do a bank reconciliation. So, use it or don't use it, but if you are going to use it, you'd want to make sure you are using it correctly and every deposit is getting tied out correctly.

Sales Order/Quote/Estimate – This is basically a pre-invoice that you'd send to a customer to establish an understanding and get approval, and upon completion of work or delivery of goods, it can be converted into an invoice. This is a non-posting entry meaning that creating an estimate doesn't by itself increase revenues or assets or have an impact on the financial statements. Some software provides the ability to generate a report of open sales orders or estimates which can be a good source of information as to a business' revenue pipeline.

Sales Receipt – This is like invoicing and receiving the payment all in one, rather than sending an invoice and later receiving the payment. If you perform a service and get paid that same day, you can use this function to reflect it. The software would typically still enable the ability to convert an estimate or quote into a sales receipt much like it would an invoice.

Credit Memo – Credit memos can be generated to reflect a return of goods or services from a customer, or a reduction in a balance due for whatever reason. Credit memos would be like creating a negative invoice and would generally get applied at a customer level, so many accounting software systems would require you to manually apply this credit (like a payment) to outstanding invoices or issue a refund.

Statement – A statement is a summary that can be generated and sent to a client showing activity like invoices and payments. Generally, you'd send a statement to a client to remind them they still owe you money and to show the total amount they owe you if you have multiple invoices outstanding. Neither QBO or Xero have the ability to "receive payment" against a statement electronically that would automatically get applied to the open invoices per the statement. It is a highly requested feature for both systems as it is very frustrating. If you have multiple invoices for a single customer, they can send you a check and you can manually apply to multiple open invoices, but for electronic payments, it is generally one invoice to one payment (currently). If you want to give your customer the ability to pay their entire balance electronically, you'd likely have to create a phantom payment on one or more invoices and edit the one invoice you'll resend and add the item with the description indicating a consolidation of invoices into the one invoice.

Expenses and Accounts Payable

Accounts payable (AP) can be an annoyance, which is why AP automation is popular. And if you deal with AP, it would definitely be worth looking into. Both Xero and QuickBooks has bill pay functionality or deep integrations. The mechanics and functionality would also be similar. For the most part you'd get a dedicated email for your AP department, which might be entrepreneur@bill.com or something like that. For vendors that you have online accounts with, you can update the notifications and settings to automatically send invoices to your new inbox, which would be like the bank sync in that it reads the documents and makes suggestions about vendor, expense accounts, dates, amounts, etc. It is relatively painless to do a quick review of your billing inbox, accept recommendations to convert the documents to a bill (it attaches a copy as well for your records) and is now in your accounts payable. You can also click and pay them without writing a check. There is typically a fee with such a feature, but again, time is money, so not having to manually open an envelope, enter the bill, write a check, and mail it is worth it. Even if you are primarily a service-based business but utilize subcontractors, if you tell them they have to email you an invoice to get paid, they will and you can go through that process for your subcontractors as well. The best part is that it tracks subcontractor payments, making it a lot easier to do your 1099MISC filing at the end of the year.

Write a Check or Create an Expense – Same impact as going through the bank sync and coding transactions, it records the expenses and deducts the amount from the bank account balance per your books. Occasionally, people create expenses or checks that never actually clear the bank, so if you are creating expenses or checks in your system, they should ideally be associated with and be able to match to real transactions as they get synced with the data feed from the bank. In the case of the check, there may be a period of time before the check clears the bank, which is where reconciling the bank accounts becomes an essential internal control function.

> For cash and accrual taxpayers, when you write a check and send it, the expense is recorded when you record the check, even if the vendor doesn't cash the check until later on. Some try and write as many checks as they can near the end of the year to get as much deductions for taxes as possible and may also try to not deposit the checks they receive until after the year end. However, just because you decided not to deposit the check doesn't mean that it is not income for tax purposes; the IRS would apply the "constructive receipt" doctrine, which means it's income when you received it, not when you decide to deposit it. Similarly, if you are pre-paying for expenditures or acquiring inventory to use for the next year, there are rules in place that could come back to bite you if you are artificially reducing your taxable income.

For the small business and self-employed, things like accounts payable are not as commonly utilized tools, especially for businesses that don't have inventory or just pay all bills with the credit card right away, avoiding the confusing process of tracking who you owe money to. Nonetheless, the tools and capabilities are there for a reason. You may not have a credit card, deal with a reasonable amount of inventory or other working capital needs, or are working on larger projects where you can't simply swipe a card and pay it off.

Bill – A bill is a document or invoice you receive from a vendor representing an amount due to that vendor for goods or services received. In accrual accounting, it would be the point in which an expense is deemed incurred. It increases expenses and also accounts payable (amounts you owe vendors). For cash basis, the expense would get recorded when the bill is actually paid.

Pay Bills – This is the action taken to record the payment of a bill. If you employ some of the bill pay automation features, there would typically be the "pay bills online" option, which electronically remits money. Otherwise, as a manual process, it is similar to writing a check—on the books it reduces the accounts payables balance as well as the balance in the checking account, and when the payment clears the bank account, it would ideally match up with the transaction entered. Alternatively, I have seen clients that write the checks, and when they clear, they would match against open bills, but it can get pretty messy depending on how frequently you pay bills, update your accounts payables, and reconcile accounts.

Purchase Order – A purchase order is an order for goods or services you send to a vendor who would then send you a bill upon completion of work or delivery of goods. This is a non-posting entry, so it would not impact the financial statements. Most software would be able to convert an open PO to a bill, as well as provide the capabilities to see a report of open purchase orders, which can provide a view of upcoming cash outflows.

Vendor Credit – A vendor credit is created when you return goods or otherwise receive a reduction in outstanding balances you owe to a vendor, sort of like a negative bill. This could be for damaged goods, a discount applied after the fact, or several other reasons. In the accounting software, this would likely be credited at a vendor level and may need to be manually applied to open and outstanding bills or be converted into a refund you receive from the vendor.

Payroll

Payroll can create some challenges for bookkeeping. The major accounting platforms do have payroll modules built right into their products, though there is typically additional charges for such features. If set up correctly and there are no changes in any of the settings, it can work great. This is especially true with direct deposit since the money leaves your bank account to pay your employees, taxes, etc. and it matches up with the real transactions that sync from your bank account.

There can be issues that arise, like if you have employees that demand a paper check and maybe you wrote the check for a few cents different than what the actual amount should be. Or it was correct but when the check was put into the ATM, it read it slightly differently and debited your account for an amount that differed from what is in the bank register. Now things don't match up so nicely and you are spending a bunch of time trying to reconcile the account. What do you do to fix it?

Additional issues can arise when settings or rates change, like if you got a new bank account, or the unemployment agency adjusted your tax rate. If not updated correctly, these systems will continue using the previous settings and creating transactions in old accounts and tax payments won't match up or will be less or more than what the true liability is, generating notices and potential penalties from the government all because you thought everything was working. As such, the true cost of the DIY systems for payroll is that you are required to be more engaged and active in monitoring the payroll compliance aspects. QuickBooks and Xero won't call you to ask if you got an updated rate notice, but some of the major payroll providers like ADP and Paychex might.

Using a payroll provider for payroll can outsource some of the headache and potential liability since they absorb the filing and paying requirements. They have a vested interest in making sure they stay on top of it and occasionally on top of you to get them what they need to keep you in compliance. They even have features for the employee that wants that paper check where they mail that person a check but the process on your end is identical as if it were direct deposit. The money goes to a trust account and the employee cashes a check from the trust account. That way there isn't the variance or the outstanding "net check" liability that is on your books; you run a payroll and all the funds and costs associated with payroll is taken out of your account at that time, no lingering liabilities.

The integration between a payroll provider and your bookkeeping system isn't always nice and neat. I've seen many clients that don't have any integration and simply call the debits from the bank account either wages or taxes. Though that does get you close, it is better to have the actual amount of wages, taxes, and other items booked correctly, especially as it will flow to the tax return and the IRS will compare wage and tax amounts with payroll tax filings—if there are significant differences, it may wonder why. The less reason you give the IRS to take a look at your books, the better. As such, setting up the integration between the two systems is a good idea. In general, it is just creating a journal entry for payroll to account for the wages, taxes, insurances, and other items and match those entries against the real transactions that debit your bank account. You can manually enter the transaction after each payroll—that generally requires a bit more knowledge and understanding of journal entries, but it can be done by the layperson if they know what reports to look at.

Inventory and Cost of Goods Sold

For a business that is in retail or relies upon product sales as their primary source of revenue, controlling inventory is essential. Sure, we don't want it just walking out the door, but this is important also from a critical financial, strategic, and operational perspective. Since retail businesses have so much value tied up in inventory, and as a general rule, one would want as little as possible without stock out (running out when a customer wants to buy it), inventory management systems are the stock in trade for this segment of business operations. The point of sale (POS) system and inventory management systems are generally tied together, so that when someone buys something, it gets removed from inventory, alerts when reorders are necessary, completes purchase orders, etc. If you don't do retail and have less than a couple dozen items to track for inventory, then the basic systems (QBO and Xero) can handle it. But if you need a POS system, you'd need to get that separately and can integrate with the core products as neither of them have a POS system as part of their product.

Don't sweat the small stuff. Sometimes I'll see clients that spend an inordinate amount of time tracking inventory or other items with little dollar value compared to other sources of income or expense. In such cases, I'd advocate to apply some judgement and discretion based on materiality, especially if you are trying to keep track of how many paint rollers you used at this job versus that job. If it is not a high value, and you will regularly consume and restock and employ it with your jobs, then it is often better to just expense it for the most part and keep it simple. You can have non-inventory items that you sell if you want to incorporate more detail or have separately stated items on your sales receipts or invoices. So, if you charge for X number of hours of service, you could also charge for X amount of items (cleaning supplies, lubricants, paint rollers, etc.). You may want to evaluate your sales tax requirements with respect to selling or charging the customer for some of those items, though.

Inventory is an asset. As such, when the company buys inventory, it is not an expense but a reallocation of your current assets—your cash goes down and your inventory goes up, but the net income stays the same. As you sell products, the cost associated with the product gets expensed as you sell it through "Cost of Goods Sold." When you sell an item, you have income and expense in the same transaction—your cash (or accounts receivable) balance goes up but your inventory valuation goes down. The functionality with respect to the bookkeeping systems would use the same mechanics discussed with respect to purchasing and payables; the big difference is the timing when expenses are recognized.

The big takeaway is that if you are in retail or need to track inventory, do it right, spend the money on a POS and inventory management system—one that can integrate with your core accounting product would be preferred.

Job Costing

Both Xero and QBO have the ability to do job costing, which they both call projects. Job costing is an important and very valuable source of information, especially to the contractor working on multiple jobs at a time. What it does is assign costs to a project so that one can determine what the job's profitability is. So, if you are working on some remodeling projects and had subcontractor payments, materials costs, permits and licensing, etc., you can track it to the project as a direct cost. If you did a good job with budgeting and bidding, then you should have sufficient profit after job costs to cover your overhead costs like office expense, rent, marketing, etc.

Manage expectations. I've seen a good amount of contractor businesses that want to do job costing and expect the software to do it for them—they end up being disappointed when it doesn't. In order for job (or project) tracking and costing to work, the business owner, or an employee with sufficient knowledge of the financial workings of the company, would need to do much of the "costing" part. Since QuickBooks and Xero might see Home Depot, Menards, or checks written to a subcontractor, they can't really discern which project it might go to if any at all. Additionally, with employees that work on multiple jobs, it can be a challenge to apportion the employee's time to the various jobs. Not that it can't be done—if this kind of output is desired, it typically requires commitment to understand the tool and develop procedures and protocols on making sure expenditures and other costs get associated with projects, especially if they are billable.

Is It Billable?

Being billable (generally) means you get to charge your client for it. Examples would include things like travel reimbursement, job materials, permits, labor and subcontractor payments, etc. What is or isn't can depend on what your engagement with your customer is. If you do a fixed fee engagement with everything included, then nothing would be "billable" since the total invoice is already determined. You may have a project base fee plus direct expenditures, or there could also be a budget that requires a change order before exceeding, etc. In such cases, you'd track your expenditures as billable to the client, and when you go to invoice the client, the system would prompt you to include any unbilled time and expenses up to that point. If you have "track billable time and expense" turned on in your accounting system, the option for the billable checkbox would be available and you could associate to a customer for billing later on.

Sometimes it can get a bit fuzzy if you are allowed allowances instead of direct expenditures, like for mileage or per diem, in which case what you spent at the gas station or Holiday Inn wouldn't match what you are allowed to bill the customer. In such cases, it would be easier to not mark those specific expenditures as billable in the bank sync and other areas and manually add a line on the invoice for the allowance amounts. That way, it doesn't mess up the bank register or other data in order to bill the client a different amount than the actual expenses evidenced.

> In certain industries like accounting and other professional services, there can sometimes be a distinction between billable and chargeable time. With more and more fixed fee and value-based billing models being employed, firms don't always "bill" for the time they employ, but as time and labor is the biggest cost center for professional services, they would want to track time in order to determine efficiency and other aspects. As such, billable time would be tracked but wouldn't necessarily be considered chargeable against the client—it would be more of an indication to determine how many "billable" hours an associate used, what the realization rate for those billable hours are, etc. Billable in such cases would more represent the practical capacity and utilization of time available for the production of services and not necessarily time that will result in greater billings, but depending on the engagement, billable time could actually be billable.

The Dreaded NSF

Yes, it happens, and more often than you might think. If you do business with consumers or small businesses, occasionally they run out of cash and the money they paid you gets recalled by the bank for non-sufficient funds (NSF). It is quite an annoyance as it oftentimes creates several additional transactions. Once the funds hit your account, it'll show up on your bank register and reconciliation; you can't just "undo" the payment in most cases. Generally, the best way to handle it when it happens is to create an item that could be called "NSF" or something along those lines. You may need to create an item and an account—the income account you create might be called "chargebacks and returns" or something similar. When the transaction taking the money out of your account comes in, if you do the "track billable time and expenses," you can mark it as billable and charge against the client. You could potentially add the NSF fee the bank might charge you as well, and re-invoice and collect. If you don't track billable expenses, you'd still associate the debit in your account as "chargebacks and NSF" (or whatever account you decided on) and would re-invoice the client for the item "NSF," which would get associated with the same chargebacks account. If there is a delay between when you generate the invoice that corrects it and the final payment comes in, then there would potentially be a variance between cash and accrual reporting for that account.

Retainers and Prepaid/Unearned Service Revenue

When you receive a customer payment in advance of performing a service, delivering a product or earning your commission, you have a retainer (or unearned service revenue, customer deposits, client trust liability, etc.). There are different ways to handle it. For some that are in particular industries like law, there are strict requirements by their state bar or other authoritative guidance on handling client funds and segregating it from other funds; banks have specific IOLTA accounts (Interest on Lawyer Trust Accounts) that are for just that. When you have to segregate the funds, it does add additional steps to the process of managing retainers. Since most of your merchant accounts will be tied to your main checking account, when you receive funds that need to be segregated, you'll have to manually transfer to the IOLTA account. If payments are for both retainer and fees earned, now you'll need to reconcile the retainers to figure out how much to transfer over and back. It is enough to sprawl a whole software specialty.

I've seen some small law firm's set up two completely separate sets of books: one for the main firm, and one just for the IOLTA. They'd never commingle. A client pays just retainer or just fees or they would bill the "retainer" account and transfer money manually. A pain in the you-know-what, but the state bar makes it seem like blasphemy if they are even one dollar off.

If you don't mind your accounts receivables having a negative balance, then you can receive payments from the customer without any corresponding items or charges, which creates a credit balance for the customer. When you invoice for work performed, you can apply that payment/credit to the invoice, which will reduce the final amount due and everyone is happy.

You may want to account for it where the customer deposits liability actually shows up on the liability section of your balance sheet, or maybe you want to invoice your customer for the retainer so they can pay electronically. Generally, an efficient and practical way to handle such funds is to create an item within your accounting system. The item can be called something along the lines of "Client Retainer" (or customer deposits, etc.). Then have that item be associated with a liability account, which could be called "client retainers" (or customer deposits, client trust liability etc.). When you use the item in an invoice or sales receipt, it will increase your liability for client retainers and correspondingly increase accounts receivable (or cash). Though the liability account is aggregated on the balance sheet, one can generate a report that is sorted by customer to reconcile the total retainer balance with the individual customers that make up the account. Of course, one can also create separate items and accounts for each client, as well as sub accounts for the IOLTA account, which I've seen such guidance from state bars. The result would be more or less the same, but it gets really cumbersome and messy when you have hundreds of asset and liability accounts to account for retainers.

With the items and accounts set up in your accounting system, when you earn the retainer and invoice your client, you should be able to use the same item with a negative amount to convert unearned to earned. For instance:

First Invoice (Retainer collection)
Retainer $100
Balance Due $100

Second Invoice
Fees Earned $100
Retainer   ($100)
Balance Due $0.00

> Cash versus Accrual – As an additional note, upon collecting deposits or retainers, when you generate an invoice with a "retainer" item, for accrual basis it increases your liability and accounts receivable, even though you haven't received the funds yet. When you receive the funds is when it would impact the cash basis reporting. I mention this as it can create some frustration in certain cases. For example, say you invoice your client to collect a retainer and then perform work, but the client doesn't pay the original invoice. Now you have earned fees, which you could bill against the retainer, but the client never paid the first invoice. If you look at retainer balances under accrual accounting, it'll show they have retainer balances, whereas cash basis wouldn't. Plus, it can be confusing to the client if you have more than one invoice open and due at a time.

Prepaid Expenses

Sometimes there may be situations that call for accounting for prepaid expenses. In a sense, it is like inventory, where it becomes an expense when you consume it. It can encompass all sorts of things like prepaid sales commissions, insurance, trade show and advertising deposits, project work in process, etc. Accounting for it may require journal entries in order to account for the usage of it. As an example, say you bought a three-year insurance policy for $36,000; the payment would get associated with prepaid insurance, then you can set up a recurring journal entry that would credit (reduce) the prepaid insurance by $1,000.00 per month and debit (increase) insurance expense, which would impact both the balance sheet and the P&L reports.

In certain cases, like if you are engaging a contractor to work on a project that requires a deposit, the payment can get associated with a vendor. This may look weird when you look at your balance sheet because it can create a negative accounts payable until you enter the bill for the vendor upon completion of the project, apply the payment to the bill, and restore the normal balance for the liability account. Much like with handling prepaid deposits from customers, you can create items and accounts and create bills and expenses that would get associated with asset accounts instead of having abnormal balances in your accounts payables.

Fixed Assets and Depreciation

When you buy an asset for the business that has a useful life of more than 12 months, you may want to account for it as a fixed asset. I say "may" because like all things, the materiality principle should apply. Just because a $10 trash can will last you five years, doesn't mean you should call it a fixed asset. Everyone is different. Some would consider anything over $500 as a fixed asset, and some $2,500. If you are going to write it off for tax purposes and strive to have your books to match your tax return, then applying that concept would make sense. You may still need to account for it as a fixed asset and depreciate it for tax purposes where you depreciate the whole cost, but as a general rule, not making things more complicated than they need to be is preferred.

Depreciation is the process of apportioning the cost of a long-lived asset over its useful life in a methodological way. As it pertains to accounting, it would generally be in a manner that attempts to best match the economic reality of the enterprise to reflect the cost of operating the business, though many small businesses either don't really track fixed assets/depreciation or do so on a tax basis, which generally is more aggressive at the cost recovery in order to incentivize consumption and economic activity.

Titles – Can you depreciate something under the entity when the entity doesn't have the title in their name? Yes, you can. Though it would be preferred that you maintain that separation between your personal life and the business, there may be situations like with vehicles that are in your name personally, but you use for business and want to deduct the costs or depreciate the cost of the vehicle. There are different ways to handle it, which will be covered later.

Most often, I see journal entries as the main way to account for fixed assets and depreciation. Depending on what it is, you may be able to avoid the journal entry. For instance, if you bought a nice copier for the office with your credit card, then the credit card transaction could get coded to fixed assets instead of an expense account. The journal entry allows you to account for aspects that are not always accounted for in the real transactions that hit the bank account. Like if you buy a car and put $5,000 down and have a car loan payable for the balance. Here, you'd need to do a journal entry to get the correct balance in the fixed assets and liabilities.

Depreciation – Depreciation is an expense and is entered as a journal entry as well. There are different ways to account for depreciation. You (or your accountant) might only enter depreciation for the end of the year when the tax return is prepared. You could schedule the recurring journal entry to account for depreciation throughout the year as well. Generally, when you don't have to report your financial statements to third parties, it's not as important to account for it in the interim as depreciation is a non-cash expenditure, and for most small businesses, cash is king.

Accumulated Depreciation – The other side of the depreciation journal entry goes to accumulated depreciation, which is a contra asset account. A *contra* account is an account that is associated with a parent account to account for things like depreciation or allowances. Contra accounts have a normal (debit/credit) balance that is opposite of the parent account. So, in the case of accumulated depreciation it would be a credit balance and the journal entry to account for depreciation would be a debit to depreciation expense and a credit to accumulated depreciation. When you look at your balance sheet report after making such an entry, it should look like:

Fixed Asset	$10,000
Less Accumulated Depreciation	($4,000)
Total Fixed Assets	$6,000

Split Transactions

You can split a transaction like an expense, check, or bill. What splitting does is associate a single real transaction with multiple categories. When you create an invoice or a bill, you can add several lines for various products or services, which can potentially impact how that transaction is apportioned out (like if a bill contained supplies and subcontractor payments, etc.). For transactions in the bank sync where there may not be a bill, expense, invoice, or other transaction associated with it but accounts for more than a single category, splitting it allows for the segregation. Maybe the $704.26 you spent at Target the other day wasn't all just for office supplies, so you'd split it to break it out further. A common example would be for loan payments that typically contain both principal and interest; I'd advise using the loan amortization schedule to split such transactions and not just guess how much of the payment is interest versus principal.

Journal Entry (also Adjusting Journal Entry) – This is the process of manually putting in a transaction (containing debits and an equal amount of credits). Occasionally, a journal entry is required as the information that the system has from bank syncs and other sources may not contain sufficient details to reflect the economic reality of the transaction; hence, the manual journal entry would be used to account for it correctly, like with accounting for prepaid expenses, depreciation, loan interest amortization, etc. Many of the third-party software programs that integrate and sync with your accounting system will be using a journal entry—like with payroll, ADP or whomever will add in the journal entry which would encompass wages, taxes, net check amounts, etc.

> Not all debits and credits are created equal. A debit may increase one account type while decreasing

another account type; each account type has a normal balance (like having a normal PH level of being an acid or a base). Here is a short list of basic account types and their normal (increasing) balance and the corresponding decreasing entry type.

Account Type	Normal Balance (increase)	Entry to Reduce Balance
Asset Accounts	Debit	Credit
Contra Asset Accounts	Credit	Debit
Liability Accounts	Credit	Debit
Equity Accounts	Credit	Debit
Revenue Accounts	Credit	Debit
Expense Accounts	Debit	Credit

PERSONNEL

There are so many compliance requirements around payroll that one basically has to hire someone just to hire someone. I don't mean they are hiring an employee just to do payroll, but more so in the sense that entities typically engage a third party like ADP or Paychex to handle payroll since there are so many complexities with it.

Do you need payroll? Before just going out there and hiring people, the first question should be whether you need to hire people. I've seen countless small businesses struggle with this. The story typically would go like this: Small business is growing and the entrepreneur is getting overworked and stressed out. They want to keep growing because they got a tiger by the tail here, so they hire someone expecting to develop a copy of themselves, only to realize that employees are not the same thing as entrepreneurs. They don't just read your mind or understand what the value chain of your organization is. So, the business owner tries and tries to train and develop this person, but fails, and now is spending a ton of time they don't have and money paying for someone that is not reducing stress.

What went wrong? For starters, it is unlikely to find someone with the same passion, motivation, ambition, creativity, competence, drive, etc., as you. Secondly, when you are going to bring on an employee, you should have a reasonable expectation of what that person is going to do and how much they'll actually be doing. Getting a 2,080-hour resource is expensive and employees don't fit in the same "wear every hat" mindset or skill set that a proprietor does.

Job Description – When you are thinking of hiring an employee, you should write a job description that can provide a basic outline of what is entailed. With a job description, you should be able to determine what the going rate for that position is, how much of this resource you might need, and more importantly, determine if you might be able to start off with temp or contracted staff rather than committing to a full-time permanent position.

Family business—another common mistake, fishing within your own circle. Some may have friends and family that may be experienced or have the right skill sets, but more often, it's a bad idea to mix business and family. Family employees can expect certain treatment or perks, and if you hire your nephew and need to fire him for cash flow reasons or because he isn't adding value, it can make those holiday dinners a little awkward when he has to move back in with your sister because you're so heartless. I know there is the temptation. I think the big one is the level of trust—new businesses don't always have the kind of internal controls that larger businesses have, so it seems sound to hire someone who won't rob you blind or blab about what's under the kimono, per se. Better to establish clear expectations for employment with someone unrelated, find the right candidate that's a good fit, and have internal controls to protect your and your customer's data that could be damaging if compromised or stolen.

Contractor or Employee

Generally, the preference is to have someone classified as independent contractor rather than employee to save on taxes and compliance costs. Government agencies can be quite aggressive about worker classification, which the government prefers to see employees to get more tax revenue and have entities absorb the liabilities and risks associated with employment. It's not just the IRS that does auditing in this area; worker's compensation departments and state unemployment insurance agencies, as well as others, will also audit independently on this, so even if the IRS chooses not to audit, that doesn't mean you are in the clear.

There are several factors that various agencies would consider when determining if you have a bona fide employee instead of a contractor. The IRS breaks down the factors into three main categories: behavioral control, financial control, and relationship of the parties.

Behavioral Control
- Type of Instructions – The who, what, where, when, why, and how. If you are dictating how they do the work, when, where, and telling them what tools to use or provide equipment or direction, it is considered more like an employee than contractor.
- Evaluation Systems – Evaluating incremental or interim aspects of a project point more towards employee; evaluating just the end result doesn't support either classification.
- Training – If you are providing training, either up front or on an ongoing basis, it leans more toward employee not contractor.

Financial Control
- Equipment – Significant investment in equipment the worker uses for their services, especially if they work with other engagements would indicate more of a contractor status.
- Unreimbursed Expenses – Contractors would typically have unreimbursed expenses; employees would be more likely to get reimbursed for expenses.

- Opportunity for Profit/Loss – A worker bound to a certain economic reality due to the amount of commitment on an engagement would be an employee indicator.
- Open to Market – Contractors should be free to solicit and engage other contracts and not be isolated to just one contract.
- Method of Payment – Employees are more often guaranteed regular wages or salary based on a period of time (hours/weeks, etc.), even when supplemented by commission. Independent contractors are paid by the job or specific deliverables within a project they are engaged to perform.

Relationship

- Contracts – Just because there is a contract that says a person is a contractor, doesn't mean someone is a contractor.
- Benefits – Providing benefits (insurance, retirement, vacation, etc.) generally would indicate more of an employee relationship.
- Permanency – Contracts are not as likely to be into perpetuity, and contracts that are presumed to continue indefinitely would be more employee status.
- Type of Services – The more a worker performs services in a manner that is integral to the business or acting in an agency capacity to the business, the more likely an employee relationship truly exists.

There are things you can do to provide some protection to maintaining your sub-contractor's classification as contractor. The best course of action would be to engage with a law firm that specializes in labor and contract law. They would ideally be a good fit for writing contracts and structuring the components of the project work to fit. Besides that, tips would include:

- Use contracts that outline the scope of work to be performed, the fee structure, and terms for payment.
- Collect W9 forms (a one-page form that can be found on the IRS's website, basically provides name, address, and ID number for your subcontractor).

- Engage with subs that have their own entity set up and carry their own insurance policies for general liability and potentially worker's compensation.
- Remember that they are not employees, which means they are not supposed to be a 9-5 person in the office doing customer service and available for all sorts of things as the needs arise. They are contractors—you engage them to do specific tasks for specific fees and would more typically be paid by the job and not by the hour (though certain consultants and self-employed professionals do work on an hourly billing engagement).
- For contracts that might require additional skills or training, you could consider having them on as a temporary employee for the period of training, and upon completion, when the person no longer would need direction or supervision, engage in contract work. Though, again, consulting with an attorney would be the best option to ensure compliance with the law.

First Things First

Going from no employees to one is probably the most difficult. It is a big commitment, takes a huge amount of time and money to develop the person, and if you're not careful, it can end up sapping the future growth of the company. Generally, with respect to retail, food service, and other areas with more causal, low-skilled employment, it's not as imperative. However, when your business is in an area with skilled/semi-skilled workforce that expects customary full-time plus benefits opportunities, it can be quite a large obligation for a small business to absorb initially. If you are looking to hire someone that can do all the stuff you don't want to and then some, consider structuring the workload into compartmentalized aspects. There is a wide array of freelance human capital available. Marketplaces like Upwork are built around the gig economy. You can also find them directly if they have their own website to solicit engagements. You just need to know what you are looking for and about how much you might need.

So, if you determine from constructing what your needs are that you are looking for 40 hours a month of support, 20 hours a month of marketing and advertising, and so on, you can fine tune the resources through contracted engagements to more precisely meet your needs without having to take on a full-time employee with all the headaches that come with it. Though the hourly rate for a contractor will often be higher than an employee, you are not paying for idle time or employment taxes and fringe benefits. Further, you have access to potentially higher specialized and more advanced skills within your targeted area of need, and you can terminate the engagement without having to worry about unemployment rate changes or wrongful termination issues.

One of the first hires/contracts might be a virtual assistant (VA), which is like a support staff person that typically works remotely. Not everything can be done remotely, but the more tasks you make accomplishable through the internet, the more tasks that can be readily automated and outsourced. Even with something like opening and processing the mail, one can set up a mail virtualization service that would automatically deposit checks and image all correspondence. With that, a virtual assistant would even be able to "sort the mail."

> Resources like employees or contractors are there to give you back time. But employees don't always have the same construct of what you expect from them. Additionally, the financial stress of having to make payroll and manage cash flow can shift the business' focus towards quantity rather than quality. I've had employees before, and I realized that I wasn't saving any time or money. As such, I decided to downgrade to deliver higher quality services and focused on finding better fitting clients rather than simply more of them.

Professional Service Providers

Many small businesses and self-employed individuals engage with outside third-party service providers to meet certain needs. Everyone's needs are different and their capacity to handle such functions internally can vary widely. Professional service firms can offer a wide array of experience and expertise in specific areas that can add a lot of value to entrepreneurs. Some of the main functions handled by professional service firms include the following:

Accounting – This can encompass a varied degree of services. There are bookkeeping businesses that only do bookkeeping, tax practices that do just tax returns and tax planning, industry-specialized firms that typically only handle a particular profession or industry area, and firms that are more of a one-stop shop for accounting and taxes. The CPA designation, which stands for Certified Public Accountant, is generally seen as a standard of quality that differentiates service providers of tax and accounting services.

Some offer monthly bookkeeping where they keep the books on their end in an isolated system, often based solely on the cash in and out of the bank accounts and don't reflect an accurate accounting of your accounts receivables or payables (which may be just fine for certain business types). For the most part, such services would reflect a cash basis financial statement and flow into the tax return at the end of the year. I generally prefer to control my own set of books (and have my clients control and retain ownership of their books) and be able to see things like outstanding receivables and payables. The collaboration can pose some challenges for certain service providers, but it all depends on what you are looking for.

Bookkeeping functionality can vary depending on what specific requirements one might have. If a person is expected to come in house, sort the mail, enter bills, reconcile receivables and such, it can limit what providers would even be willing to bid on such work. You may need such functionality, but again, the more you can digitize, virtualize, and compartmentalize into tasks that can be accomplished remotely, the greater efficiency and transparency as well as better pricing the enterprise can expect out of that service area. The rates for bookkeepers can vary—some price by the hour, others on a fixed fee, some based on the number of transactions, but most would be comparable.

Mix and Match – You may prefer to do it yourself. If you are confident about keeping your own books and don't really want to get a bookkeeper, but just want to get a CPA to do the taxes at the end of the year, there is a firm out there with your name on it. You may also want to have a bookkeeper only business do the bookkeeping and get a CPA to do the taxes, which is also a very common structure.

A common occurrence I see is the small business owner whose books are "so simple," as they would exclaim, and would either prefer to do their own books to save money or insist upon a very low fee because they are so simple. I have seen quite a few cases in which the clients professed to have super simple books, but when I had a chance to review them, they realized they weren't so simple or were not being done correctly. This limits the ability to provide higher level services for the client if they are responsible for the books and would make the relationship unprofitable for the firm to do them at bargain rates. After being burned a few times, I learned to, as Ronald Reagan put it, "trust but verify," in that I would bid based on what the prospect is telling me but explain that if the scope is materially different, I would adjust the fee accordingly. Though one may assume or feel their books are super simple, there may be more to it than just telling your QuickBooks where to code a few transactions, especially if you are invoicing customers, using purchase orders, estimates, billable time, or any other functions beyond the most basic bookkeeping aspects. So managing expectations is important. If you are convinced you are super simple or not risky, that doesn't make it so; the same would apply to legal, insurance, and other aspects. We engage professional service providers not to just turn a knob but to apply professional judgement and solve problems that are not completely homogeneous, because if it were so simple, then a robot or other canned service would be a better fit to solve the problem and not a professional service provider.

In general, many small businesses (excluding the tiny businesses that generate less than $50,000 per year) can expect the total amount spent on bookkeeping/accounting/taxes/payroll combined would be in the 1-3% of your gross revenue. So, a business with revenue of $250,000 might expect to spend $2,500-7,500 in annual fees to cover all their bookkeeping, accounting, taxes, and payroll services.

Taxes, Tax Planning, and Consulting in general – Many small business owners are often looking for more than someone to just do the books. Taxes, and more specifically tax planning, are sought after though not well articulated in developing a relationship with an accountant. As technology and other factors have created a more standardized pricing model for certain productized offerings (like bookkeeping, tax return preparation, etc.), there is pressure to price accordingly, but know that just because one is a lower price doesn't mean it is the better value as you may not be comparing apples to apples. I think of the airline model, where carriers continuously reduced aspects of the ticket price in order to win on price, which is why many flights nowadays may have you pay to select your seat, pay for a meal, pay for wi-fi, pay for checking a second bag, and so on. Not that accountants are airlines, but when you are looking for a packaged solution, make sure you understand what is included in the package. Does tax planning mean they will reply to your email when and if you ask them a question or is there a structured process and clear deliverable on that subject, how many hours per year of consulting is included, etc.? Sometimes it can be difficult to tell, and if a firm isn't really doing much beyond bookkeeping and tax returns but is charging you for consulting and other higher value services, what you may really be buying is fairy dust.

There is a sweet spot where you are not paying for fairy dust and also not getting the bottom of the barrel. You can have a phone conversation or initial consultation with more than one CPA or ask for referrals. Generally, there should be the feeling that it's a good fit, that the person will solve the problems you need solved, and that they aren't gouging you in the process.

Legal – There comes a time when we may need the services that attorneys provide. Many law firms have areas of law they practice in. This would be your first consideration. What is the legal issue at hand? Is it contracts and UCC (Uniform Commercial Code) law, labor and employment, real estate and lease issues, etc.? If you engaged an attorney to set up your entity, bylaws, operating agreement, etc., they would likely be the first stop in the journey as you would already have some rapport with that person. For the most part, lawyers are pretty good about knowing what their limits are and would refer you to an appropriate resource. With a good rapport already established, they would ideally want to see you get good legal services and not just feed some referral network, but nonetheless you'd still want to do your due diligence. Review the firm's website and information available about the practicing attorneys. How long have they been in practice? Do they handle litigation in their practice? What areas of law do they practice? You could even go so far as looking up public records that would be available on the state bar's website to see if there were any corrective action taken against the firm or practitioners. Additionally, reading some reviews from real people in the world whether it be on Yelp, Google, or another source can potentially provide some more insights.

You don't have to wait until there is a legal issue to consult with an attorney. I know they can be expensive, but preventative action is far cheaper than corrective action. Examples would include employment contracts, subcontractor agreements, leases, or other documents regarding business the entity is engaged in. Having an attorney review and prepare legal documents before they are put to the test is one of the best insurance policies money can buy.

Marketing and Advertising – There is big business in marketing and advertising. Seems like as soon as your business has a phone number, it keeps ringing, and on the other end is a company that mentions the word "Google" and how they'd like to help you fix issues on your site. I generally found that, with respect to advertising and marketing, the entrepreneur needs to take an active role in building their vision and brand. One should be proud of their website and business cards. If you treat them as just an afterthought or footnote, what does a prospect think? Relying upon a third party to build some side website using canned templates and keywords that don't articulate what makes you stand out may not be what one is looking for. Not that they are all bad, but be warned there are many less than ideal operators and, in my experience, the less the value of service, the more aggressive they are and will call and email and make unsolicited attempts to get you on their hook.

There are well-established and legitimate firms that can be engaged with respect to branding, marketing, and advertising, including your web and social media presence. There are different sized firms, some of the more established and reputable firms may be geared more towards the regional and mid-size businesses. Like other professions, there are one-stop shops than can do much of everything. On the other end of the spectrum would be one-man band operations that can do specific objectives in a more limited fashion. In general, the more reputable and sizable the company, the more expansive and capable their services are and correspondingly the fee structure. Some do have a billing structure that is derived from your ad spend if you are spending enough. So, if you spend $3,000-5,000 per month on your advertising budget, a firm could potentially absorb that function and, using their expertise for placement, keyword selection, and other factors, get you a higher quality result for about the same amount of money because they know how to make ad spend dollars go further and collect a spread on the efficiency.

Besides the professional service providers in the space, there are, of course, the less professional services that offer the canned website with stock photos and advertising campaigns that generate poorly qualified leads, all while costing a bunch of money for limited results. Usually operated out of India in some war room, they mention that they are a "Google preferred partner," but when you ask if they are Google, they continue to mention Google without actually admitting they are not Google. Maybe others have had good luck and it could potentially work for the businesses like an HVAC company that does emergency call service. With that type of business, the customer is under duress, so whatever pops up first with correct spelling on the webpage and appears reasonably close to them will get the call, and once you get the call you have the job. I am by no means trying to throw emergency service HVAC companies under the bus, but there is a great deal that goes into building a solid business of reputation, referrals, and repeat business that clickbait wouldn't help build—just making an example.

Insurance – We all need insurance. However, what policies and coverage can vary. Having an agent you trust is insurance in itself—though we need insurance we don't need excessive coverage. Not all insurance companies or independent agents carry all policies, but with a good agent, they can underwrite policies that are in their wheelhouse and connect you with those who can meet the rest of your needs. Many policies are on marketplaces, so for the most part, the prices of policies should ideally be similar, but it doesn't hurt to get quotes occasionally to double check. General liability coverage for a small business is typically quite affordable and would be under $1,000 per year for a policy that can provide $2 million of liability coverage depending on the size and scope of business. Some landlords for commercial space require such policies. If you are part of a profession that has a society or association, there will oftentimes be a partnership with a company that can underwrite policies for its members; the preferred rate on such policies can sometimes pay for the cost of membership alone. As I've mentioned before, self-employed individuals will also generally need to get life insurance and long-term disability insurance as a minimum level of risk mitigation for being self-employed.

Be honest with your insurance agent. The last thing you need is to be denied a claim because you were not completely honest in your application. Though some policies have a statute of limitations for false application information, like two years in some cases; so, if you die within two years and they determined that you were a smoker and you failed to acknowledge that on the application then they could say you lied and refuse to pay. It is better to have the right coverage based on honest application information from the onset of coverage. Otherwise, it could just be the perception of coverage, and a misperception of actual coverage is not a wise strategy for proper risk mitigation. And this is what insurance provides—an assumption of risk that a particular event may occur, however unlikely, for if it does, you wouldn't have the wherewithal to absorb the burden of the event alone.

Freelance – The list for professional service providers, companies, firms, etc. could go on and on. We live in an exciting time of decentralization and multitudes of marketplaces that creates many more options for the entrepreneur than ever before. Small businesses and the self-employed are now able to access in much finer granular fashion the services that best fit the needs they have along with providing the potential to serve in such capacities as a self-employed entrepreneur. What is really exciting is that many of the functions available through freelance contractors are ones that just a few years ago were basically inaccessible for the typical small business. Finding someone with particular skills is difficult by itself and even more so to find that person who is also willing to work for only eight hours a month. Now with freelancing and especially marketplaces for freelance resources, the ability to find that person exists, enabling a small business to get the marketing, HR, or other services in proportion to their needs.

Freelance resources would include things like web development, marketing and advertising, virtual assistants, supply chain management consultants, and just about anything else you might be able to imagine. Getting a freelancer is typically going to have a higher price tag than hiring a part-time employee—they need to make money too, after all. That higher price tag is nothing compared to the cost of getting a full-time employee and hoping they can do the bookkeeping, marketing, HR, bill pay, support staff, and everything else because unless you found a magician, you're not likely to find that superstar for an affordable price.

Employment

When you have employees, even if it's just yourself, you have to worry about payroll. It wouldn't be so bad if it was just paying people, but it isn't. With payroll comes all sorts of additional compliance tasks such as the following:

New Hire Reporting

Within a short period of time after hiring an employee (20 days), employers are required to remit new hire reports. It is designed to identify people that have child support, non-custodial parents, detect welfare and unemployment fraud, etc. Most payroll platforms would handle this reporting. For employees that you have with a garnishment, there is separate termination reporting in order to let the applicable agency know not to expect any more garnishment payments.

Worker's Compensation Insurance

Many states exempt self-employed, owner/officer businesses from having to cover themselves for worker's compensation coverage, but check with your state's requirements to be sure. Some states even allow you to have a couple employees before coverage is mandated. Generally, conservative states would be laxer about mandating coverage while the more liberal states are more aggressive. Worker's compensation covers workplace injuries (medical bills as well as disability payments to workers unable to return to work for a period of time). The rates for coverage can vary based on your industry. Office and clerical businesses would have a much lower rate than roofers or other industries that have a greater likelihood of injury. The traditional model was to underwrite a policy based on estimates as far as amount of payroll and worker classification types, which would be paid up front or over a fixed period of time. After the policy period, an audit would be done to reconcile estimates with actual payroll data.

The worker's comp audits can be pretty straightforward or very disruptive depending on the circumstances. If you engage with subcontractors and issue a good amount of 1099s, they'll likely want to see that each one of your subs had coverage or coverage exemptions during the period they were a sub, that you collected their documentation, and issued 1099s in addition to your payroll data. The main reason for this is when it comes to worker classification, the classification could come after the fact and could possibly assign liability to your policy. As such, carriers are sometimes a bit nervous about engaging companies in more injury-prone industries with practices that rely upon subcontracted labor. Sometimes it may be unclear as to the subcontractor question, and maybe there was a junior producer that sent the policy through underwriting without doing the due diligence, gives you a great price, and doesn't even mention subs; be careful and ask to make sure. If they are going to charge you more for the policy, it is far better to know up front and make a decision than to have an audit conducted where they show you the fine print. You may end up paying more anyway, but now don't have a choice in the matter.

Many of the large payroll providers like ADP, Paychex, and Intuit/QuickBooks have pay-as-you-go policies, where they partner with a third-party broker that underwrites a policy from a company like Travelers or another major carrier. The policies and pricing should be relatively the same since it is in a marketplace. The major benefit is no major upfront investment in the policy, and ideally, you'd be able to avoid the audit as well since the payroll data is shared after each payroll which then translates into the premium that you pay alongside your payroll. Sometimes there are hidden fees where they may charge you a convenience fee to remit and share the data. It could be as high as $15 per payroll, so again know what you are getting and all the details. They'll get you all warm and cozy thinking you've saved a bunch of money not realizing that you are paying like $400 a year just for them to share information with themselves.

Though the pay-as-you-go option would be preferred, sometimes they decline to underwrite a policy. This could be for a number of reasons associated with how they calculate risk. Maybe they anticipate a greater likelihood of subcontract labor in your industry, or there could be a claim from the past that has your name on it. I've also seen them declined because the principal officer's credit rating was too low. Sometimes it doesn't take much for them to perceive a deviation from the cookie cutter mold. If that happens, you'll just have to get a policy directly from an insurance company that can underwrite it.

Unemployment Insurance

This is similar to worker's compensation insurance in that many states allow for owner-officer closely held businesses to be exempt from coverage, but check with your state to be sure. Additionally,

SUTA (which stands for State Unemployment Tax Act) is an insurance, and the costs an entity pays are correlated to the risk associated with a particular industry or employer if a history exists. Industries with higher turnover and layoffs would have higher rates. Employers that establish a history of stable employment will often see their rate decline, and likewise when entities terminate employment that results in unemployment claims, the rates and costs go up for that entity.

Unemployment insurance can be expensive. I've seen it cost over 8% of gross wages. The amount of wages subjected to the insurance (taxable wage base) can vary between the states as well—some follow the federal (FUTA) wage base of $7,000 and other states can be as high as $45,000. Though your state may have a higher taxable wage base, the rate may be lower due to greater amounts of contributions (broadening of the risk pool). When employees reach the base for the year, the rest of that year no longer has unemployment insurance contributions for that employee.

Federal unemployment insurance works in conjunction to the state's unemployment programs. If you are exempt from state unemployment insurance coverage, that doesn't mean you are exempt from federal unemployment taxes which is 6% of the first $7,000 of wages paid to an employee. When you have state unemployment insurance, you get a credit for federal unemployment, so unless you don't have state coverage, you wouldn't pay 6% to the feds. Federal unemployment is reported annually, and most state unemployment reporting is paid and filed quarterly.

The S corporation is a very popular structure for the small operating business. One of the requirements is paying reasonable compensation to the owner/officers of the business. That reasonable compensation—which is often reported through traditional payroll mechanisms—can be exempt from some state's unemployment programs. Not having state coverage increases the amount paid for federal unemployment insurance with little benefits. Not that we plan to fail, but at least if you elect coverage from your state's unemployment agency, there is the possibility to file a claim and collect benefits if things don't work out for your business. There are special rules for the self-employed and owner/officer businesses like a waiting period after a business termination or requiring coverage for a number of years before being eligible, but it may be worth it. Do the math. It may actually be cheaper to get state coverage (after considering the FUTA credits) and have actual coverage rather than to pay $420 a year for nothing.

Unemployment can be a bit of a bear in that it's not as smooth sailing as the normal payroll taxes but is directly attributed to payroll. Some states have consolidated agencies (or at least the appearance of consolidation) to make it easy to set up, file, and remit payroll and unemployment taxes. Other states have completely separate agencies with outdated web interfaces and restrictive mechanics on just getting things set up to have a third party like ADP handle the process—and not all payroll providers are good about onboarding unemployment. Like many aspects of small business compliance, it is up to the business owner to verify that their compliance aspects are being handled correctly. Outsourcing payroll and payroll-related compliance aspects is generally an efficient way to handle it, but double check after a quarter end to make sure that the fed, state, and unemployment returns and taxes are being filed and paid.

Social Security and Medicare Tax

These taxes are imposed both on employer and employee. Currently, the social security rate is 6.2% for employee and 6.2% for employer up to the wage base (2019 wage base is $132,900). Medicare is 1.45% for employee and 1.45% employer and there is no cap.

The Additional Medicare Tax is imposed on individuals who earn over $200,000 and households over $250,000 per year. Employers are required to withhold the 0.9% employee-only tax when wages exceed $200,000, even if their household won't actually be liable for the tax—as in, their household income is under $250,000 but above

$200,000 from one spouse's wages.

Federal, State, and Local Withholding

Though many small businesses feel like these are business taxes when they pay them, they are employee-only taxes. It is individuals pre-paying their federal, state, and local individual income tax along with the employee portion of social security and Medicare obligations through salary reductions called withholding. The employer is responsible to remit these taxes after payroll in a specified time period. Your deposit requirements are based on the volume of taxes withheld and paid within a period of time—the larger the volume, the more frequent the payment. State and local deposit frequencies would generally follow the federal requirements but could deviate a bit.

Other Taxes

Depending on your state or jurisdiction, there may be other taxes that are imposed on payroll. For instance, California has SDI (State Disability Insurance) tax, which is a deduction from employee wages, and ETT (Employment Training Tax), which is an employer-paid tax. So be cognizant of additional potential obligations. Most states are pretty good—when you go to set up a relationship and register for tax types, they would typically have FAQs and other quick tips and suggestions to help ensure proper compliance. After all, it's their job to educate the public for an efficient process of tax collection and promote future compliance with applicable laws and regulations.

Trust

Payroll taxes are no joke, especially withholding taxes (those deducted from employee's checks) as those taxes were paid by employees and technically held in trust by the entity to pay to the government on their behalf. Mishandling funds, borrowing against the funds for cash flow purposes, not making the deposits on time, or simply making the funds disappear is a big no-no. The IRS and other agencies will assess massive penalties for failings in this regard, and having an LLC or other entity will not protect you from the liability, even if the business goes belly up. Officers and owners of the business at the time of the failings can and will be assessed personally liable, and these debts can survive bankruptcy, so play it safe. If you can't trust yourself with the trust tax money, then I'd suggest utilizing a payroll provider that impounds the taxes for you so it's not a temptation.

Impounding

Many payroll providers will impound tax obligations when you run a payroll. Impounding is collecting the payroll taxes from the entity at the time of a payroll run and paying them when they are due, which could be a few days to a few months from the time the money was collected. For most small businesses, having the taxes taken out at the time of running a payroll can be smart because it removes most of the liabilities associated with payroll that would otherwise creep up on you, probably when you don't have the money in the bank to pay them.

Burden Rate

Now that we have an idea of what the liabilities associated with payroll are, we can do some simple back-of-the-envelope calculations to figure out the burden rate. The burden rate is an allocation of indirect costs that can be added to direct costs like "gross wages" in order to determine what the actual cost to the business is (or the fully burdened rate). As an example, say you want to hire an employee at $15 per hour, and let's say that your worker's compensation rate is 3%, your unemployment rate is 3%, the social security rate is 6.2%, and Medicare is 1.45%. This would give us a burden rate of 13.65% (if you wanted to be conservative, you could round up to 15% or another logical number). With that, we could calculate what that employee fully burdened would cost:

Gross Rate of Pay $15.00
Burden Rate   13.65%

Fully Burdened (Gross Rate * (1+burden rate)) = $17.05 per hour.

This was a very simple example, and the rates for various aspects could be drastically different. Additionally, benefits like retirement contributions and health insurance would also need to be added in if the business provides them. Understanding the true cost of employees is critical. Many small business owners get overwhelmed by the excessive burden that is imposed on the employer beyond just paying people. This is a contributing factor to why many businesses prefer to just give someone a 1099 and avoid much of the taxes and compliance costs.

Pay Types, Frequency, and Overtime

There are several ways and forms of compensation—the most common types are hourly and salary. Hourly, as the term implies, computes pay based on the number of hours worked at a particular pay rate. Salaried employees are paid a fixed amount of compensation over a period of time, regardless of the amount of time or effort exerted for their employer. Salaried employees would generally fall within the "exempt" category, meaning they are exempt from overtime and minimum wage requirements. Generally, you must pay exempt employees over certain thresholds. States can have differing amounts for what they consider sufficient to be exempt, so you'd want to verify that the employment would meet the requirements to truly be considered exempt.

When an employee is not exempt, they would be "non-exempt" and would of course be eligible for overtime (1.5 times the hourly rate) for hours worked over 40 hours in a workweek. However, workweek doesn't necessarily have to correspond to a calendar week. If your work week is Thursday to the following Wednesday, then that would be the time period calculating overtime.

Many small businesses work with part-time employees but have regular and fixed scheduling. A common question I get is whether you can have a salaried part-time employee. The short answer is no, but you could of course just have an hourly (non-exempt) employee with a regular fixed schedule. It is a method referred to as a fixed salary for an agreed-upon set number of hours worked per week. It would not change the exempt/non-exempt status, so there could be complications. However, if the employer and employee have a clear understanding and expectations, then having employees that regularly and consistently receive the same number of hours a week through payroll should be acceptable.

Payroll frequencies can of course vary—biweekly is a very common schedule (every other week), but one could also do weekly, monthly, or semi-monthly (twice a month, usually something like the 15th and the last day of the month). The semi-monthly frequency can get a bit fuzzy in calculating overtime pay since the pay period encompasses more than two weeks. The general rule is to calculate whole weeks (seven-day periods, as in Sunday to Saturday) as normal, so anything over 40 hours for a non-exempt employee would be considered overtime. For the weeks split between two pay periods, you'd calculate the total number of hours. If there are over 40 hours, then there would be overtime due to the employee and would typically be paid on the later payroll.

As an illustration, let's say the pay date of the 30th is in the middle of the workweek that goes from the 27th to the 3rd of the following month, and the employee worked 44 hours for that week. The four hours of overtime would get picked up and paid out on the payroll for the 15th of the following month. It can still get a bit unclear, like if the first week had 28 hours worked in the first three days, would those get paid out as all straight time? And if the overtime is determined on the over 40 rule, then yes, it would be all straight time and the next payroll would have 20 hours of straight time and four hours of overtime. Some states may require overtime for any time worked over eight hours in one day, so check with your particular state to ensure compliance with not only federal labor laws but also state ones.

Commissions, Bonuses, and Profit Sharing

Providing commissions and bonuses can create incentives to increase productivity, morale, loyalty, retention, and esprit de corps among others. How one structures such compensation can vary between industry and between employees within the same industry or company. For commission-only employees, there are exemptions to the FLSA (Fair Labor Standards Act) rules. One can structure minimum salaries or draws to satisfy the minimum amount allowed for exemption. They can also engage outside salespeople (who don't work at one's regular retail location), among other strategies. Generally, commissions would be based upon transactions like sales.

Bonuses likewise can take many forms. Some can be quite complex with different tiers, pools, algorithms, and other aspects. Generally, the desire is to align employee behavior with the strategic goals and vision of the company and to reward employees for their loyalty and continued engagement in the enterprise. For the most part, in smaller businesses, bonuses are completely discretionary and can be as arbitrary or transparent as desired. Bonuses can have required minimum withholding requirements—many employees are shocked when they see 25% is withheld for federal taxes. Your payroll platform should be able to calculate it correctly, and many are capable of doing a net-to-gross bonus as well (where you indicate you want to give your employee a net check of $5,000 and it runs the bonus payroll, which might cost the company closer to $7,500). Explaining it to the employees would be left to you to blame Uncle Sam.

Profit sharing, like bonuses, can be discretionary as well. For employee distributions not in a retirement account, it would be treated much the same as a bonus. Generally, profit sharing is done in logical allocations like number of hours worked in the period or gross wages paid. So, if you are doing a $10,000 profit sharing payment amongst several employees with an aggregate number of hours worked of 5,000, it would be $2 per hour worked. One could also base it on gross wages in a similar fashion. Additionally, 401k and other retirement plans also allow for discretionary profit-sharing contributions to employee's accounts, which can be a nice feature since the company gets to deduct the contribution for taxes currently and the employee can defer the taxes to be paid until retirement. The retirement plan allocations of profit sharing do have more rules from the IRS and DOL, but they would generally be with the comp-to-comp method (employee's total compensation divided by company total compensation times profit sharing total equals employees profit sharing contribution).

When you have commissions, bonuses, and/or profit-sharing arrangements, it is good practice to document the arrangements to avoid confusion and frustration. Of course, creating documents and written communication to employees can also encumber the company to commitments, even if it was meant to be less formal. So, if you tell employees that X amount of productivity will result in X amount of bonus and you don't pay that out, some may take that as breaking promises. Likewise, if one states that 10% of profits will be distributed to employees in bonuses once a year and you had a profit, it could potentially create some legal risk. Many small businesses are very informal with their bonuses and profit sharing and remain guarded about affixing large commitments to the entity. Even if commission structures aren't written, if there is a consistent calculation and then you change the formula, that too can be considered a reduction in compensation allowing employees to potentially walk off the job and collect unemployment.

Reimbursements and Allowances

In the world of the small business, it is often an understanding that employees may have to use their personal vehicle, cell phone, home internet, or other personal expenditures for the benefit of the business. Employers are not required to provide reimbursement or allowances to employees, though employees could also refuse to allow the employer to use their personal assets for the business—but then they may not be seen as being much of a "team player." As the terms imply, a reimbursement is a direct recovery of expenditures incurred by the employee. The employee would submit documentation to substantiate usage and would receive reimbursement from the employer. Reimbursements are not taxable income to the employee and the employer does get to deduct the expenses. Reimbursement can be in the form of mileage, typically using the IRS standard mileage rate guidance that is published every year (58 cents per mile for 2019). With cell phone and internet use, there isn't a standard rate per minute or gigabyte of data utilization.

Generally, with respect to phone/internet, an allowance of a fixed amount would be appropriate.

The main consideration with allowances and reimbursements is the determination that the policy falls within an accountable or non-accountable plan. The requirements for an accountable plan are not too stringent. For the most part, if you communicate to your employees how it works, require that there be a business connection with respect to the expenditure in question, document and retain substantiation for the expenditures, and not provide allowance or reimbursement in excess of actual cost or utilization, you should be good to go. A non-accountable plan is one that doesn't provide those controls, and in such cases, the allowances would generally be considered income to the employee. Entrepreneurs don't always want to spend time collecting receipts. Though it is not typically a large amount, if audited and you don't have an accountable plan, the auditor could throw out the expenses and create additional assessment for you later on, which could add up to substantial amounts in the aggregate.

Sometimes small businesses have a non-accountable or informal arrangement to give an employee a few hundred dollars a month in lieu of having a health insurance plan in place since health insurance is generally unaffordable for many small businesses, but they still need to attract and retain quality people. Those payments, like with other non-accountable plans, would be income to the employee. As such, the easiest way to address would be to create an additional pay type in the payroll platform to include the addition of a fixed amount of taxable income on top of their hourly or salary pay.

The main takeaway is that if you're not interested in maintaining an accountable plan, then consider committing to a non-accountable plan in which the employees would have taxable income but would still be getting reimbursement—as long as someone has taxable income in a transaction, it is a lot easier to justify the tax deduction for the business.

Benefits for Employees

Small businesses that have fewer than 50 full-time equivalent (FTE, as in the total number of hours divided by 2,080) employees generally are not required to provide benefits to employees. Some local jurisdictions do mandate sick leave and other aspects, but otherwise, it's at the discretion of the small business owner to decide what kind of compensation and benefits package is right for their business.

Setting up benefits for your workforce generally would involve third parties in order to make sure you are doing it correctly. Plus, with the technology and scalability of today, it can often be cheaper than trying to do it yourself. Benefits can cover a pretty wide swath of different aspects, from retirement accounts, health insurance, cafeteria plans with pre-tax spending accounts, transit passes, or other perks. Many of the benefit options for small business owners will be covered in the benefits chapter later on. It can get complex, as you might imagine. Things like insurance may have shared cost allocations between employee and employer, some are completely employee funded like pre-tax spending accounts, and some can be completely employer funded but may still require the recognition of taxable income like with life insurance over a certain threshold.

It takes many small businesses years before they are able to set up and maintain certain benefits for their employees. A common one that is relatively inexpensive would be a SIMPLE retirement plan— some have no fees to set up and administer to the employer and assess small fees at the participant level per mutual fund in their own accounts. The employer simply matches their 1-3% of the employee's gross wages if they are participating and deposits the funds on a regular basis. Combine this with some allowances or "in lieu of health insurance" payout, and a small business can still be a competitive employer. Beyond that, an employer would typically want to seek outside assistance through their payroll platform or others to get the kind of benefits package that fits their needs for attracting and retaining employees.

At-Will Versus Contract

Most states follow the at-will doctrine, which holds that without a contract, employment can be terminated by either party for almost any reason. Employment contracts, whether in writing, orally, or potentially implied, have certain conditions that would be required in order to terminate employment without it being considered a breech. If you are going to use employment contracts or non-compete agreements (which restrict employees' ability to use information gained from employment, solicit your clients, or other restrictions during and for a period after employment), you'd want to have an HR professional or lawyer assist in drafting the documents so that the execution matches your desired expectations. There has also been a good amount of at-will agreements where employees are restricted with certain regards but are not provided protections or additional compensation beyond the job offer itself. But again, when you are engaging actions that you intend to have legal standing and protections, don't just Google or Rocket Lawyer your way into a lawsuit—get professional advice first.

> Just because you have a non-compete or an at-will employment agreement doesn't mean that you are rock solid untouchable. In many jurisdictions, non-compete agreements with employees, if written too restrictively and not providing any consideration or assurances for the employee, can potentially be thrown out by a judge as many feel that non-compete agreements restrict trade and economic activity, but it would depend on the facts and circumstances.

Termination

It happens. Sometimes you get a dud and you need to fire someone. It's not fun for either party, but if it needs to be done, then rip that Band-Aid off and move on. Even if the employee has earned their termination, it seems like less friction to dismiss the person without cause, which does enable them to collect unemployment and potentially increase your UI rate. Large businesses with HR staff and legal teams can afford to go the distance and have all the evidence they need to substantiate terminations with cause.

The entrepreneur doesn't always have the time to have an unemployment case be heard by a judge and present facts and findings with the he-said-she-said circus; they have a business to run while the newly unemployed seems to have plenty of time. Ideally, such situations would be avoided; but if you are going to contest an unemployment claim because you terminated someone with cause, then you'd want to show that policies and procedures are in place and followed, along with documentation to substantiate the "cause" someone was fired for.

Many payroll platforms and HR solution sets have termination checklists so that if you have to give them their final paycheck within 24 hours, pay out vacation or other fringe benefit accounts, etc., you'll be able to make sure your bases are covered for the most part.

Human Resources

Human resources (HR) can encompass a variety of functions. As many small employers don't have the resources to have a full-time, part-time, or even a contracted resource for HR, many payroll platforms like ADP, Paychex, and others have add-on services to provide some of the services commonly affiliated with HR departments. These include standardized job descriptions, offer letters, onboarding and termination checklists, employee handbooks, and more. Employee handbooks, which can be in digital or paper form, are a set of company policies and procedures as it pertains to employment relations—some provide additional language such as mission, vision, and corporate cultural components. Written policies and procedures of this sort can create obligations as a side effect; like if it says that employees must be given a written reprimand prior to dismissal or other procedural aspects, then it creates the requirement to follow the doctrine. Many of the handbooks that are created through platforms are mix and match, plug and play, constructed with canned content like dress and appearance, tobacco use policies, EEO language, etc.

Zenefits, which is a platform all on its own, has a growing user base. The basic components of the platform are free, and they have an ever-increasing knowledge base and HR resource library. They are built with the goal of selling benefit functions for small employers, like transit passes, vacation and sick time management and requisitions, insurances, flex spending accounts, and more. They broker the policies and generate income from such products, which allows them to have a mix of free and paid services. They do have a payroll module and are working to expand functionality to all states. They have some great features to look at, such as employee onboarding and document retention—you can create employee offer letters that are digitally signed by the employee and they would self onboard and complete their own w4 and direct deposit information which eliminates steps in the process. Though it may not integrate with all outside payroll platforms, it is still a nice function to have a low-cost HR suite that retains documents and manages certain aspects for you. They even have deep integrations with the Google G-suite, so once an employee is onboarded, their email and provisioned access to certain systems would be centrally managed through the platform, and likewise upon termination could be deprovisioned centrally, providing the capability for immediate isolation of the potential threat to the enterprise.

HR functionality bridges more than just job descriptions and vacation policies. As a small business grows, their needs likewise grow with it. Demands to recruit and retain skilled people for the business requires competitive compensation and benefits, which may require HR functions to have the right package in place. Even if there isn't an HR department or an outside HR provider, the business would still have HR functions when they have employees, such as performance reviews, periodic compensation analysis, job description evaluations and revisions, and more. Though it would be nice to set it and forget it, a business in motion should strive to continuously improve its process and be committed to the programs and policies it puts in place or it can be difficult to maintain employee engagement. While small, an out-of-the-box or canned solution set might be a good fit, but as one gets more than a couple employees, it would be wise to consider enhancing the HR aspects to evolve with the business.

Payroll

When you need to run payroll to pay people, get a payroll solution. Don't try to use a spreadsheet and manually remit taxes and filings—just don't do it. Really, with the options available, there is no compelling reason I've heard not to use them. Some banks even provide a payroll platform for virtually nothing if you have deposit or credit relationships with them.

There is no shortage of payroll providers out there, the largest being ADP. The main accounting software packages for QuickBooks and Xero both have payroll modules onboard with the software, which can be a good place to start the evaluation. If you use an accounting software and don't have benefits or need other auxiliary functionality, that can be a reasonable solution at least initially. However, as mentioned previously, not all providers are the same and if you want to outsource the liability and responsibility over payroll taxes, you'd want to make sure the features and functionality fit your needs.

Paying employees through direct deposit is the standard practice and it makes life so much easier to just take the money electronically and be done with it. Sometimes there are employees who don't have a bank account. Checks may also be needed for things like child support or other garnishments as payroll platforms don't always have the ability to electronically remit to every agency electronically. All the payroll platforms have some form of paper check functionality. Some tell you how much to write a check for, while others will mail you the check for your signature and you then hand it to the employee. There is also the option with some for direct drafting of checks that go directly to the employee, so you don't have to write a check but it is still drawn on the business bank account. Another alternative is where the checks are drafted from a trust account, so the money is taken out of your account at payroll and clears the trust account later on.

Once you have a payroll platform you are committed to, many of the processes will be pretty similar with respect to onboarding. You'd set up your bank accounts, input the employee data and pay rates, payroll schedule, and you're off and running. Then, every payroll, you'd key in the hours (or it would import from a time and attendance app or plugin) and run the payroll, which would take money out of the business bank account for wages, taxes, etc. Then, after the quarter end, you may be prompted to click a button to acknowledge or sign payroll tax returns to electronically file them; same with year-end returns and you're pretty much set.

Most payroll platforms provide electronic access to pay stubs, so you wouldn't need to print pay stubs every two weeks. Employees can access, download, and print the stubs themselves if so desired. Many providers also offer the option to deliver a hard copy of the W-2 to employees as well. Though they may charge for the feature, it is a nice time saver to use—otherwise, you can print and hand or mail a copy of the W-2s to employees to ensure they receive it. When providers do it, the envelope would typically have the statement "Important Tax Return Document Enclosed" which extends the mail forwarding timeframe if the employee moved and ensures it gets returned to the return address if unable to deliver.

BENEFITS

Being an entrepreneur can come with certain perks. Part of the lure of self-employment is the added benefits that you get by being an entrepreneur. Though there are many aspects where one might get tax deductions for things that would otherwise be personal, it is important to not let the tail wag the dog. Being deductible doesn't make it a good investment. Even though you get to "write it off," the savings is primarily based on your tax bracket which may be less than 30%. You'd still be spending the other 70% in real cash outflows, so I advocate for doing what is in the best interest of your long-term goals both for the business and personally. When opportunities come up that are a good investment for the business and you just so happen to enjoy it, then it's a win-win, but don't go buy an SUV in December solely because you want to reduce your taxable income.

Medical

The self-employed health insurance deduction is an "above the line" deduction for the entrepreneur. Above the line refers to deductions that are allowed in arriving at adjusted gross income; below the line would be deductions that may be allowed from adjusted gross income, as in itemized deductions. The preference is to get as many above the line deductions since you'll still be able to get the standard deduction from adjusted gross income. We'll cover taxes more in depth later. The premiums paid for health and dental insurance along with portions of long-term care insurance are deductible up to the amount of self-employment earnings.

The deduction is after determining your net income/loss for the business, so it is not a business deduction but a personal deduction that is allowed due to your self-employment income source. The copays, office visits, prescriptions, and other out of pocket costs are still deductible but only as an itemized deduction. Since the new tax reform was implemented, this means that you'd need to itemize deductions and exceed 7.5% of your gross income before the first dollar of medical cost becomes deductible. Due to this, if your business is expected to generate sufficient net income, it would be more beneficial to select plans that provide better overall coverage with less copays and out of pocket costs since the premiums for the self-employed are fully deductible and the out-of-pocket costs are only partially potentially deductible. The more you can shift to the definitely deductible category, the better, even though the cost of the monthly premiums would of course be higher.

The deductibility of health insurance premiums includes the self-employed (sole proprietors and entities that are taxed as sole proprietors), partnerships (not as a limited partner, must have self-employment income), and as an S corporation, but the rules for the S corporation are that the premiums should be included in the wage income from the corporation. Even if the corporation doesn't pay the premiums directly, the company can still reflect the cost of the premiums as an increase in the shareholder's W-2 income. If the shareholder paid the premiums out of their personal funds, those payments would, in a sense, be reflected as capital contributions to the entity (need to be at least on paper reimbursed by the entity). With the increase in wage income, it reduces the net income that flows through to the shareholder while the increase in wage income provides a corresponding increase in personal income, so it is a wash until it gets reflected as the self-employed health insurance deduction similar to if you didn't have the S corp entity. I know, it is a bit convoluted to do such roundabout mechanics in order to get a tax deduction, but those are the rules for getting the self-employed health insurance deduction for an S corp owner/officer.

Don't want to pay a ton of money up front for health insurance premiums? Another option is to couple a high deductible health plan (HDHP) with a health savings account (HSA). The rules are that you are covered by a HDHP, can't have a non-HDHP or be enrolled in Medicare, and you cannot be claimed as a dependent on someone else's tax return. A high deductible health plan, as the name implies, has higher deductibles. A deductible is the amount that a participant (covered person(s) under the plan) is expected to pay before the insurance will pay a claim. The minimum amount that a deductible must be in order to be considered a high deductible changes every year. With the HDHP, you can now open up an HSA and make contributions, which are deductible, above the line, and the funds can be used to cover copays, out-of-pocket costs, deductibles, and other medical costs. With an HSA, it is not a use-it-or-lose-it fund—if you don't spend all the money in one year, it remains in the account for medical expenses later on. The HSA contribution limits change every year as well. There is also the additional catch up contribution for those 55 years of age and older. If your household doesn't use the medical system that much, the HSA and HDHP option can provide adequate coverage and a good amount of tax savings, along with accumulating savings for medical costs which can be applied in the event there is a medical need.

Retirement

Saving for retirement is critical and is one of the best deductions out there, especially if you are in a higher tax bracket. The best thing about retirement contributions is that not only do you get to "write off" the cost of the contributions, you get to keep the money. Sure, when you take the money out in retirement, it is taxable income, but the time value of money is a valuable thing. Your tax bracket today may be different from your tax bracket tomorrow. Tax rates change, the amount and character of income and its related taxability changes, and of course the cost of your lifestyle today may be very different than in retirement. Generally, the expectation is one's household needs will be less in retirement, considering that one would have less mortgage payments, less costs associated with transportation, food, wardrobe, and other work-related expenditures, etc. Though some aspects may increase in retirement, such as healthcare, the overall expectation would be a lower cost of living.

It is very difficult to determine which way tax rates might go in the future. If tax rates go up, it is possible that even with a reduced amount of income later on, the effective rate could be higher than when the deductions were taken. Roth investment vehicles allow investments to grow and be withdrawn in retirement tax-free, though the contributions do not provide the current benefit of a tax deduction, so you'd be using after-tax dollars for the contributions. Effective tax rate changes are a risk, but don't let the mere potential of not getting a steal of a deal deter you from saving for retirement. It is far easier to save for retirement when it has the added benefit of reducing your current tax burden, but one can usually allocate a portion to traditional (deductible) and a portion to Roth (non-deductible) vehicles to alleviate concerns of potentially higher tax rates to come. There are options one can take alongside traditional retirement plans, such as life insurance policies and investments in real estate among others, to supplement income streams and diversify cash flow sources along with enhancing the ability to mix and match taxable and non-taxable income to help mitigate and manage taxes in retirement.

Of course, a small business or self-employed individual is not required to set up, fund, and maintain a retirement plan. If the IRA contribution limits are sufficient for your needs, then you could just do that, which is the most simple and painless option. However, if you want to put more than $6,000 (2019 limit) per year into a retirement account, then you'll need to set up a plan to provide the vehicle for increased capacity.

For small businesses and the self-employed, there are four main retirement plans: Simplified Employee Pension (SEP), Savings Incentive Match Plan for Employees (SIMPLE IRA), Self-Employed 401(k), and a traditional 401(k). Yes, there are several other retirement plans that exist like 403(b), 457(b), and Deferred Compensation plans among others, some of which are a part of a legacy from traditional defined benefit plans of the past. Defined benefit plans are plans that provide for a benefit in retirement that is based on factors like years of service, high earning period, and other aspects that are not dependent upon the amount of assets accumulated by the employer or employee. Since the 1970s, there have been much less private sector pension plans due to increased scrutiny and funding requirements placed upon them after the government was basically on the hook for bailing out underfunded plans when companies went through bankruptcy and left pensioners out on a lurch. State and local governments were exempted from the additional requirements as can be seen from certain state's pension plans being very much underfunded. Depending on circumstances, it is still possible to set up cash balance and other defined benefit plans, which can potentially provide for hundreds of thousands of dollars in deductions and wealth accumulation in a single year. Generally, such circumstances are limited to a pretty small pool of entrepreneurs like lawyers, architects, and other small practice type businesses that have highly compensated proprietors of a certain age and have sufficient and regular cash flow and reserves to meet such continuous obligations.

Additionally, there are a couple plan types that can be set up but wouldn't be a logical choice given the other more typical plans. The MyIRA is one that can be set up which basically allows employees to allocate a portion of their after-tax net check amount into a Roth IRA that goes into the government "G" fund which is very low risk and low return. Once a MyIRA account gets to $15,000, it has to be rolled over into another Roth IRA account and it has the same contribution limits as a Roth account and doesn't provide an option for employer contributions—as such, it would make more sense for employees to set up their own Roth accounts and skip the MyIRA process altogether. Additionally, there is a SIMPLE 401k plan, but that has the same contribution limits as a SIMPLE IRA plan and comes with additional compliance requirements, so one would be better off just having a SIMPLE IRA or an actual 401k plan as there wouldn't be much benefit to choose a SIMPLE 401k plan. As such, the focus for most small businesses is on the four plans previously mentioned.

Saving for retirement is extremely important, yet in my experience, many small businesses are not doing so. Especially considering that many small businesses choose to be structured as an S corporation in order to save on employment taxes, those employment taxes would have eventually contributed to a larger social security benefit later on in life, so curating your wage and profit income to reduce the amount of your social security taxes today does have a potential downside tomorrow. At a minimum, you should strive to put into retirement the amount you're saving on employment taxes as a result of your entity structure, and possibly more. Your older self will definitely appreciate your younger self's decision to start saving.

One of the biggest factors in small business retirement plans is the presence of common-law-employees, which is a non-owner, non-spouse. When you have employees and want to set up a retirement plan, the rules are basically that "what's good for the goose is good for the gander," in that it becomes a bit more difficult to have a plan that is extremely generous to the owner without also being very generous to employees. I've never seen it where an employee was willing to take a lower wage amount in exchange for much larger retirement contributions either. Generally, the wage is what the market forces determine it should be, so when you add in very generous retirement plans, the burden to the entity and the perceived value to prospective employees would not be in line with actual market conditions. It is quite difficult as it is for the small business to remain competitive with pay and benefits, and so the main conclusion is that if you have employees, plan on having more traditional retirement plan options that receive a majority of the funding from employee deferrals rather than employer contributions or profit sharing.

SEP – The Simplified Employee Pension, also commonly known as the self-employed pension, is one of the most straightforward retirement plans out there. As far as simplicity, the SEP is about as easy as it gets: typically low to no administrative fees, no filing requirements, flexible annual contributions, and simple calculations for determining contributions. SEPs are employer-funded, meaning there is no employee contribution (though individuals can still contribute based on regular IRA rules).

The employer funding is discretionary, which provides some flexibility. If it's not a good year for the business, it can decide to skip the SEP contribution. Due to the fact that the employer funds contributions, most small businesses that have employees other than themselves and relatives typically wouldn't choose the SEP. For a small business owner, if you wanted to make sizable contributions to your own retirement plan, it requires that the same allocation be applied to other eligible employees. There is the possibility to have a SEP for a couple years after getting an employee and excluding the employee, but check with your financial institution or fund custodian to verify if that is desired.

The SEP can be a good option for the self-employed, especially when the tax status is as a sole proprietorship. They can be set up and funded after the year end but before the due date for the tax return, which provides some after the fact tax reductions, and with the extended period of time can also help with cash flow since the self-employed could potentially have until October of the following year to fund contributions for the prior year while still enjoying the deductions in the prior year. The contribution limit is 25% of compensation up to the annual max for defined contribution plans ($56,000 for 2019), although for the self-employed sole proprietor, the calculation works out to be 20% of the net profit less the deduction for half the self-employment taxes to determine the max. So if you made $100,000, the max SEP contribution would be about $18,500.

SIMPLE – As the name implies, SIMPLE plans as very simple and straightforward. For the most part, it is a collection of individual retirement accounts that is funded through employer and employee allocations. Many investment companies, for instance Vanguard, don't charge anything to the entity for establishing or maintaining the plan, but do assess annual fees at the participant level which may be on a per-fund basis. This means if an employee wants to have 10 different funds in their IRA, then they'd have a higher maintenance fee than an employee who just wants one. The employer contribution can be 1-3% of each eligible employee's compensation, with either a match of 1-3% or a contribution with or without any employee contribution of 2%. The employee can elect to defer up to $13,000 (2019) from their wages, ($16,000 if over 50 years of age).

The SIMPLE plan was designed to provide an alternative to the more complex 401k plans and alleviate the need for non-discrimination testing and annual tax return filings. No annual filing is remitted for a SIMPLE plan, though the employer is required to fill out and maintain a copy of the annual contribution form that sets the contribution rates for the next year (although many small businesses probably don't fill out the form or make changes very often).

For a business that has common law employees, the SIMPLE plan is a great tool. It is very cost effective—for the most part, the only cost is whatever is elected to be the company's contribution and that contribution goes into the employee's accounts and not spent on administrative fees to maintain a complex 401k plan. If you don't plan on putting more than $13,000 or so into your own retirement account (potentially double if your spouse is an employee as well), then the SIMPLE provides a great vehicle for your retirement planning goals as well as a decent benefit option for employees.

Self-Employed 401(k) – Pretty much all of the investment companies out there have a self-employed 401(k) plan, which may be called other synonyms but should have very similar features. It combines the benefits of a traditional 401(k) plan with an aggressive profit-sharing component. Because of its unique benefits, it is generally not available when the business has common law employees as it no longer would be sufficiently simple to avoid the "highly compensated" and "non-discrimination" rules that come with a 401(k) plan, but with just owners and their spouses, it is probably the best option available. Generally, there is very low cost for set up and administration, and as a 401(k) plan, it would have many of the same functions as plan adoption agreements, annual form 5500 filings and so on. However, with the absence of regular employees, the compliance aspects can be more or less automated making it an affordable and very attractive product for the self-employed.

With a W-2, the calculations are pretty straightforward. Employer max contribution is 25% of compensation, which would be what the wage amount is. For those that are taxed as a sole proprietorship, the calculation would be the same as a SEP contribution, which is 20% of the net profit less the deduction for half of the self-employment taxes. But that is just the employer or profit-sharing contribution. As a 401(k), there is also the employee deferral, which is $19,000 for 2019. What this means is that a self-employed sole proprietorship with $100,000 of net business profit could put around $37,000 into a retirement account in a single year and also reduce their taxable income by that amount. The overall max would be the same as other defined contribution plans at $56,000 for 2019, which would include both employer and employee portions.

A popular mechanism for the entrepreneur is the S corporation structure, primarily used as a means to reduce the amount of self-employment taxes. It also provides for the ability to put sizable amounts into one's retirement accounts without having as much exposed to self-employment taxes. From the previous example of $100,000 net profit, if that were structured through an S corporation which had $50,000 wages to the owner and $50,000 of profit, the owner would still be able to put over $30,000 into their retirement account while not having as much in self-employment taxes.

401(k) – As one of the most prominent vehicles out there for retirement plans, the 401(k) enables the kind of features that are not possible with the other plans. This includes features such as minimum participation age, or service requirement prior to eligibility to participate in the plan, along with vesting schedules for profit sharing contributions, and more. Some of the unique features can come in handy, especially when one relies upon a more variable and transient workforce. Having a service requirement allows for the owners to continue to have a decent retirement plan structure for themselves while also potentially avoiding the requirement to set up and contribute to participant accounts that won't be employees for more than a few months. There are safe harbor plans, which ensure compliance with the applicable rules and regulations—such plans may reduce the ability to have vesting and participation schedules, so check with the plan sponsor to make sure the features you want are part of the plan before setting up.

As the 401(k) can get quite complex, much of the factors would be addressed when you go to set one up. Annual compliance includes the annual form 5500 tax return as well as non-discrimination testing and other obligations. Some of the plan sponsors and/or custodians can have their own fees. The sponsor and custodian may not be the same company. The sponsor is the organization that assists in setting up and maintaining compliance, and the custodian would be companies like Vanguard, Fidelity, or others where the participant accounts and the money is actually kept. Where there is a separation, it can occasionally create some headaches when it's time to file the annual reports and compliance tasks as you'd be required to go to two or more different sources to look up reports and manually key in data to complete certain functions. You may also have to review definitions and other aspects in order to have the payroll and other reports segregate aspects as needed, such as who is considered a highly compensated employee, etc.

The cumbersome and complex aspects are what help organizations like ADP and Paychex since they do offer 401(k) and other products, and with all the data and information at their disposal, they can maintain the compliance environment. But a business can also end up being held hostage and on the hook for all sorts of fees they didn't realize, and then have to pay thousands of dollars to untangle the relationship. The "one-stop-shop" payroll providers offer integrated solutions to alleviate the headaches of having to figure out and maintain compliance aspects, though they are not necessarily best in terms of performance, flexibility, or fees.

Simpler is better unless there are strategic reasons for adding complexity. One such reason is wanting to retain key employees, so having a vesting schedule or more complex or differently weighted profit-sharing calculations can incentivize employees to stick around for five years to keep their portion of the profits they've earned. In the absence of strategic justification for complexity, the less centralized, greater flexibility, higher performing and lower fees, the better. Some custodians (Vanguard, Fidelity, Schwab, etc.) can provide for self-directed accounts and offer very low fees at the entity and plan level so employees can decide what investments their retirement funds go towards.

How much education and responsibility the entity has with respect to investment performance can be a bit of a grey area. There have been class action lawsuits against some larger companies that ended up being required to pay into the participant accounts because they didn't provide for better performing fund availability. For the small business, such concerns would be very unlikely, but regardless, avoiding potential conflict by providing higher quality vehicles for employees should be the goal—after all, a 401(k) plan is set up for employees so they'll be happy, stick around, and be more engaged employees, and if your plan gives them the option of what funds they want to have, can they really blame you for not picking the funds for them?

Business Before Pleasure

Business doesn't have to be boring, you are allowed to enjoy things and still get a tax deduction, providing there is a business connection. Of course, there are many aspects that live in that grey area of business versus personal and how much should be considered business as opposed to personal, but having an understanding can help maximize the benefits available. One of the main criteria for business deductions relates to its "ordinary and necessary" use for business, which means common and accepted as well as helpful and appropriate for your trade or business. Arguments could be made for and against just about everything: did you really need paper clips when you already had staples? The IRS would not likely split hairs on such ridiculous aspects, but in certain cases, they could. A more likely challenge might be that you may need the internet, but you didn't need the triple play package with ESPN and Showtime. Use common sense; don't get too greedy with trying to subsidize your personal life and there shouldn't be an issue.

Phone, Internet, Computers, and Peripherals

Some of the common items include your cell phone and internet service. As one needs a phone to operate their business and fewer people have landlines, the cell phone is definitely an ordinary and necessary business expenditure. Having games, apps, use of social media, and so on, does not negate its use as a business deduction. This would include not only the service agreement, but also the cost of the phone itself. For the most part, cell phone for business usage can generally be 100% a business expense if you use it for business.

We can't run a business nowadays without the internet, so it would seem to me that the internet should be 100% deductible, even though you may also use it for Netflix. Since you need it, and because it is ordinary for businesses like yours, the full deduction should be appropriate. That doesn't mean that the TV service or add-ons would be deductible, so if you've got a comprehensive service agreement, I would advise separating the internet service from the less businesslike items. Some incorporate their telecommunication costs into their utility figure when calculating their home office deduction as opposed to splicing their Comcast bill to figure out what was business or not, which may be easier and, depending on circumstances, could yield a similar result.

Much like the cell phone, computers and the related peripheral equipment that go along with it are essential business tools. Computers and peripheral equipment are no longer considered listed property for tax purposes. Listed property as a class gets a bit more attention from the IRS due to the fact that it is equipment used for personal purposes, even though for deductibility it is being claimed for business. The IRS does consider vehicles, along with recreational and entertainment property, as listed property unless it is only used at a regular business establishment. That business establishment can include a qualified home office. The computers, furniture, and other acquisitions for business can provide business deductions that help save on taxes. Depending of the value, if under $2,500 for a single item like a computer, it can generally be written off, even if it is expected to be used for more than a year. Items over that amount for tax purposes can be written off either immediately through an accelerated depreciation method or over time through another allowable cost recovery methodology.

Home Office

A "qualifying home office" is defined as having regular and exclusive use or is the principal place of your business. The home office deduction has always been an area of great interest to many and for good reason: it's like getting a subsidy for your home. The IRS has two main methods for calculating the home office deduction. The more recent safe harbor method is the simplified option, which says you multiply your home office square footage by $5 on up to 300 square feet to arrive at what your deduction is. Though it is simple and easy to use, often the long method can produce better results.

There can be some grey area as with many things, such as if you are a chiropractor and have a retail location with an office where you primarily conduct business, the IRS may apply a higher level of scrutiny for your home office deduction versus a self-employed consultant that doesn't have a commercial office space. Some of the more aggressive cases I've seen were those in which the taxpayer had a regular office and also claimed the home office deduction and would deduct all miles in between since he was going from office A to office B. While going from work location to work location is deductible, commuting isn't, so the IRS would want to see greater justification if they selected the return for audit.

No one likes the idea of being audited. So many of my clients and prospects are terrified of getting audited, and there is a general perception that the home office is a red flag. Though the IRS doesn't publish their audit selection algorithms, in my experience, red flags are more egregious and noticeable than having a home office. One of the biggest red flags is a taxpayer that has substantial income and wealth from one source and then has a small business that just never seems to make any money year after year. As for the home office, as with many aspects that could potentially highlight oneself as a red flag, statistics and reason should be the rule. The IRS and other agencies have business and labor statistics from thousands of similar sized businesses within certain industries. So when a business shows expense categories (including the home office deduction) that are outside of a standard deviation from the pack, it is more noticeable.

Additionally, if you are playing by the rules and are able to document and substantiate your position, then you should strive to have the correct tax liability. You shouldn't have to pay more in taxes for a false sense of insurance that being more conservative might provide.

The long method of calculating your home office deduction is based on an apportionment of expenditures. Though the simplified method may be simpler, in years in which the business shows a net loss, you would need to do the long method in order to carry the expenditures forward to be used in a year with a net income as the short method is a use-or-lose method and doesn't allow you to go below zero. Additionally, as many will be using the standard deduction with the new tax reform ($12,000 for singles and $24,000 for married filing jointly for 2018), using the long method can enable achieving deductibility of a portion of mortgage interest and real estate taxes in addition to the utilities and other direct office expenses. When you itemize your personal deductions, the amount of "business use" would reduce the amount of personal deductions by that amount as we are not allowed to "double-tap" deductions. But when using the standard deduction we don't have to subtract the business use amounts from the personal itemized deductions because we are not itemizing.

SAMPLE HOME OFFICE DEDUCITON CALCULATION		
	Simplified Method	Long Method
Sq Footage of Office	80	80
Sq Footage of Home	1600	1600
Business Use %		5%
Land Value		35,000
Building Value		110,000
Utilities		2,400
Repairs/Maintenance		150
Mortgage Interest		5,100
Real Estate Taxes		1,650
Other Expenditures		250
Rent		
Total		9,550
Business Use Total		478
Depreciation		141
Home Office Deduciton	$400	$619

Depreciation is taking the business use portion of the home's value at the time it began its usage as a home office and deducting it for tax purposes over a period of time allowed by the tax code (39 years). The depreciable value is the building value and not the land value, so you'd need to separate them out. If the current value of your home is higher than your purchase price of the home, then you'd use your purchase price; if your home's value is lower, you should use the lower value as your basis for depreciation. Once you begin depreciating a portion of your home, you'll need to keep track of it, which can usually be accomplished with your tax returns.

Depreciating your home office would not exclude you from being eligible for the exclusion of gain on the sale of your personal residence, though you would be required to recognize as income the amount of depreciation taken. In certain situations, depreciation deductions can be a timing difference where you are deducting costs now and may have to recover those deductions as income in a future year when you sell the house if the sales price is higher than your adjusted basis. If you eventually sell your house for less than you paid for it, depreciation that you've taken may not need to be recaptured (depending on the numbers) and thus a portion of the otherwise non-deductible personal loss has become deductible through the use of the home office deduction. If instead of selling your home you simply no longer use it for business, it is not a deemed distribution or an immediate taxable event, though you would still need to maintain your depreciation records for when you do sell the house.

Not a homeowner? You can still take a home office deduction so long as you have a qualifying home office. As a renter, you would be able to use your rent expense along with the other costs in determining your home office deduction and you wouldn't need to worry about keeping track of depreciation records since you wouldn't be depreciating anything.

S corporation or other non-sole proprietorship entity structure? Don't just pay rent to yourself—that is not advisable. The more appropriate method would be to have an accountable plan. This means there is a methodology pertaining to items that have a business connection, are documented and records are maintained by the entity, and are not in excess of the costs. There too is some grey area as to what is considered a reasonable time to remit such expenditures. For a one-person S corporation, it would be a bit more of an annoyance to have to go through the exercise 12 times when calculating and recording the expense on the company's books once a year before preparing the tax return should suffice. When taking the home office deduction in such a way, keep it to direct costs and avoid trying to get depreciation. Additionally, with items like real estate taxes and mortgage interest, if you itemize your deductions and those items reduce your taxable income, you would need to reduce your personal deduction by the amount the "accountable plan" paid you for such expenditures so you don't "double-tap" the deductions.

Meals and Entertainment

Getting a tax deduction for meals is like using a coupon wherever

130

you go. The new Tax Cuts and Jobs Act of 2017 did make some significant changes to Meals and Entertainment expense deductibility. At a high level, expenses that are deemed "entertainment" are no longer deductible. So, taking a client to a ball game, an orchestra, the opera, etc., would not be deductible anymore. In addition, the cost for transportation, parking, and other ancillary expenditures related to an event deemed entertainment is also not deductible. Similarly, and though it wasn't as much of a change, it is clear that expenses related to membership dues and fees are considered entertainment as well and would not be deductible. This would include country clubs, sporting clubs, hotel clubs, airline clubs, golf and athletic clubs, etc. There are exceptions for professional organizations—those dues (not including the portion allocated to political activities) would be deductible, such as your state or national society of [fill in the blank with your profession], the chamber of commerce, rotary club, and so on.

Sponsorships can be deductible but would need to get apportioned between the fair market value (FMV) of the meal, FMV of entertainment, and the remainder being classified as sponsorship. This could be for things like charity dinners, golf outings, etc. The sponsorship which promotes business is certainly a business expenditure, but the perks received in exchange for the sponsorship need to be subtracted from the total cost of the sponsorship in order to determine the deductible portion.

Meals with clients and prospects are still 50% deductible. The main requirement is that business be discussed during the meal. You should maintain a log to substantiate your meals expenditures. A simple method for maintaining your log can be your calendar. By putting some details into the description of the calendar event, like who you are meeting with, what will be discussed, and the location of the meeting, you are able to provide the record needed for not only the meals expense but potentially the mileage expense as well if you are not using another method to maintain a mileage log.

Deductible meals would include meals with clients, prospects, and coworkers so long as business is discussed. Celebratory meals such as a holiday party are still 100% deductible, in addition to business promotional events such as an open house with snacks and beverages provided. When taking a 100% deduction on meals, as you might expect, a greater level of detail and justification in the documentation should be kept as that would be a prime target in an audit. So, if you have an open house or other 100% deductible event, keep a log of whom you invited and notes on the purpose of the event. Additionally, meals while traveling for business are 50% deductible, and you don't have to meet a client, prospect, or coworker for the meal to discuss business since the trip itself provides the business justification. That 50% would apply to the total of direct costs for meals or to the applicable per diem rate (discussed later).

Travel

Being able to receive tax deductibility for traveling is a nice perk when you can get it. Not as good as a free trip but a close second. What is considered travel can be somewhat subjective. Generally, it constitutes being away from the general area of your tax home for a period longer than a day. Your tax home is the entire city or area where your main place of business or work is located, not necessarily the place you call home. So if you live in one area and work in another that requires you to stay in a hotel during the week and you return on the weekends, the IRS says that your workplace is your tax home and the food and lodging costs associated with working away from your residence are not deductible in that example. Most people live and work within the same general area, which makes it much easier to determine when you are traveling.

As travel contains significant elements of pleasure, there is a high degree of scrutiny the IRS would apply when examining such expenditures. Additionally, there is great desire from the taxpayer's perspective to have subsidized vacations. But keep in mind, there are many rules around travel expenditures—you can't just spend 20 minutes passing out a business card at a coffee shop somewhere for it to be considered business related. I've had clients that put just about everything they can on the business, including vacations. Some may justify it with the argument that "because my wife and I are both employees, it makes it business related." Having a couple that are both employees of the same business, and even if on your trip you discuss business and make elaborate new marketing plans, it doesn't make it what the IRS would consider "ordinary and necessary." Even some of the more legitimate justifications like conferences, shareholder meetings, continuing education seminars, and others can be put under the microscope. The government would likely argue that though elements of business were present, the extravagant and exotic destination was beyond what would be reasonable. This is the main premise for certain aspects: would a reasonable, prudent businessperson who owned the company pay to send you on a work trip to Barbados, not as a reward for good performance but as a normal course of running the business and driving profits?

The main requirement for deductible business travel is to have a bona fide business purpose for the trip. Incidental or ancillary services and functions like entertaining customers or checking emails and typing notes aren't enough for it to be considered a "business trip." A business purpose could be things like taking on a project in a different area that requires you to be at that location, conferences and seminars, continuing education events, etc. There would be some grey area, for instance, if you were to travel to solicit new business and needed to present a proposal and secure the project. Even if you didn't secure the new business, if you maintain records of the business purpose and the activities performed while traveling, it can be deductible if it's in the same line of work.

The expenses that can be included in a deductible business trip would include all the necessary expenses that brought you there and back from the location. This includes airfare, train tickets, taxi and Uber fees, baggage and shipping, car rental, lodging, meals, laundry expenses, tips, and other expenses associated with travel. The IRS, as you might expect, has special rules relating to travel, so keep that in mind. Just because there is a conference or seminar on a cruise ship, doesn't mean the entire cost of the "business trip" is deductible.

Check the allowable rates and compare to actual costs so you understand and can make an informed decision as to what the actual cost and benefit of the decision is. Travel can have both business and personal elements, and in general, the personal portions are not deductible. There are many rules related to the business/personal travel expenditures and how to correctly apportion costs.

Per diem is an allowable method that enables you to deduct the rate prescribed by the GSA (General Services Administration) in lieu of actual receipts. The GSA publishes per diem rates every year that are applicable for the following fiscal year. The government's fiscal year is October 1 to September 30, so it is quite likely that the rate for per diem on your tax return will not be the same for the entire year. There are different rates for different areas; a single state could have several different rates, as well as special rates for transportation workers and other circumstances. In addition, there are different categories for per diem separated into lodging, meals, and incidental expenses. Per diem usage can get quite complicated and there are numerous rules as well as examples. See the GSA website for specific rates for locations and allocation between different expense categories. See the IRS's publication 463 for the specific rules related to travel, entertainment, gift, and car expenses for more specific guidance.

For the most part, one should know that with per diem usage, it is possible to get a higher deduction for business travel expenses than with direct costs, especially if one is a bargain hunter that can keep the actual costs under what the per diem allowances are. The big takeaway is to keep records, document everything, and maintain your calendar. You don't want to get to tax time—or worse, audit time— and then make guesses. It is possible to switch between methods (actual versus per diem), but if you can't determine the actual cost and category (lodging, meals, and incidental expenses, etc.), it becomes difficult to do a simple analysis and establish that you used the per diem method for January through August and then used the actual expense method from September through December and so on.

Vehicle

A nice benefit to the self-employed and small business owner is the deductibility of vehicle expenses. The vehicle doesn't have to be owned by the entity in order to enjoy the benefits, the main requirement is that you use your car for business. Though many claim a 100% business use percentage, if you don't have another vehicle for personal purposes, that could potentially be a bit high, but it all depends on the circumstances.

There are two methods the IRS allows for deducting vehicle expenses: the standard mileage rate or actual expenses. As implied by the name, the standard mileage rate, much like the per diem allowance method described previously, prescribes a per mile rate for deductibility. The rate changes every year (2019 rate is 58 cents per mile). To use the standard mileage rate, it must be used in the first year the car is available for use in your business. You can use the standard mileage for leased vehicles, but you would need to use that method for the entire lease. You can't switch from the actual expense to the standard mileage method, but you can switch from the standard mileage to the actual expense method (aside from leased vehicles). Regardless of method chosen, one should keep records. There are numerous apps that can help automatically track business mileage, even the main accounting software packages incorporate mileage trackers.

> When I was an auditor with the Department of Revenue (before switching sides), the presence of a vehicle that was claimed as 100% business utilization, especially when the taxpayer didn't have another car for personal use, was like a bonus. Though it wasn't the main justification for examining a return, when added to one or more other factors, it created a better chance of getting an assessment from the audit. I would ask for the mileage log, which generally didn't exist, and when combined with other pieces of information, it became difficult for the taxpayer to justify a 100% business use.

The actual expense method would deduct actual vehicle costs. These costs can include all the items you'd imagine like gas, maintenance, insurance, other vehicle related expenses, and depreciation. Depreciation is one of the big deductions for a vehicle expense. Like with the home office deduction, it is the recovery of the vehicle's cost over a period of time. Since congress didn't want to subsidize the wealthy people's super fancy cars, there are limits and specified maximum depreciation allowable per year, so if the vehicle costs more than a certain amount, it may take longer to recover the cost for tax purposes than its useful economic life. Depreciation, and especially accelerated depreciation, is why you see and hear of small business owners rushing to buy a new truck or SUV near the end of the year. There are aspects like bonus depreciation and Section 179 expensing that were written into the tax code during economic downturns in order to incentivize spending and spur growth that somehow have a tough time getting unwritten from allowable small business benefits. As such, in certain circumstances, it may be possible that buying a new SUV meeting certain requirement and being used primarily for business, the initial year deduction could be over $30,000.

Clients will often ask me around December about buying an SUV for the business, along with other potential purchases and write offs. My first question is, "Have you maxed out your retirement account?" Even though I will typically know the answer, the goal is to help my clients think long term and not just make impulsive decisions just for tax write offs. If it makes economic sense to get a vehicle or other purchase for the business, then great. Sometimes the timing could be off a bit and, yes, it would still make sense to speed up the acquisition in certain cases. But if you are spending money just to reduce the amount of taxes you have to pay, that isn't always the best strategy. Besides, retirement contributions can provide the same tax deduction as buying an SUV with the exception being that it doesn't depreciate in value as soon as you send the money.

Much like the limitations on depreciation expenses, there are also special limitations on vehicle lease expenses in order to limit abuse of the tax code by the wealthy. The limits do change over time, so confer with the applicable IRS publication before signing the lease to make sure you'll receive the full benefit from the lease. Leased vehicles can still do both direct costs or mileage—instead of depreciation, you'd get the actual lease payment itself. You would lose the accelerated depreciation that is available when buying, so the recovery of cost would be more linear, but that could also be preferred, especially if you anticipate higher earnings and taxes in future years.

Value of Benefits

Much of the value derived from being a small business owner or self-employed individual is in the form of deductions. Those deductions are not the same value to everyone since different taxpayers have different tax rates. From a general perspective, if you have an idea of what your marginal tax rate is, then as a simple calculation, multiply the deduction by the marginal tax rate to get what the savings are. It can be a bit more challenging if it is the first year in business. But if you have been in business a year or more, you can look at your previous year's tax return to get an idea of what your marginal tax rate is by taking the total taxes (federal/state income taxes, self-employment taxes, etc.) and dividing by total income before adjustments and credits. Alternatively, you could make an educated guess at a nice round number like 35%; it won't be spot on but can get you close enough to make decisions. The actual value won't be fully realized until you prepare and file your tax return, and by then, the tax law could have changed a bit anyways.

In a sense, the benefit is that by sharing personal aspects (cell phone, computer, home office, vehicle, travel, etc.) with your business, you are still likely the only beneficiary of the components in question, but the cost to you personally is reduced. What used to be $100 per month for a service personally now has an economic reality cost of closer to $65 per month. Looking at the world with such a perspective can of course be dangerous, where your business credit card becomes the ultimate discount card. But with some self-control, one can have their cake and eat it too.

TAXES

Taxes are probably the single most frustrating, anxiety causing, and confusing aspect of entrepreneurship. If it weren't for the tax aspect, I'd probably have far fewer clients. With taxes often representing the largest single economic outlay for a small business owner, having an understanding and strategy to minimize taxes pays huge dividends. Even with respect to the bare minimum of meeting requirements for filing and paying by the due dates and avoiding penalties and interest alone can provide the resources to pay for an accountant to figure it all out for you.

A large part of the confusion and frustration come from the fact that being self-employed means that there isn't an employer that provides benefits, withholds taxes, and gives you a W-2 form at the end of the year that encompasses the majority of your income along with tax withholdings to do your personal taxes. Even though many small business owners are employees of their own small business and give themselves a W-2, the complications add up quickly, so the W-2 you give yourself doesn't always cover all the taxes that you may be liable for unless you do the math and make reasonable projections.

Income is the basis for the calculation of taxes. Though tax law can encompass an extremely wide and diverse amount of content, the focus here will be on ordinary income from a small business and self-employment. I will not be covering everything, as it would not be beneficial to you, the reader, or do justice to the content. There are literally tens of thousands of pages of tax code and related content—entire professions and advanced degrees in the subject are not able to cover all the potential topics within their specific disciplines.

Taxes are calculated and determined through filing tax returns. There are two main taxpayer types: C corporations and individuals. Trusts can be subject to taxes similar to corporations depending on circumstances, but generally, taxes are paid by individuals or corporations. Partnerships and S corporations don't pay federal income tax, rather those entities aggregate the income (or loss) and pass along the proportion of the total allocable to each partner, shareholder, or member of the entity, and the taxes are determined and paid at the individual (shareholder) level.

Basis of Accounting

Before getting right into taxes, we'll need to revisit the two main methods of accounting, which are cash basis and accrual basis. Cash basis records income and expenses when the cash moves. Accrual basis records income when earned and expenses when incurred. In some instances, there could be little difference between the two, like for a retail operation that pays for everything with cash. There would be differences when there are timing differences between earning income or incurring expenses and actually receiving or paying cash. A small business that completes services and invoices their customer and carries an accounts receivables balance would have a different net income between cash and accrual basis reporting. Similarly, if receiving a bill for services, supplies, etc., there too would be a difference. That difference may be insignificant, or it could be material.

> **Credit Cards** – Using a credit card results in a recognition of expense at the time of the transaction regardless of cash or accrual basis. Even though logically it would be very similar to ordering supplies

or inventory and receiving a bill and paying later, using a credit card does enable both cash and accrual taxpayers to recognize the transactions for tax purposes.

Inventory would be accounted for tax purposes relatively the same regardless of basis of accounting. If you are in the retail business or otherwise acquire goods that are resold, you would have a value of inventory; there are different methods for determining inventory valuation and the corresponding cost of goods sold, but for the most part, being cash or accrual basis, there would be the requirement to account for inventory. So you can't just buy $100,000 worth of inventory in year one and write it all off for tax purposes—the write off for that inventory would be reflected as the goods are sold when they are actually sold, hence the term cost of goods sold. There are of course situations like inventory obsolescence, shrinkage, and other events that enable the write down of worthless inventory.

Fixed assets and other capitalized costs would have similar treatment between cash and accrual basis, and the deduction for capitalized costs would be reflected through allowable cost recovery methods the IRS sets as prescribed by congress. Depreciation and the cost recovery of capitalized assets can get quite complex; we'll cover more on that later, but for now, the main point is that the rules would be virtually the same for cash and accrual basis taxpayers.

Just a timing difference? In a simple sense, it is more or less a timing difference since eventually the economic reality over the life of the business or asset in question should be the same. But the time value of money can be huge. Plus, your tax rate in year one is not necessarily going to be the same in year two or 10. It may be difficult or nearly impossible to predict the future—if so, the decision would be much easier to make. As we all want to get the most bang for our buck, the ultimate goal would be to minimize taxes and maximize wealth accumulation.

Additional complexities arise with the fact that most small businesses are pass-through entities. This makes one's marginal tax rate on their business income very different depending on other factors besides the method of accounting or even the net income of the business. For instance, if the business owner's spouse had a high paying job in year one and then left the job to take care of the family in year two, even if the business had identical income, the effective tax rate would be drastically different between the years.

Many small businesses are cash-basis taxpayers. This could be for simplicity, perhaps they have receivables from customers that they don't want to treat as income until they collect, or perhaps the accountant made the determination for them. From a simple analysis, if your accounts receivables are bigger than your accounts payables, then the cash basis would likely result in deferring more income than expenses resulting in less taxable income for that year. Going from one basis to another is allowable, but in certain instances, you may need to get permission from the IRS by filing Form 3115.

Income

Not all income is treated the same. Even if your business has investments that generate interest, capital gains, dividends, or other investment income, those items should be separately reported on your tax return and not accounted for as ordinary business income. This is especially true with long-term gains and qualified dividends as they generally have preferential tax treatment. Capital gains that are long term have a holding period of over one year. Qualified dividends are dividends that are generally from domestic corporations in which the stock is owned for 60 or more days prior to the ex-dividend date. If your business is structured through an entity like an S corporation or partnership, the process of preparing and filing the entity's tax return would account for items like investment income, rental income, and others as separately stated items that flow to the personal return and are nicely formatted on a shareholder's K-1 form. For businesses structured as C corporations, it is generally not advised to engage in significant investment operations, as much of the preferential treatment enjoyed by individual taxpayers is not present for C corporations.

When you set up your accounting system (if applicable) is generally where the classification and categorization for tax purposes originates. In accounting, we have a saying that "tax follows book," meaning that the tax impact generally would correspond to the economic realities of the business. Some of the more obtuse items would include inventory and cost of goods sold. If you are in the retail business and carry inventory, you would ideally have an inventory and point of sale system in place, and in a perfect world, such systems would integrate with your accounting software so that when it is time to do the taxes, what the "books" say are your cost of goods sold and ending inventory valuation should be accurate. Though, you should conduct regular inventories and adjust accordingly.

For prepaid expenses and unearned revenue—when you pay for something in advance of its utilization or receive money in advance of delivering a product or service—the actual recognition as an income or expense item may be rightfully deferred. The IRS does have a 12-month rule, so if you pay for something that will be fully utilized or realized within 12 months, then, especially for cash-basis taxpayers, the deduction is generally allowable. Unearned revenues like retainers or customer deposits can be deferred for the accrual-basis taxpayer and are not as easily deferred by the cash-basis taxpayer since one has received the cash.

There may be situations in which significant portions of unearned revenue show up on a tax form like a 1099 from Kickstarter. In such cases, it is important to report it correctly on the tax return which may require attaching statements to the return explaining why it is not included in income for the particular year. In the absence of properly reporting unearned revenue, the IRS may adjust your return to include the amount they believe you omitted and send you a bill with penalties and interest. Even if you are able to later provide the documentation and justification, it is a real headache and takes a lot of time and causes anguish in the process.

Expenses

Most expenses for a small business are fully deductible when the cost is incurred. Common items would include office supplies, rent, insurance, interest, salaries and wages, etc. The tax forms that are used to report business income/expense have a collection of common categories and a catchall "other deductions" line where expenses that don't fit the other options would go. Generally, I try to have as much as possible align to the built-in categories as having an unusually large amount of deductions in the "other" category can raise eyebrows. It's not necessarily a red flag, but because agencies use algorithms and AI in their selection process for audit, having less in the free form and customized categories could potentially reduce some exposure.

Most items should align to the tax forms from the bookkeeping categories. If, when setting up the accounting system and chart of accounts, the end of year taxes was a consideration, then it should make it much easier, especially if you plan to prepare your own tax returns. Some of the grey area can arise from aspects like vehicle expenses, travel, meals and entertainment, charitable contributions, political contributions, etc. As mentioned previously, vehicle expenses can either be direct expenses or mileage and you can't always switch between the two. Also, with travel, travel meals, and incidental expenses, there is the potential to use per diem allowances as deductions in lieu of actual expenses. In such cases, it is possible that the deduction for certain expenses exceeds actual cash outlays, which is nice since you get more deductions than your cost, but it can also throw your books off since the tax return would have more deductions than your books say.

Items that are separately stated and/or non-deductible also can cause some confusion as they may not cleanly show up on the tax return and reconcile back to what money actually left the bank account. Common items that are non-deductible or not reported on the main business income/expense schedule for tax purposes would include charitable contributions, officer life and disability insurance, political contributions, expenses deemed to be entertainment expenses, principal portion of debt payments, federal income tax payments, personal expenses, owner draws, etc.

Larger expenditures and purchases are often reported as capitalized assets and the cost is depreciated over time. The basis for depreciation is the purchase price plus or minus any adjustments in getting the asset to work for the business. The total cost may oftentimes include the initial loan, like a vehicle purchase with a car loan, which may have a trade-in allowance from a previous vehicle, a down payment, sales tax, title fees, etc.; all such aspects would be incorporated into the basis for depreciation.

Depreciation

Depreciation is the cost recovery for assets that have greater than one year of useful life and/or would have a cost of over $2,500. The IRS has tables and lists of all sorts of items and what method of depreciation is available. It can vary considerably; most small businesses would have assets in the seven years or less category and use a double declining balance method as the default. The available methods include either the straight line method or declining balance method. Straight line method is the simplest and easiest to figure out; basically just divide the cost by the life to get what your depreciation is. For example, a $15,000 asset with a 15-year life would have $1,000 per year in depreciation expense. The double declining balance recognizes much more depreciation in the first years and less in the later years. It basically takes twice the straight line method in the first year, and for the remaining years, it would take the remaining cost to be recovered, divide by the total years in the schedule of depreciation, and double it. I don't know of anyone that prepares returns with paper and pencil anymore and would be shocked to see someone manually calculating and reporting depreciation in such a manner. The software you are using should be able to calculate it for you.

What's the point? Well, it contributes to decision making. No one likes the idea of paying taxes, and as the goal is to pay the least amount of taxes over time, being able to control how much depreciation is taken in year one versus year three can help in the game of arbitrage. This is especially helpful if you have a reasonable expectation for what your income is over the next year or two. As tempting as it is to maximize deductions for the current year, if you are in the 12% tax bracket and know you'll likely be in the 22% bracket next year, the smart play is to shift as many of the deductions as you can to that year, even though it might mean paying more taxes for the current year.

The IRS also has conventions. Generally, the half year convention would be applied for most items like cars, computers, furniture, etc., which means, regardless of when in the year you bought something, the first and last year for depreciation is half what it would be without consideration for the convention. So, in the previous example with a $15,000 asset depreciated over 15 years on the straight line method, if the half year convention was applied the first year, $500 would be the depreciation expense, and $1000 per year for years 2-15, followed by a final $500 in year 16. There is also the mid-month convention, which is generally applied for real estate, so it would calculate depreciation down to the month of acquisition and split that month. The mid-quarter convention, designed to prevent taxpayers from buying everything on December 31 and getting to depreciate half of the first year, the IRS requires all the assets purchased in that year to be on the mid-quarter convention when 40% or more is bought in the fourth quarter. There are ways around it like electing bonus depreciation or S179 expensing on those assets, reducing the total depreciable basis of assets purchased in the fourth quarter.

With the new Tax Cuts and Jobs Act of 2017, there is greater flexibility to enjoy immediate first year recognition of expenses for depreciable assets. Bonus depreciation and S179 expensing are allowances that enable the immediate cost recovery (tax deduction) for up to the entire cost of property placed in service. There are differences between bonus depreciation and S179 expensing as far as what property type qualifies, limitations, and so forth. Now even qualified improvement property (which is improvements to real property except for enlargement, elevators/escalators, or major internal structural framework projects) can potentially be written off in the first year. Also, the new flexibility loosened up some of the rigid requirements stating that certain assets be bought brand new in order to qualify. Now as long as it is new to you and bought from an unrelated party, it should qualify for accelerated depreciation. Not all states can afford to be as generous, so depending on where you live, there could be the requirement to "add back" portions of the accelerated depreciation for state tax purposes and maintain two depreciation schedules. Most tax software, if you use the same one every year, should be able to maintain your depreciation schedules for you.

Net Operating Loss (NOL)

You may have heard the term "net operating loss" or NOL. A NOL arises when the business shows a loss that is not fully absorbed by other income in that year. In such cases, a portion of the excess loss is carried forward to be applied against future earnings. No longer is a loss allowed to be carried back to previous years, and the use of an NOL can't offset more than 80% of your taxable income. Since most small businesses are pass-through entities where the tax and potential NOL is determined at the individual taxpayer level, the calculation of the NOL and how much gets carried forward will depend on the circumstances; the business may show a loss, but the taxpayer may not have a NOL. Generally, the tax program will calculate it for you and maintain the schedule of allowable losses in the future. The main takeaway is that if you have a bad year that creates a negative income year, you will eventually be able to use those losses in future years.

Passive Activity Loss

Not every business is an active business. With pass-through entities, the owners are entitled to a share of the income or loss from that business. However, if you are not an active participant in the business, then the losses may not be allowable in that year. The bulk of passive activities are rental activities which are inherently passive. Even though people who own a duplex or other dwelling they rent will tell you there is nothing passive about it, the IRS says that it is passive. One is allowed up to $25,000 of passive activity losses in which there is active participation in a year to offset other income, provided their household income is under certain thresholds. Active participation is less stringent than material participation, to have active participation one may simply demonstrate that they make managerial decisions like approving tenants and making deposits and/or expenditures for the activity.

Besides rental activities, operating businesses can be considered passive as well depending on the person. For example, if you own a part of a business but don't do any of the work, then it would be an active business for the owners that work the business but a passive activity for the owners that are just investors. The IRS has material participation tests that include things like the number of hours worked in the activity along with other factors to determine if you would be able to deduct a certain amount of the losses against other income. Such passive losses, even if allowable, may be limited based on household income.

With passive activity losses, they get bottled up and carried forward if they are not used to offset other income. Once the activity is disposed of, the bottled-up losses would get released and utilized on that year's tax return.

Owner Draws

Paying yourself out of the business can come in different forms. One of the most common is through owner draws, which can be called a number of things like distributions, disbursements, stipends, dividends, partner payouts, and so on. Draws are what an owner uses to pay their personal bills. Draws are not deductions. Occasionally, I'll see clients that classify draws as an expense item, which is not correct. Draws should generally be classified as an equity account and show up on the balance sheet. A draw is a return of capital or distribution out of the retained earnings of the business. Retained earnings is the aggregate net income/loss of the business since the beginning of the business. As most small businesses are pass-through entities, the business doesn't pay taxes, but the owner does. Since the owner paid taxes on the net income already, a return of that net income or of the capital they originally injected into the business to get going is not a taxable event to the owner.

> As a pass-through entity, the net income of the business is taxed to the owner regardless of whether

they take money out as draws or not. This is often an area of confusion because an entrepreneur that is good about keeping business and personal separate will know how much money they took out of the business, which may be much less than the amount that is taxed. Like if a business made $100,000 in net income, but the owner only took $60,000 in owner draws and salary, the owner will get to tax time and be a bit frustrated at the tax system when what felt like $60,000 of income is being taxed like it is $100,000. The difference can be for many reasons like investments in working capital, undepreciated assets, or other items that are usually quite necessary for the business. Financing a business out of retained earnings can be a painful lesson.

Shareholder Loans and Basis

Another common form that money going to the owner(s) of a business can take is through shareholder loans. This is particularly common in S corporations. When an S corporation has more than one owner, the rules are that distributions be in pro rata proportion to ownership, which can create some frustration. For example, if an S corporation has two owners, one with 80% ownership and one with 20% ownership, distributions would need to follow that allocation. It doesn't matter if the 20% owner did more work or earned more of the profit. In order to have disproportionate disbursals, it would need to be in the form of compensation on a W-2 or 1099 to the owner for services rendered (which would generally be subject to employment taxes), otherwise the excess distribution would likely be deemed as a loan from the corporation that would need to be recovered at some point. Failure to follow the rules of S corporations could result in termination of S corporation status, which, if the option is C corporation or S corporation, the preference is generally to be an S corporation and avoid the double taxation.

Another common justification for shareholder loans for S corporations comes into play with respect to basis. An S corporation's debt does not provide basis to the shareholder. Basis is determined at the shareholder level. Loans and even credit card balances at the end of the year, if in excess of assets, creates a negative equity situation. When this occurs, the losses can be suspended due to a lack of basis, and in the case of distributions, it becomes what is labeled a distribution in excess of basis, which is taxable income. To remedy this in order to take losses on their personal return and not have to pay taxes on distributions, a common tactic I'll see is to reclassify distributions as a loan to shareholder, which is an asset; thus, reducing the negative equity and increasing assets to restore a positive equity balance, at least on paper.

Partnerships don't have the same issue as they can specify in their partnership agreement that there will be disproportionate profit/loss, capital, or other special allocations in addition to the use of guaranteed payments to partners. Plus, partners have capital accounts that go up and down and don't need to necessarily be in pro rata proportion to their ownership interest every year, so partners can take disproportionate draws; the capital accounts would get reconciled and whatever tax consequences sorted out upon liquidation of the partnership or withdrawal of a partner.

Keeping track of capital accounts and basis is important. For most small businesses, it is relatively simple and straightforward: cash goes in, cash goes out, etc. It becomes a bit more complex and essential to track for partnerships with unrelated parties, entities formed and capitalized with assets that have built in gains, or something more complex than a plain vanilla setup. For instance, a partnership is formed where partner A contributes $100,000 and partner B contributes land with a current value of $100,000, but a cost basis of only $10,000; or with one party contributing capital and the other party contributing labor. It can get way more complicated considering tiered partnerships, partially depreciated assets, unrealized receivables, inventory (aka, "hot assets"), and more. Many tax programs can track capital and shareholder basis accounts, which, when utilized, helps ensure that there aren't basis issues along the way and that the capital accounts reflect the economic reality from a tax perspective.

Tax Credits

Tax credits, not to be confused with deductions, are nice perks when you can get them. A credit is a reduction in the actual tax liability, and a deduction is a reduction of taxable income that determines tax (like spending money on office supplies). The dollar value of a credit is worth more than a deduction, but that doesn't mean you should bend over backwards to get a credit. There are a number of credits that a small business may be eligible for. They cover various aspects from employing veterans to biofuel bladder cells. Many came about as special earmarks to legislation and policy to carve out special treatment or to create economic incentives for things like carbon dioxide sequestration. It would be exhausting for both you and me to list them out here. Many of the credits would get reported on the General Business Credit Form 3800, which is something of an aggregation for business credits, so even if the particular credit requires certain documentation or a specific form, it often would flow into the Form 3800 and then flow into the master tax form (1040, 1065, 1120, 1120s, etc.). It wouldn't hurt to peruse through the general business credit form and the web pages the IRS publishes pertaining to business tax credits to see if one or more applies and what the requirements are. Most of the names for the credits describe what the credit is for, like "low income housing credit," so you should be able to identify which credits to read more about without too much effort. Again, I would advocate for doing things that make sense for business first, not just because there is a deduction or credit associated with a particular transaction. Don't just hire an ex-convicted felon because you'll get a small tax credit for it—hire the right person (rent in the right location, use the right equipment, etc.) for the business.

Qualified Business Income Deduction

The new tax reform enacted in late 2017 cut the corporate tax rate to 21% along with reducing individual rates. With most small businesses organized and operated as pass-through entities, rather than further reducing individual rates, a deduction was created to reduce the effective tax rate of pass-through income to achieve some parity with the corporate tax rate. The deduction is limited to 20% of taxable income adjusted for capital gain/loss of the owner. Earned income (wages, guaranteed payments) are excluded from qualified business income (QBI). The limitations can get a bit complicated; if you are married and file a joint tax return (MFJ), and your household income is below $315,000 (or $157,500 for all others), then the deduction would not be limited due to income.

Example:
Joe owns a plumbing business and files a tax return as married filing jointly. Their household income includes $200,000 of business income from the plumbing business and $100,000 of wages from the same business.

A	Wage income	$100,000
B	Business Income	$200,000
C	Total Income	$300,000
D	Standard Deduction	-$24,000
E	QBID (B*20%)	-$40,000
F	Taxable Income	$236,000

If your income is above the thresholds, then the deduction is limited to the greater of either 50% of the total W-2 compensation paid by the entity or 25% of W-2 compensation plus 2.5% of unadjusted basis of assets (the alternative method). The limitation is phased in (or proportionally applied) as one exceeds the threshold ($315,000 for married filing jointly, $157,500 all others) for the first $100,000 ($50,000 for all others) over the threshold.

Special restrictions apply to service professionals. Bad news if you are in the field of medical services, law, accounting, actuarial science, performing arts, consulting, athletics, financial services, brokerage services, etc. The deduction is allowed under the thresholds and phaseout of limitations. So, for MFJ under $315,000, full deduction is allowed; over $415,000, no deduction is allowed; and in between those amounts, a portion of the deduction is allowed. For not MFJ, under $157,500 is fully allowed, over $207,500 is not allowed, and in between a portion is allowed.

With the new qualified business income deduction, it creates a unique consideration into tax planning. As the common logic was to default to the S corporation and save on self-employment taxes, it may not be the best choice in all cases. The QBID is typically higher for the self-employed business as opposed to the S corp, but the sole prop typically would have much higher self-employment taxes. This means that the overall impact of electing S corporation status isn't as simple anymore.

Self-Employment Taxes

For new entrepreneurs, self-employment taxes can be a shock, especially for those in the lower tax brackets that enjoy some of the deductions and credits available to them. The reason being is that with self-employment taxes, it can be quite possible to have little to no income tax liability and still have a considerable self-employment tax liability. Take, for example, a taxpayer that makes $50,000 a year in self-employment income, is married filing a joint tax return, and has one kid that qualifies for the child tax credit; their federal income tax would likely be less than zero, but their self-employment tax liability would be over $7,000. If you are a household of three living on $50,000 a year and didn't make estimated tax deposits, getting a tax bill of $7,000 would be quite devastating.

What makes self-employment taxes so punishing is that the entrepreneur pays both the employer and employee portion of social security and Medicare taxes. To make matters worse, for those new to self-employment, there is no employer that is withholding any taxes, so one gets to tax time and can have a very rude awakening if not prepared.

To calculate self-employment taxes, one must first have an idea of their net self-employment income. This net income is reduced by certain items like the home office deduction, vehicle expenses, and depreciation, which may be difficult to get exact until the tax return is prepared, but nonetheless, an educated guess will get you to a rough number. With that number, if it is under the social security tax cap ($132,900 for 2019), the calculation isn't too bad. Take your anticipated net self-employment income, multiply by .9235 (which accounts for the employer portion of self-employment taxes), and take that number and multiply by .153 (15.3%).

Example:
Bill, a self-employed person, anticipates making $100,000 in net self-employment income after accounting for anticipated depreciation, home office, and vehicle expenses.

A Net Self-Employment Income $100,000
B *.9235 $92,350
C *.153 = Net SE Tax $14,130

The employer portion of self-employment tax is a deduction for both income tax and self-employment tax. When self-employment income exceeds the cap for social security, it is still relatively simple to calculate, but you'd do two calculations and separate the social security portion from the Medicare portion.

Example:
From the previous example, assume Bill makes $200,000 in net self-employment income instead of $100,000; the calculation would be as follows:

A Net Self-Employment Income $200,000
B *.9235 $184,700

Since Line B's result is over the threshold ($132,900 for 2019), the calculation would be the sum of two calculations, one for social security and one for Medicare.

C 132,900 * .124 (SS Tax) $16,479.60
D 184,700 * .029 (Medicare) $5,356.30
E Net SE Tax $21,835.90

Additional Medicare Tax – This is a tax that impacts individuals that make over $200,000 or married filing joint households with earned income of over $250,000 ($125,000 for married filing separately). It is an additional 0.9% tax on the amount over the amounts listed above. There is also a net investment income tax that was created alongside the additional Medicare tax—it has the same floor as far as income, but applies to investment income (interest, dividends, capital gains, etc.). The calculation uses a modified adjusted household income which may be slightly different from the common adjusted gross income term seen on your tax return and applies a 3.8% tax on investment income when household income exceeds the threshold amount.

Employers are required to withhold for the additional Medicare tax when the employee exceeds $200,000 in wages, regardless of their filing status. There could be some situations in which one spouse makes $250,000 and the other spouse is a stay-at-home parent, so they wouldn't have an additional Medicare tax liability, but the employer would nonetheless withhold on wages in excess of $200,000. In such situations, it would get credited on their tax return and potentially refunded depending on their return.

Guaranteed Payments and Partnership Income

There have been many tax court cases addressing aspects of partnership income. Specifically, the allocation of income that is subject to self-employment taxes. In general, a partnership (or an entity that is taxed as a partnership like an LLC) would have at least one partner that is a general partner and may also have persons deemed as limited partners. Aside from partnerships that are formed and organized for the purposes of rental activity or investment activity, operating businesses that are partnerships should have one or more persons who bear the brunt of the self-employment taxes, at least that is what the IRS would like to see.

The LLC or limited liability company was proliferated after the last major tax reform in the mid-1980s. It created a unique entity in which the members of the LLC are both participating managers and limited owners as far as their liability exposure—it sounds like the perfect vehicle when one can be a general and limited partner at the same time. Well, the IRS didn't really like the way that some taxpayers decided to be taxed. The issue would come about where a member of the LLC would allocate the earnings from self-employment in a very deliberate and discretionary way. This may be by having guaranteed payments to the partner, but then have their profit participation be considered a limited partner's profit interest, or creating multiple ownership interests for the same person, etc. Guaranteed payments are payments to a partner. They are deductible as an expense to the partnership and are considered self-employment income to the partner. The receipt of guaranteed payments is not an owner draw and doesn't have the same impact on the partner's capital account. Unlike wages or salaries, the entity does not absorb or pay any employment tax liabilities associated with guaranteed payments; it is all on the partner at the individual level.

> To avoid red flags with the IRS, when you are an operating business organized as a partnership, at least one partner's income should be deemed as self-employment earnings. This would include not only guaranteed payments, but also the partner's profit participation; creating multiple partners for the same taxpayer would mean that all of that partner's interests be classified as self-employment income.

What makes matters extra complex and confusing is that entities are formed, organized, and have legal standing within a particular state's legal code, whereas federal tax law attempts to ascribe taxes in an aggregate and individually applied manner based on the entity's economics as defined by congress. Though entities are formed at the state level, most states follow the uniform act that provides the framework for the states to follow. Partnerships can have special allocations and unique arrangements, but that doesn't mean one is given license to engage in evasive tax strategies. But, in general, with special allocations, as long as there is economic substance behind it, taxes will be applied in a manner consistent with such special situations.

> Special allocations can be something of an enigma. Partnerships can amend their partnership agreement every year if they choose to and change their allocations and other aspects. Where trouble can arise is when the apparent justification and economic reasoning behind adjustments and special allocations seems to point solely to the avoidance and shifting of tax liabilities. For example, in a partnership with two

partners—one wealthy and in a high tax bracket and one in a lower tax bracket—the partnership could allocate more of the income items to the lower taxed partner and more of the expense items to the higher taxed partner. However, attempting to flip flop it when the higher taxed partner is in retirement and at a lower bracket may raise more than just eyebrows, and the IRS could collapse such transactions and recalculate taxes based on the economic reality they determine to be correct.

Estimates and Withholding

Making quarterly estimated tax payments is a part of life for the self-employed. The due dates for quarterly estimates fall on April 15, June 15, September 15, and January 15, which applies to the Quarters 1-4, respectively. The amount of the estimates can vary with the net income of the business. The safe harbor rules are that you pay either 100% of the previous year's tax or 90% of the current year's actual tax if you are able to determine; if your income is over $150,000 ($75,000 for married filing separately), then the safe harbor is 110% of the previous year's or 90% of the current year's actual tax.

Generally, the IRS will expect one-fourth of the total tax estimate on the due date of each quarter. If your income fluctuates or has seasonality, there is the possibility of employing the annualized estimated tax worksheet in order to provide some variabilization into the estimated tax payments to better match the cash flow of the business.

Withholdings (which are federal and state individual income tax obligations that are withheld from employee paychecks and remitted to the federal and state agencies on their behalf) are generally considered received evenly throughout the year. Sometimes I'll see greater reported wages and withholdings in the last month of the year, which would then evenly be applied as though it was received throughout the year and thus offsetting the absent payments that were not made. If you have a spouse who has their own W-2 job, that can be an excellent tool in assisting in tax planning. It is generally advisable to have the W-2 earner increase withholdings and take maximum advantage of employer provided benefits like flex accounts, insurances, retirement, etc.; even though it reduces take home pay for that spouse, you and your spouse are one taxpayer, and in reality, one economic entity. Sometimes it can get a bit hairy when there isn't as much commingling of financial assets in a marriage, but it is just math after all; it can be figured out so that each party is made whole from any short-term sacrifice that benefits the other party.

Businesses that elect to be taxed as an S corporation can use the additional compliance requirements of reasonable compensation to manage their tax liability through the withholdings of the owner/officer payroll. Since one of the main reasons that the S corporation is used is to mitigate self-employment taxes, the owners will typically have both wages and profit distributions. The challenge is to incorporate the tax effect from the entity's profits into payroll. Officer-only payroll products are available through a variety of service providers. With a payroll module, there is often much customization, though the default settings are typically insufficient to absorb their total tax liability. The reason is that the withholding calculators that come with a payroll product are designed for traditional employees, so simply selecting that you are married or single wouldn't withhold enough to cover the impact of the business's profits. Fortunately, one can elect to withhold more than what the calculators would otherwise calculate, which is what would typically be needed in order to not have to also make estimated tax payments or have to pay penalties and interest for not paying enough in estimates.

Is the S Corporation the Right Choice?

That can depend on a number of factors. The main benefit comes from the reduction in employment taxes, so that at least a portion of the business's net income can potentially avoid being subjected to self-employment taxes. As an example, a single taxpayer that makes a net income of $100,000 a year would have a total federal tax liability of around $24,000 as a sole proprietor. As an S corporation with the same net income split between profit and wages, that taxpayer would have a total federal tax liability (including employment taxes) of just over $20,000 or about $3,000 savings as an S corporation. Though the increased cost of compliance (payroll, corporate tax return, etc.) may erode some of those savings, the benefit can add up so long as one is cognizant of the added costs; don't just save money only to pay an accountant.

As one's income and reasonable compensation requirements can vary, so too would the impact of such a comparison. In general, if the business has a net income of over $40,000 and can choose between S corporation and sole proprietor, it would be a good idea to run the comparison. Less than $40,000 and much of the savings would go right to the accountant to meet your compliance requirements. As the overall net income exceeds $150,000-200,000, the benefit is not as lucrative since the self-employment taxes are drastically less as the net income exceeds the social security wage cap. However, there are a lot of businesses in that sweet spot, so it may still make good sense to elect the S corporation.

The big question would be, what impact does the reduction of one's social security wage base have on one's future benefit? Since the social security benefit uses 35 years of data and applies an index factor to approximate common size monthly units and then has a progressive algorithm that has a diminishing return on earnings in their calculation, it is very cumbersome to even figure out. There is a decreased marginal utility for paying social security taxes beyond a certain point. The numbers change every year, but as a general rule and providing it doesn't conflict with reasonable compensation requirements or retirement funding goals that need a larger wage base, if half or less of the social security wage base ($132,900/2 = $66,450 for 2018) is in compliance, then that would be a reasonable target to shoot for. Going over that amount wouldn't be as beneficial because of the progressive (or regressive, depending on how you look at it) way social security benefits are calculated. But, again, I am not advocating anyone cheat or do something inconsistent with the law—you would still need to justify reasonable compensation requirements. Also, if you are going to reduce your self-employment taxes, it would be a good idea to take the savings and put into a retirement account if you are not already maxing out your accounts.

Entity Taxes

Many states have taxes and fees assessed at the entity level, so even though a business is a pass-through entity that doesn't pay federal or state income taxes, there may be fees, assessments, or other charges that some states levy. Many states label them as a "minimum fee" which levies a fee when filing an entity tax return. The fees can vary, and some states are worse than others. California's minimum fee collects about $800 per year at a minimum, and if the income exceeds certain thresholds, it can be much higher than that. Other states, including Texas, have a gross receipts tax that collects taxes based on revenue. Many states also demand that nonresident withholding or composite taxes be paid. Composite tax is a return filed by a pass-through entity that calculates the shareholder/partner's respective share of that state's income and tax and remits tax to that state on behalf of the shareholder/partner. Especially when operating in more than one state, there can be a cumbersome set of compliance tasks that various states employ to ensure they get their share of tax revenue out of the economy.

Let's Get Personal

With the vast majority of small businesses being pass-through entities, the impact and tax consequences of the business are determined at the individual taxpayer level. While that avoids the double taxation of having a C corporation, it makes figuring out taxes for a typical small business no small matter. Two businesses with identical results can have very different implications on the owners depending on their households. Aspects like being married filing jointly or single, having children that provide the child tax credit, etc. all contribute to the calculation and consideration for the tax impact of entrepreneurship.

When both spouses in a household work or are self-employed, it can be a frustrating exercise to explain, especially when there is segregation of expenses and finances within the household since, for tax purposes, they are one economic entity and not two. Often, the working spouse with a W-2 doesn't like the idea of having to increase their withholdings to cover the taxes of their spouse, but it wouldn't really be fair to put the entire burden on the self-employed spouse either since that would mean that the working spouse gets to enjoy all the deductions, credits, and the lower tax bracket and the self-employed spouse is left with taxable income and a higher marginal tax rate to contend with. As such, having a basic understanding of how taxes work can help be more transparent and develop equitable apportionment of the household's liability for taxes. Most tax programs have the ability to do a comparison for filing status that can do a simple comparison and separation of the spouse's income and deductions.

Every year, the brackets for taxes change a little reflecting the cost of living and inflationary adjustments. Here are some tax tables to see the basic tax brackets; shown on this page is the capital gain brackets and on the following page is the income tax brackets.

Long-Term Capital Gains and Qualified Dividends Tax Rates for Taxpayers with Taxable Income in the Specified Ranges*			
2018	0%	15%	20%
MFJ/SS	$0 - $77,199	$77,200 - $478,999	$479,000 and up
MFS	$0 - $38,599	$38,600 - $239,499	$239,500 and up
HoH	$0 - $51,699	$51,700 - $452,399	$452,400 and up
Single	$0 - $38,599	$38,600 - $425,799	$425,800 and up
E&T	$0 - $2,599	$2,600 - $12,699	$12,700 and up
2019	0%	15%	20%
MFJ/SS	$0 - $78,749	$78,750 - $488,849	$488,850 and up
MFS	$0 - $39,374	$39,375 - $244,424	$244,425 and up
HoH	$0 - $52,749	$52,750 - $461,699	$461,700 and up
Single	$0 - $39,374	$39,375 - $434,549	$434,550 and up
E&T	$0 - $2,649	$2,650 - $12,949	$12,950 and up

* Additional 3.8% tax imposed on the lesser of the individual's Net Investment Income or the excess of the individual's MAGI over certain thresholds ($250,000 for married couples filing jointly or surviving spouse, $125,000 for married couples filing separately, and $200,000 for all other taxpayers).

2019

If Taxable Income Is:

Over	But Not More Than	The Tax Is	Of the Amount Over
Married Filing Jointly:			
$0	$19,400	$0 + 10%	$0
19,400	78,950	1,940.00 + 12%	19,400
78,950	168,400	9,086.00 + 22%	78,950
168,400	321,450	28,765.00 + 24%	168,400
321,450	408,200	65,497.00 + 32%	321,450
408,200	612,350	93,257.00 + 35%	408,200
612,350		164,709.50 + 37%	612,350
Married Filing Separately:			
$0	$9,700	$0 + 10%	$0
9,700	39,475	970.00 + 12%	9,700
39,475	84,200	4,543.00 + 22%	39,475
84,200	160,725	14,382.50 + 24%	84,200
160,725	204,100	32,748.50 + 32%	160,725
204,100	306,175	46,628.50 + 35%	204,100
306,175		82,354.75 + 37%	306,175
Head of Household:			
$0	$13,850	$0 + 10%	$0
13,850	52,850	1,385.00 + 12%	13,850
52,850	84,200	6,065.00 + 22%	52,850
84,200	160,700	12,962.00 + 24%	84,200
160,700	204,100	31,322.00 + 32%	160,700
204,100	510,300	45,210.00 + 35%	204,100
510,300		152,380.00 + 37%	510,300
Single:			
$0	$9,700	$0 + 10%	$0
9,700	39,475	970.00 + 12%	9,700
39,475	84,200	4,543.00 + 22%	39,475
84,200	160,725	14,382.50 + 24%	84,200
160,725	204,100	32,748.50 + 32%	160,725
204,100	510,300	46,628.50 + 35%	204,100
510,300		153,798.50 + 37%	510,300
Estates and Trusts:			
$0	$2,600	$0 + 10%	$0
2,600	9,300	260.00 + 24%	2,600
9,300	12,750	1,868.00 + 35%	9,300
12,750		3,075.50 + 37%	12,750

The income tax on your personal tax return forms the basis of how a small business will be taxed. As mentioned previously, not all income is treated the same.

Income Types

Business income is ordinary income, which may sound boring but is one of the major classifications of income. Ordinary income is non-capital gain income, which includes wages, tips, interest, ordinary dividends, rental income, etc. Not to be confused with earned income, which is also ordinary income but has the added component of being subject to employment taxes (social security and Medicare) such as wages, self-employment income, partnership interests as a general partner, etc. Ordinary income is taxed using the regular tax tables.

The other major category of income includes long-term capital gains and qualified dividends, which are taxed at capital gain rates and range from 0% if you are in the lower two brackets (10% and 12% brackets) to 20% in the higher brackets, with most middle income households falling in the 15% long-term capital gain rate. Capital losses are allowed to offset other income in the amount of $3,000 per year and the remaining amount can be carried forward.

Tax exempt interest or dividends, as the name implies, provides income that is exempt from the regular tax tables, though it may have an impact in the calculation of state income taxes as well as the alternative minimum tax (AMT). The AMT was simplified and restructured with the latest tax reform—it is designed to ensure that high income earners pay a minimum amount of tax and are not overly advantaged by certain aspects of the tax code. Far fewer people will fall into the AMT situation now that it has been reformed, but the main takeaway is that though there are sources of income that have preferential treatment for the regular taxes, it may end up not being able to provide the entire benefit anticipated if AMT kicks in to recalculate your taxes. On the following page is a table showing what the AMT threshold and exemption amounts are.

AMT Rates for Individuals

| | AMTI Threshold | | AMT Rate |
	2018	2019	
Single, MFJ, HoH	$0 - $191,100	$0 - $194,800	26%
	$191,101 or more	$194,801 or more	28%
MFS	$0 - $95,550	$0 - $97,400	26%
	$95,551 or more	$97,401 or more	28%

| | AMT Exemption | |
	2018	2019
Single, HoH	$70,300	$71,700
MFJ, SS	$109,400	$111,700
MFS	$54,700	$55,850

Depreciation Recapture and Multi-Classified Income

As discussed previously, depreciation is an expense reflecting the recovery of cost for an asset with greater than one year of useful life. Since the expense for depreciation is an ordinary expense item, when you sell an asset that has been depreciated, there may be the potential for the recapture of depreciation, which would be taxed at ordinary rates and the balance of gain allowed to be taxed at more preferential capital gain rates.

Additionally, the tax code allows for 1231 gain/losses, which come from depreciable business assets that have more than one year of service. They have the unique attribute of enabling the preferential long-term gain treatment for gains, and on the flipside, allow fully deductible ordinary loss treatment for losses. The gain portion would typically be in excess of the original purchase price as depreciation recapture would still apply. There is a lookback provision, so taxpayers may have to net 1231 gains/losses that span several years, but otherwise, it is a nice feature for small businesses that employ depreciable assets.

Example 1:
Bill Taxpayer owns a business and used his truck for business. The truck cost $30,000 originally, and after a few years, he

trades in the truck for a new one and is given a trade-in value of $18,000. His adjusted basis (original basis plus adjustments less depreciation) is $14,400 at the time of the transaction, meaning he had $15,600 of depreciation.

His gain on the sale is $3,600 ($18,000 - $14,400) and would be classified as ordinary income because of depreciation recapture.

Example 2:
Bill also owns a machine press used for business that also is being depreciated for tax purposes. His original cost is $100,000. He used it for over a year and decided to sell it; at the time of sale, his adjusted basis in the machine press is $80,000 and the sale price is $110,000.

In this case, Bill would have both ordinary income of $20,000 (depreciation recapture) and $10,000 of long-term gain. This property would be considered 1231 property that has unique attributes and benefits.

Example 3:
Same facts as Example 2, except let's say the sale price was $70,000 instead. In this case, there would be an overall loss of $10,000. Since this is 1231 property, Bill would get to deduct an ordinary loss of $10,000, though Bill would need to keep track of his 1231 losses and could potentially be netted against 1231 gains later on.

Knowns and Unknowns

The best way to determine taxes is to prepare a tax return. That, however, doesn't help much if you want to know in July where you are at for the year. Figuring out taxes without actually preparing a tax return can be a complex and confusing exercise. But with some realistic assumptions and projections, we can get close enough for horseshoes and hand grenades, or so the saying goes. After all, it is just math—the numbers may change a bit here and there, but the calculations are relatively constant. It starts with taking the knowns into account, then incorporating the unknowns.

The best place to start when constructing the knowns would be your previous year's tax return and making adjustments as necessary. Things like wages, investment income, adjustments for self-employed health insurance and student loan interest, etc. With respect to deductions, since the new tax reform increased the standard deduction to $12,000 for individuals and $24,000 for married filing joint returns and limited certain deductions, the majority of taxpayers will take the standard deduction. Even if you may exceed the standard deduction for purposes of making predictions, using the standard deduction is a good safe estimate that ensures a level of conservatism.

Anticipation of tax credits plays a role in figuring out what liability to expect. A couple common credits include the child tax credit, which is worth $2,000 per child under 17 years old at the end of the tax year. The income limit phase out begins at $400,000 for joint filers and $200,000 for single filers, so the majority of those with children will get to enjoy this perk. Another common credit is the child and dependent care credit which is based on up to $3,000 worth of daycare type expenses per child on up to two children. The credit amount is based on income and can vary. Other more specific credits and unique considerations would likely be known to you and, of course, should be incorporated into projections.

With an assembly of what the knowns are, the big unknown is usually the business, how will it be taxed, what rate should be applied, etc. If you do a reasonable job of keeping the books or at least have an accountant or bookkeeper to help you track it, then the task becomes much easier. With the year-to-date information, one can extrapolate the entire year's information. This can be done in a multitude of ways, but one should strive to be as accurate as possible. If your business slows down in the fourth quarter, then that should be taken into account, which would otherwise be overstated in a straight line extrapolation; and of course, the opposite would also potentially create issues if, for example, you do more business in the fourth quarter. You would then likely understate in the projection what the year's net income will be without that additional adjustment.

Example:
Bill Businessman, a sole proprietor, wants to figure out his tax liability for the year. It is July and he has his January-June books done showing he made $60,000 for the year so far. If he extrapolated his net income for the year without any adjustments, it would be approximately $120,000.

$$\$60,000/(6/12) = \$120,000$$

If Bill is aware of adjustments, he should incorporate them into the assumptions. For instance, he should take into consideration if $20,000 of the net income came from a project that was a one-time thing and not reflective of a recurring business trend, or if the business drastically slows down in November, etc. The point is to get close without trying to split hairs; Bill just wants to know about how much should be set aside for taxes, and/or what his options for reducing that might be while there is time (and ideally money) available to take action.

You may not have any depreciation expense or may be in the habit of writing off as much as you can as fast as you can, which makes it much easier since you wouldn't have to try and figure out how much depreciation expense you might have this year versus next year. Similar to other items like vehicle expense, it may not be clear in the interim what the total expense for the year will be, so using an approximation works for making a projection. This is what a projection is—an educated guess. Some items like home office, depreciation, vehicle mileage, and others may only be on the books for the end of the year. Just something to keep in mind if making a projection and the easiest way would be to incorporate into the projection by subtracting from an extrapolation.

Continuing from the previous example, say that Bill Businessman looked at his previous year's tax return and books and sees that in December, he booked $3,500 in home office expenses, $10,000 in vehicle mileage which will be similar to this year, and knows that he bought $15,000 worth of equipment this year that he'll be able to write off and intends to do so. With that, his updated projection would be:

$$\$120,000 - \$3,500 - \$10,000 - \$15,000 = \$91,500$$

S corporations and Partnerships can add additional layers of complexity in making projections. Some of this stems from the fact that the entity can adjust certain things like officer salary/guaranteed payments, which impact not only what the net income from the business will be, but also the owner's personal taxes as well. This is especially true with respect to S corporations as the profit portion is typically not subjected to employment taxes, whereas the wage income that comes from that same entity is. This can be something of a relief in many cases because the business will be absorbing and paying the employment tax obligations concurrently, making the individual tax projections much simpler. Nonetheless, as the entity and owner are in reality one economic entity, taxes paid by the entity are paid by the owner. As such, a desired outcome from a projection isn't just what the individual tax liability might be, but more so to determine what the total amount of cash needed for tax purposes, including income tax, employment, tax, etc., regardless if paid by entity or individual.

The goal is to take what is unknown and assign a value based on reasonable expectations so that we can make projections. When the owner is an employee of the entity and there are payroll taxes and other compliance costs paid by the entity, one almost needs to do multiple projections to get to the bottom line—one for the entity that incorporates the payroll costs and one for the owner's personal taxes. Though it may seem like a lot of moving parts, in reality, the business should already have a level of separation from the owner anyway. So, it would be just making a cash flow projection for the business for the rest of the year, which then combines with non-business-related information in order for the owner to determine their personal tax liability (or asset if overpaid).

Example:
Entrepreneur LLC, an S corporation, is owned by John Doe. He wants to do a projection to see what his taxes might be

for the year. As of the end of June, the business has a net profit of $50,000 after all expenses, including wages to himself that amounted to $36,000 with $7,200 paid in federal withholding; he expects the rest of the year to be consistent with the first half of the year.

His projected business information that would flow to the personal tax projection would be:

$50,000/(6/12) = $100,000 net income from the business

John Doe's anticipated W-2 for the year would be:

$36,000/(6/12) = $72,000 with $14,400 ($7,200/(6/12)) of estimated federal withholding taxes paid.

So, on John's personal taxes he would anticipate $172,000 of income and have $14,400 of withholding and could then incorporate the other items like spouse wages, child tax credits, etc., and could also factor in amounts paid with payroll for employment taxes to determine total tax related cash outflows.

Brass Tax

With a reasonable expectation for the components that make up what will be taxable income, deductions, credits, and other items, we can put together our mock tax return. I say "mock" tax return because that is basically what making a projection is. If the year were done, we'd simply prepare an actual tax return. If you use tax preparation software to prepare your own taxes, you can use that software to do much of the calculations to prepare a mock return as well. Just know it'll be slightly different due to the changes from one year to the next. Some programs also incorporate projections and analysis to quickly and easily inject variables into a "next year scenario," which makes much of the work less taxing.

For entrepreneurs taxed as sole proprietorships, though there isn't the added complexity of the corporate tax return or payroll for the owner of the entity, there is self-employment taxes, as well as the deduction for self-employment taxes. Regardless, starting with anticipated business income, one can determine about what their taxes will be. Such projection exercises can be done just about any time of year, and ideally, even before a year begins, it can be beneficial to get the ball rolling with setting money aside for Uncle Sam.

Example:
Jack and Jill are married taxpayers filing a joint return. They have one child under 17 and have $3,000 of child care expenses. Jill has a W-2 job earning $50,000 per year with $7,500 of withholding, and her job provides health insurance. Jack is self-employed, anticipates about $80,000 of business income after approximating vehicle, home office, depreciation, and other unique expenses.

Wages	$50,000
Business Income	$80,000
Deduction for ½ SE Tax	($5,652)
Adjusted Gross Income	$124,348
QBID	($14,870)
Standard Deduction	($24,000)
Taxable Income	$85,478
Income Taxes	$10,684
Child Tax Credit	($2,000)
Child Care Credit	($600)
Income Tax Liability	$8,084
Self-Employment Tax	$11,304
Est. Withholdings	($7,500)
Remaining Tax Liability	**$11,888**

With this information, they would have an idea of their taxes for the year and could make arrangements. This could be to increase Jill's withholding or Jack could have about $1,000 per month set aside for taxes, etc.

Even though the S corporation adds a level of abstraction, one can incorporate into relatively simple projections. I typically like to start with the same starting point as far as anticipated net income for the business without regard to wages to the officer.

Let's use the same facts as the previous example, except that Jack's business is an S corporation. He determines that a reasonable compensation for him is $50,000; before paying any wages to himself, he would project the same $80,000 of business income. But now he can adjust his withholdings from his officer salary to meet his tax liability. For simplicity, we'll say that the employment taxes are 15.3% of his wage income, or $7,650, of which half is withheld from his wages as an employee and the other half is deducted on the business return. Before setting his withholdings, their taxes would be projected as:

Wages (Jack)	$50,000
Wages (Jill)	$50,000
S Corporation Income	$26,175
Adjusted Gross Income	$126,175
QBID (20% of S Corp Inc)	($5,235)
Standard Deduction	($24,000)
Taxable Income	$96,940
Income Taxes	$13,203
Child Tax Credit	($2,000)
Child Care Credit	($600)
Income Tax Liability	$10,603
Est. Withholdings	($7,500)
Remaining Tax Liability	$3,103
Add:	
Employment Taxes:	$7,650
Total Tax liability	**$10,753**

Now Jack would be armed with a reasonable projection that he could use to make decisions. And in this particular case, I would say the most logical course of action would be to incorporate the estimated tax liability of $3,103 into the withholdings for the $50,000 of wages he'll be reporting through his S corporation. That $3,103 would get paid alongside the $7,650 of payroll taxes.

Since our two scenarios take the same data set but alters it with the use of the S corporation, we can run a comparison that shows about an $1,135 benefit as an S corp. Though the reality would be less since there would typically be additional compliance costs for corporate tax return filing, payroll fees, and potentially unemployment taxes that would erode the miniscule benefit for being an S corporation in our examples.

Taxes are not something that many people get excited about. I've had clients that wait to the last minute to file simply because they don't want to have to think about the fact that they will likely have to pay in. Not thinking about it doesn't make it go away, and in many cases, only makes it worse. As an employee, we can just set our withholdings and forget it. As an entrepreneur, it is essential to not only address taxes when they are due, but to project and predict far in advance. Such knowledge helps to be more prepared and make better decisions, and better decision making is what leads to success.

OPERATIONS

Don't worry, I'm not going to tell you how to run your business. Operations is typically the area of expertise for the entrepreneur; after all, they are the heart and soul of the business they are running. When one goes into self-employment or starts a small business, there is generally a solid understanding of what the business does or intends to do. From chocolatiers to real estate agents, delivering a product or service is the core of operating a business. Though some businesses are relatively simple without a significant artisanal touch, many small enterprises rely upon the capabilities of the proprietor to deliver a product or service. One doesn't become an expert just because they opened a shop—generally, the skills and knowledge exist first. These are what form the core competency and competitive advantage for the business to exist and succeed.

What does operations mean or entail as it pertains to a small business? Many of the clients I encounter manage much of their operations in their head. An entrepreneur just knows what needs to be done, when, for whom, etc. Documenting and mapping out a system and flow of functions seems unnecessary and a waste of time to many since they know what needs to be done—why even write it down? The value of having a structured methodology for managing your operations isn't simply the creation of a redundant reminder or unnecessary checklists. It comes in the form of efficiency and scalability. When you actually write out the steps in a process to deliver a product or service, you can determine unnecessary or redundant actions, enhance quality control, and increase the speed of delivery. Plus, in the consideration of growing the business, being able to tell an employee what needs to be done and having the system in place to communicate the flow of resources works out a lot better than expecting people to read your mind.

I, like many small business owners, have experienced the realization that employees can't read minds. It's not like as an entrepreneur we actually expect people to read our minds, but to a certain extent, I have made the mistake and assumed an employee can see the big picture and what is going on, and then expect them to take the initiative to contribute to solving problems and adding value to the business without being explicitly instructed to do so. Nope. Unless you are able to find an exceptional individual, many employees will need direction, supervision, and oversight. That does consume some of your time, but the goal is to develop the person to alleviate the constraints on your time, which takes time to get to that point. It is incredibly difficult to develop people to be valuable members of the team without effectively communicating what needs to be done, how to do it, when it needs to be done, and how one is to know they did it right. The best way to do that is to document your processes like workflow, employ checklists and internal controls, map out a value chain and other tools and strategies so that people don't have to read minds. They can read words and interpret images, and that is reasonable to expect one to be able to do.

Workflow

Workflow is the nuts and bolts of the business. It is the flow of work and or resources needed to deliver the product or service to the market. A simple workflow for a self-employed Uber driver might be to turn on app, select and secure open jobs, and drive people to where they want to go. For most small businesses and self-employed persons, it isn't that simple. Even with respect to the self-employed working with a single contract like a business analyst. Though their workflow would likely not have as much involved with external factors like solicitation, engagement management, billing and receivables management, etc., there would still be a set of expectations their client has; such expectations can vary considerably with respect to timing, quantity, and quality.

There are numerous software applications that are dedicated to workflow management. This would be the preferred route to managing operations and workflow, as trying to use pen and paper is a tiring process rife with human errors. For the most part, with software you can create projects, tasks, notes, and all sorts of other data and content; schedule the timing of work to coincide with other necessary resources and availability; and of course, incorporate checklists to ensure the work is meeting the customers' expectation and desired end result. Software, though an invaluable tool, can also mask the various steps, necessary or otherwise, that contribute to the products and services being delivered. For the most part, the projects and schedules are sort of a shell that indicates work and blocks off time but doesn't always delineate the actual functional steps in the process, as listing every little tiny step would be exhausting.

I've gone through a few different tools for managing workflow. One of the big challenges with software in general is that it doesn't always align to the physical reality of the world it is there to manage. Adjusting processes and practices to fit a toolset doesn't always pan out, as we have certain tasks and sequences for a reason, such as completing tier one work then routing the work to the next level for review and quality control. It seems like a common logical arrangement, yet you'd be surprised to find out how many workflow tools don't have many quality control aspects baked into the product, which can be frustrating and one of the reasons for going through several software products to find the right one. Software is supposed to help us scale and enhance quality, but sometimes internal controls are sacrificed in exchange for ease of use and flexibility within the application. Even in the selection of software, it is good to have a map of what one's workflow processes are in order to determine if a proposed software will be able to manage and if it can be adjusted or configured to make it fit.

Flowcharts

Flowcharts can be an excellent way to map out workflow. A business can have several charts for different processes. One may have a flowchart for the sales and intake process, one for productivity, one for other activities, and so on. There are entire books and other resources on building flowcharts. They can get incredibly complex, especially if there are many variables and decision points within a process. Mapping out a basic set of tasks doesn't require fancy software; a pencil and paper can work, along with most spreadsheet software programs. The goal of drawing out the flowchart is to see the interrelated and sequential nature of functions, which can highlight tasks that can potentially be eliminated, or done in conjunction with other steps, potentially done by a lower level staff member, etc. In addition to the visibility and forward-looking functionality, like being able to see at Step 5 that one needs to order certain materials and have it in place for Step 10, rather than waiting until you get to Step 10 and having to stop production in order to get the required materials to continue.

In an ideal world, the projects and tasks that are created in your workflow management software would correspond to a flowchart of some sort. Flowcharts can help fine tune the process of bidding on work as well as help to identify the variables and decision points within a process. So when one is soliciting and securing new work, such decisions can be incorporated into the bid, reducing the probability of having to incorporate too large of an overhead allowance and losing the bid and not as likely ending up eating one's shirt from a project consuming non-billable resources.

Checklists

Checklists can provide a significant value to an operation. I use them for just about every structured task. It is a great internal control function. There are a number of apps and software available that do just checklists. Much of the workflow management software is built around a series of tasks and projects that are checked off when complete. It ensures that one acknowledge that certain functions have been completed. This is very important—the cost to a business for missing just one small item can be huge, not even considering the additional costs to reputation and lost future sales.

> If I didn't have checklists, it would be possible for me or other employees of my firm to give clients a copy of a tax return and all their source documents back

and potentially miss a very important step like efile the tax return. Sure, they received a copy of the tax return and think everything is fine for a couple weeks, but when the client doesn't get their refund or gets letters demanding payment or for them to file a return, it could get pretty ugly. So before being able to complete the work, the checklist must be completed, verifying that the tasks on the list have also been completed. Eventually, we may have deeply integrated software that can automatically determine that certain tasks are completed without having to manually check things off, but for now, the checklist is a critical component for quality control.

Value Chain

Why does a customer or client choose you over your competition? What makes your product or service more valuable than the next? Is it the scented thank you cards you send them after an initial meeting? Perhaps it's the fact your service includes a follow up and after-the-fact warranty service as part of the promise. Discovering your value can be difficult—we see things in a certain light with a certain perspective. A welder may place a different value on certain aspects of the project than the client. That doesn't mean to not do quality work; it means communicating and articulating value may be a part of your job. Not everything can be visible or understood inherently. Even with respect to less complex work like cleaning, if you are chemical-free or use materials and processes that may be more expensive or require more time to achieve the end result, without communicating that, your client or prospect is left not comparing apples to apples.

One should consider their value chain, which is a set of activities performed in order to deliver a valuable product or service to the market. Though the concept around value chain can get inordinately complex, the simple viewpoint is to look through the eyes of a customer, client, or prospect and determine which components of a product or service have perceived value and which do not. The process of determining, defining, and mapping out a company's value chain has immensely valuable information and helps shape operational directives. The ultimate goal of having a value chain is that your operations focus productivity on the components of perceived value.

Not everything can be broken down into nice and clean objects. There are many aspects in which the customer doesn't see or realize the who, what, where, when, or why, and so places little value on certain activities, but nonetheless, the activities contribute to or are integral as a sequential process or building block towards that valuable component. Also, processes that enhance quality control are important and valuable contributions to the final product or service, regardless of what a customer perceives as value. Often the customer wants a quality product or service at reasonable prices. Quality can be subjective, and it isn't always about utility—all chairs allow one to sit, but a Herman Miller chair is more than a place for our butts; that "more" is special and unique, and has many facets that come together to create the perception of value.

Capacity

Capacity is incredibly important. The biggest resource limitation is time. We can only do so much in a fixed amount of time. As much as we'd like to believe we can do eight hours of project work in a day, the truth is typically less than that. As mentioned previously, total capacity and practical capacity are very different. Many companies employ variable relationships with their subcontractors and employees to shift the risk of inefficiencies, cost of idle time, and other aspects onto the employee/sub. An employee or sub may not even realize it, but when compensation and payment for services and work performance is tied to production, it isn't so the employee can make twice what they would be able to if they were salaried. It is to ensure that labor costs are tied directly to the project value so the company can protect their profit margin against inefficiencies and other scope creep (expansion of work without a corresponding expansion of value).

Production-based compensation can be a good tool to control labor costs, but it can also backfire in the sense that incentivizing production can come at the cost of quality. Since the employees or subs are not paid for quality, their economic behavior would likely be geared towards productivity alone. This could result in a less than ideal perceived value from the customer with less repeat business or referrals. But if one can ensure quality control and happy customers while limiting the risk of exploding labor costs, then it may be something to consider.

A big misconception about capacity is that it is linear, as in, simply adding more resources in a similar proportion will yield the same relationship of capacity and overall revenue and profit figures. Unfortunately, there is the law of diminishing returns, which holds that for each additional input, the corresponding return or output is marginally less than the previous input. This means that if your revenue per full-time equivalent (FTE) employee is X, adding an additional FTE will not by itself increase revenue by that same amount. This happens for many reasons, but the simplest analogy I've heard was like picking apples. First, you collect the low hanging fruit and everything is good, but as you go up the tree, the cost to collect the additional fruit increases. As another example for other business models that are not in the fruit-picking business, it could be that at a certain level, maybe there is someone who is good at bidding out and securing profitable jobs; as the capacity increases, the demand to secure more jobs increases as well, and the ability to obtain as many profitable jobs decreases.

Unfortunately, in business we can't always put the cart before the horse—we can't always secure the jobs and revenue before we build the capacity to deliver the product or service. If we could, life would be great. The risk associated with starting and running a business would be far less if we didn't have to exert inordinate amount of resources just for the possibility that we might be able to extract some value out of the economy. Sometimes, for the self-employed, it can work out nicely if offered a contract before one even leaves their full-time job. Of course, when that contract ends, the cost of that unused capacity (the proprietor's time) will come to roost as we can't stop the mortgage bill and other living costs from coming in just because we haven't secured another gig yet. Having sufficient capacity to meet the production demands but not so much to sap the business's profitability can be a challenging balance. Having a good sales and lead generation process in place can help ensure you are able to deploy the capacity you have and aren't left holding the bag.

FINANCE

Far too many entrepreneurs fail to grasp the importance of finance in the small business world. Yes, capitalism plays a role even for the small business. So many small businesses fail simply because they were undercapitalized, which is another way of saying they ran out of cash. Planning and preparation along with managing one's expectations are critical in being able to go the distance. Plans don't always pan out, so having a dash of resilience in addition to being conservative in one's optimism will greatly help to align projections with a more realistic and accomplishable outcome.

Besides the good old "sweat equity," there are two main forms of capital: debt and equity. As might be implied, debt capital comes from loans, notes, and other forms in which the entity or individual is a borrower and is expected to return the principal with interest. Equity comes from owners who make contributions (can be cash, equipment, or other assets), as well as retaining profits in the business once operating.

As described in earlier sections of the book, determining how much money you'll need to run the business is absolutely essential. It is probably the biggest mistake I've seen from entrepreneurs. It's hard to run a business when you are constantly running out of cash, racking up bank fees, getting penalized for late tax payments, being denied vendor credit, etc.

The main components of finance and managing finance for a small or large business revolve around time and cash, or rather cash flows. Initially, there will typically be cash outflows to pay employees and rent, buy supplies and equipment, etc. The cash inflows would come later from sales and further on from retiring equipment. One aspect that few new business owners understand is the concept of working capital.

Working capital is current assets less current liabilities. Current assets would include not only the cash in the bank account but also things like inventory, accounts receivables, work in process, etc. Current liabilities are the short-term obligations like accounts payable, credit card debt, etc. Where many entrepreneurs get into trouble is with the fact that though the business may be able to anticipate profit over time, in the short term, the business is left holding the bag in the sense that employees, vendors, credit cards, and other obligations will need to get paid before the cash comes in, especially if you give customers time to pay, as in due in 30 days. As a result, many entrepreneurs have a hard realization that a certain amount of cash is needed as an investment in working capital. This doesn't help pay for your household bills, but it is essential for a healthily functioning business.

Doing a bit of math can help figure out financing needs. Ideally, by this point, you have an idea of what the costs to run the business are and would know what kind of equipment and inventory you'll need as well. If you also know about how much sales on credit there will be, you can get a rough approximation for capitalization.

For example, say the business has $10,000 of monthly expenditures (rent, payroll, owner's needs, etc.), will need to have about $5,000 worth of supplies and inventory available, will have about $30,000 of equipment, can generate $15,000 of revenue per month, and will have most sales on credit with 30 days to pay. If you want to have two months of working capital to cover expenditures along with the other needs, you would need:

$$(\$10,000*2)+\$5,000+\$30,000 = \$55,000$$

Though the simple calculation didn't include the collection of sales, which would likely be collected starting in month two, if we subtracted that from the total, the business would run out of money within the first 30 days. No, that doesn't mean that one needs to have $55,000 before starting the business—there are options for obtaining the capital besides equity, like by financing the equipment purchase, for example. However, if you wanted to be properly capitalized without debt, then having the money available to put into the business would make sense. Debt capital reduces the amount of equity capital needed but also increases the amount of monthly cash outflows to sustain the business (through principal and interest payments). Time is the biggest factor when one considers finance. We can take all the activity of a business over the life of a business and mash it together—it may look great, but time is money. Though you can generate sales and earn money, the cost to generate that money often comes due before the sales comes in, and that is what working capital is for.

Cost of Capital

Capital, and capitalism, is like the carbon cycle. Capital has to come from somewhere and will eventually be returned to the universe possibly with different owners (or custodians). As many entrepreneurs struggle with having enough capital, calculating what the business' cost is and differentiating between debt and equity capital may seem unnecessary. In any case, even equity capital can be considered borrowed in the sense that one is borrowing from other opportunities in order to make the small business a reality.

Though finance professionals would have far reaching and much more complex calculations as to what is the cost of capital, we'll stick with relatively simple concepts. Let's say a small business is born. It needs $100,000 in capital (for working capital, equipment, etc.), and after paying for all expenses including owner's salaries, the business will generate $20,000 a year in profits available for distribution to owners. That sounds pretty nice, and a simple calculation will tell you that the return on assets (ROA) is 20% (return/average total assets). If the business is capitalized with just equity financing, then the return on equity is the same 20%.

Here is where we might take a look at leverage and its implications. Given the facts of the scenario, let's say the entrepreneur can borrow $50,000 for the business and pay 10% interest on the debt (we'll assume interest only payments for simplicity). With debt, the total return would be reduced from $20,000 to $15,000 because of the interest payments. Likewise, the return on assets would be reduced. But, the return on equity, which is now $50,000 instead of $100,000 has gone from 20% to 30% from the leverage; not bad at all.

Of course, one might also take into consideration the fact that just because they can extract more leverage and increase the return on equity of the enterprise, if the capital being released doesn't have a place to go that can generate reasonable returns, is it really that great of a move? Generally, if you can redeploy into the business to expand operations, take on additional projects, or even just place in investments that are likely to provide a higher return than the cost of debt, it may be worth it. Fortunately, many entrepreneurs who need capital typically don't have enough without debt, so there is no "excess" capital to worry about.

Regardless, the cost of capital is an important consideration with respect to small business finance. Understanding where capital comes from, its cost, and the ability to maximize the return on capital is like putting your grinding stone on steroids, because the economic return to the proprietor isn't just from spinning the stone, but also from financial management of the resources involved in delivering a product or service.

Vendor Credit

If the business relies upon supplies, inventory, or other purchases, it is possible to incorporate to a certain extent the credit extended with such transactions. Vendor credit is an allowance of time to pay from when a bill is received. For instance, if you order some supplies or inventory and it arrives on the 15th of the month along with the bill stating due in 15 days, that provides 15 days of float, which can help ease cash flow crunches. Additionally, some vendors may provide discounts on early payment with terms like 2% discount if paid within X number of days. Taking advantage of such discounts can add up to significant returns. Though not all vendors allow for credit and some demand payment on delivery.

Sales on Credit

Sales on credit, which is a common occurrence, provides your customers and clients the ability to pay later than the date they receive the invoice from you. Sure, it sounds nice to only accept cash up front, but then there could be a lot of lost business by doing so. Sometimes the project or invoice amount can be rather large, so expecting a full payment up front may be impractical or unreasonable. Sometimes the customer may be receiving funds from third parties like insurance proceeds or grant money and doesn't actually have the money in hand but is going to have it eventually, etc. In any case, providing sales/services on credit can be a good way to secure the job and increase revenues, but it also comes with side effects like bad debt expense and cash flow crunches. With sales on credit, you are providing credit to the customer by giving them time to pay. Most small businesses don't charge for this credit, even on past due balances, as it is difficult enough to get the customer to pay and adding additional charges may not improve the chances of collection.

Bad Debts

As mentioned previously, bad debt expense is the recognition that a portion of your accounts receivable are not collectable. It is such a frustrating process to do all the work to earn revenue, make several attempts to collect only to realize that you won't be getting any money from your customer. To make matters even more painful is when you have employees and other direct costs, as you've already paid and incurred expenditures in delivering the product or service, so not being able to collect isn't just losing something you didn't have, it means that you also paid real money for nothing.

Bad debts are no joke. Many strive to avoid bad debts by requiring deposits, retainers, credit card pre-authorizations, etc. My focus has been on longer-term relationships built around a recurring monthly fee, which avoids the process of invoicing customers and hoping they pay. I've had my fair share of non-payment and recognition of bad debt expense. As much as we'd all like to treat everyone the same and provide the "benefit of the doubt," one does develop a certain vision where you just know when you meet with someone whether they are more likely not to pay you. In those cases, you might increase your fees to account for the added risk and require larger portions up front in the form of a retainer or deposit. No, it isn't fair, and the people that are most impacted are generally going to be those with the least ability to afford it, but when you are in business, you are not running a charity. Non-profits and government programs are there to serve without consideration of profit. I (and many entrepreneurs) have a family to feed, mortgages to pay, etc. Unfortunately, that means you need to protect your interests and resources, especially your time as you will never get back the time you wasted on a client who doesn't pay. That being said, one can of course do pro bono work, but then there is the understanding up front, which is very different from getting stiffed.

Why do so many small businesses struggle with bad debts? There are many factors that contribute to a disproportionate impact on smaller businesses. For one, many people know small businesses don't have the resources or systems in place to do much about it. When does a business establish a relationship with a collection agency? Usually after they have customers who don't pay. The best defense is a good offense; this means structuring your processes and procedures up front before you begin work, ensuring you have a solid understanding with your customer about expectations and fees, having contracts and proposals that are legally binding, so that when it is referred to collection or an attorney, it has a greater chance of achieving success, requiring deposits, and other actions help reduce the probability and damage that a deadbeat customer can cause. Small claims court and other legal actions can be expensive and consume time that an entrepreneur doesn't have without the guarantee of success. Large businesses have actuaries and legal teams and can destroy people's credit and cause real pain to force people not to skip on the bill; even if some of the actions cost more than the benefit, the deterrent effect makes it a solid investment. A small business has to be more guarded as recourse is much more limited, so strive to avoid bad debts, and if at all possible, avoid carrying accounts receivable altogether.

Factoring

Sometimes you need cash, and not 30 days from now—right now. Many small businesses, especially in certain industries, like trucking, engage factoring services to help with their cash flow crunches. Factoring is selling or pledging your accounts receivables to a third party for a fee, much like a payday loan. Generally, the factor (third party buying the accounts receivable) requires guarantees. So if you sell $100,000 of accounts receivable and some of them don't pay, you would be required to replace them. The factor isn't absorbing the risk of non-payment. The fees for factoring can vary. It may seem small like two to four percent, but one should translate that into a common language in order to compare to other financing sources. Total factoring fees over the course of a year divided by average accounts receivables.

> Example:
> Say you have an average accounts receivables balance of $20,000 (it may go up and down but will average $20,000) and factoring receivables over the course of a year costs $4,800 (2% factor fee).

> $4,800/$20,000
> 24% APR

This was a simple example. I've seen some exceed 35%. The calculation can get more complex if your customers are allowed more time to pay like 60 to 90 days or for factoring arrangements with more complex calculations like receiving 70% of the face value of the receivables while still being levied a 2% factor on the full-face value, etc. In any case, the rates are generally going to be at or higher than credit cards, but when you need cash and can't access capital through banks or other traditional sources, what can you do?

I have seen entrepreneurs that get into factoring and end up in an endless cycle where they are constantly selling tomorrow today. The small business owners that get trapped into the factoring game are generally those with less financial understanding, less than stellar credit, and of course, insufficient assets to provide a healthy level of working capital for operations. This, to me, puts the entrepreneur in a position of duress with little options—since banks don't like risk, they can't get a loan and are left with factoring receivables or loan sharks.

Loan Sharks

Yes, there are loan sharks that prey on small businesses. They have names like Kabbage, Ondeck, WebBank, and others. Many have similar operating and promotional practices. Generally, they offer fast financing, providing unsecured debt using what they call straightforward and clear pricing, sometimes even labeled as "simple interest." For the most part, they will collect money on a weekly or even daily basis.

Some of the merchant account providers like Square and PayPal offer loans with fixed fees and recover the principal and interest by holding back a portion of future cash inflows. They may not be the exact same as the loan shark's terms, but they too make some really nice profit on the operation when you take into consideration the duration of the loan, the principal borrowed, and the fees paid for the loan. Like with factoring, the devil is in the details.

Example:
Take for example a loan offer of $10,000 with simple interest of 10% which will be paid off evenly over six months—what is your actual interest rate that you are paying?

Average Debt – Since you are paying the balance down evenly throughout the term of the loan, the average debt will be $5,000 (($0+$10,000)/2)

The total interest is known at $1,000.

Since it is for six months, we can extrapolate the annual interest rate as follows:

$$\$1,000/\$5,000/(6/12) = 40\%$$

I know there are times when a small business is in need of cash, but paying 40% interest is pretty painful. Not all of them are that high— some are lower and some even higher. The reason these sharks exist is because so many small businesses are started without sufficient capital, and the owners may not have the best credit rating. Even if the owner has decent credit, banks are a bit more conservative about small business loans, especially if the business hasn't been around for several years. In the absence of traditional providers of finance, the loan sharks are free to prey upon these new entrepreneurs with impunity. Knowing that the interest rate is at or above credit card rates, wouldn't it be easier to consider a credit card instead?

Revolving Debt

Revolving debt can be a valuable source of financing if managed properly. Revolving debt for the most part includes credit cards and lines of credit. They are revolving in the sense that one doesn't need to apply more than once and is allotted a credit limit which can be drawn upon, paid down, and drawn upon again in a revolving fashion. The benefits include flexibility, both in terms of access to capital as well as in repayment. Many entrepreneurs are nervous about credit cards and revolving debt in general, and rightfully so— we have been conditioned with horror stories of how being detached from our perception of money and the frictionless swipe of a credit card can quickly get out of control. But if one understands and appreciates what capital can do for the business and can utilize it for good, then revolving debt can be an incredible resource. Consider a business with no other debts that generates enough income but much of their sales are made on credit, and the business ends up having to wait for customers to pay them. Without access to capital, it might run out of cash, but by simply shifting the timing in which cash is utilized to settle expenditures to better match the timing of the cash inflows, everyone is happy.

Time is one of the biggest benefits of revolving debt. When the card is swiped, or the line of credit is drawn upon, the business has between 30 to 60 days before it would need to be settled to avoid paying interest. It is probably the only way (other than borrowing from your parents) to get short-term financing without having to pay any interest.

Another big potential benefit is the rewards; many cards nowadays are keen on incentivizing you to keep using the card by rewarding you for using it. Rewards can vary—some have confusing points, some with airline miles, and some with easy to understand cash back bonuses. You can get as high as 2% back on purchases (possibly more in certain categories and additional bonus opportunities). Of course, being a small business owner, one also can appreciate the other side of the equation since most businesses are charged somewhere between 2.5-4% in transaction fees for accepting credit cards. Much of that charge goes right back to the purchaser in the form of rewards, like being required to discount your products and services. But as a purchaser, you would be wise to maximize your utilization of capital. With the reward points, and providing you pay the card off before the interest sets in, not only are you getting free short-term financing, you are also being paid to use it. It is for that reason that I have as much as possible put on reward cards, even when I have the cash to pay up front; I then simply pay the entire balance when due.

The drawback of revolving debt is that interest rates are typically higher than with a term loan, so if you are carrying a balance or in need of more intermediate to long-term financing, then revolving debt may not be the best fit. The rates are typically variable and will go up and down with market forces. Additionally, your credit can be impacted from over utilization. The calculations can change, but generally, if you carry a balance of over 30% of your credit limit, it can reflect negatively on your credit score. Of course, if you have cash, you can simply pay down the card before it is due to keep from being over that amount while still enjoying the rewards. If you have decent credit, the financial institutions will generally provide enough of a credit limit, so it shouldn't be an issue unless there are larger purchases.

Additionally, I have seen entrepreneurs that do get into a hot mess from revolving debt, primarily because of poor cash flow management and an expanding personal lifestyle that saps the business of financial resources that would have otherwise been available to pay off the short-term debt when due.

Term Loans, Secured and Collateralized Debt

Most banks big and small have small business financing products like term loans. The SBA (Small Business Administration) has specific guidelines and requirements that help shape some of the small business financing options that exist. For the most part, the SBA isn't underwriting the loan itself but establishes an enhancement or endorsement for the loan product that meets its specifications, like insurance—this provides a guarantee of a certain portion of the principal if the debtor (the entrepreneur) isn't able to pay.

Some banks are better than others when it comes to SBA financing. Most of the large banks have dedicated people or departments that handle SBA-related financing. Term loans are not all SBA notes either; sometimes it can be more of a pain to go through the SBA process and meet their stringent requirements. As such, banks will typically have term loans that are not SBA loans. They can be secured or unsecured.

Secured debt means the debt is being backed by an asset, which could be a house, a car, or some other type of collateral. This can also be called collateralized debt. As secured debt provides the lender with some recourse, the overall risk to the bank is less than with unsecured debt, so typically, the rates would be lower. Debt used to purchase equipment like vehicles, bobcats, and other titled tangible property would typically be underwritten as secured/collateralized debt. Sometimes, notes are underwritten where a specific asset isn't pledged, but the entity itself may be pledged as the asset, which would stipulate that selling the company would constitute the requirement to settle the debt prior to disbursing funds to the seller.

Additional requirements of term loans that are common include insurance, such as life insurance and general liability insurance; just in case you die, they want to make sure that the life insurance proceeds pay off the loan first. Banks may also require on an annual basis (or more frequently) copies of the business tax return and owner's personal tax returns, as well as financial statements that may need to be prepared by a CPA.

Term loans, as the name implies, provide finance for a specified term, like seven years or even longer. Like a mortgage, term loans would generally have regular payments that include principal and interest, typically on a monthly frequency. The interest rate can be fixed or variable (will go up and down with market forces). Though large businesses can issue bonds that can span decades with semi-annual interest-only payments, small businesses generally don't have access to such financing.

Notes and loans can be a good source of capital. If the business is in need of longer-term capital, then a loan is typically a good choice. The monthly payment is predictable for cash flow purposes, the interest rates are generally lower than short-term financing arrangements, and the amount of capital available will generally exceed that of other products; if you need more than $50,000, a loan or note would be the main choice typically.

Unconventional Capital

Getting creative can have benefits in business. Take, for example, a business that needs some capital, with the choice between loan sharks, factoring, and revolving debt, the result is generally going to be a painful realization that capital isn't cheap. However, what if you could borrow from your 401k plan? That would potentially provide the capital needed, the interest is deductible as a business expense, and the interest income is deferred into the 401k plan. Not all plans are the same—some would have limitations on loans or require it be for current employees only. You may have to set up a 401k plan with your new entity and transfer the funds over in order to execute a loan transaction. The loan would typically have a maximum of $50,000 and that would be if you have at least $100,000 in your 401k plan, and you would need to pay it back within five years. So it's not a done deal or even a simple and easy way to get capital, but with some creativity, it can provide valuable resources at reasonable rates.

Most small businesses are organized as pass-through entities to avoid double taxation. But if the goal was to use retirement assets to provide equity capital financing, then a C corporation would be needed. This would include self-directed IRAs, as well as similar operations. There are a few companies that assist with such structures, such as Benetrends. Self-directed IRAs and 401ks are plans that retain the tax deferred status of being a retirement plan while providing a certain amount of discretion, like investing in a small business. There are many rules and restrictions—even setting up the self-directed plan can be cumbersome. Then, depending on what the money is to be used for, there could be some real issues and additional taxes levied if the Department of Labor or the IRS deems certain transactions are not consistent with the tax-deferred status. If done right, the result would be that the 401k or self-directed IRA plan is an owner of the C corporation; you could also be an owner of the C corporation. The upside is that now there is money in the business that can be used for working capital and other needs; additionally, if the business is worth a great deal more money later on and you sell it, the gain is typically deferred in the retirement account until you draw on it in retirement. The downside is, of course, the double taxation; any profits get subjected to corporate taxes, and any money you get from the business will be in the form of wages, dividends, or other taxable compensation. In addition, for certain structures there may be a requirement that you are not in control of the entity, like if your own self-directed IRA owns the corporation, it would not be viewed favorably if you are the board of directors, the president, the only employee, etc. though in such circumstances you can work for the entity, there should be someone unrelated that can potentially fire you.

Personal Credit

Your personal credit is very important when it comes to financing your business. Much of the potential loans, notes, and lines of credit are to a certain extent tied directly to a business owner's personal credit rating. You should have an idea of what your score is and what might be on your credit report. Everyone is entitled to a free credit report once a year and can go to annualcreditreport.com to get their report. That report doesn't necessarily include the score. There are numerous places in which a person can get their report and all three credit agency scores, though most would charge for such services. Many credit card companies include the credit score as part of their normal monthly statement, so one wouldn't need to pay to get their score if you have a credit card that reports it. Additionally, through personal finance apps like Mint and others, you could obtain your personal credit score and repair service options.

One's score is the result of several factors. The three agencies have slightly different information sources, so the respective FICO (Fair Isaac Corporation) score may often be slightly different from one another. For instance, a relationship with one creditor, vendor, or financial institution may report to one, all, or none of the reporting agencies. As such, the information used by one agency may be slightly different from another. Additionally, financial institutions may prefer or require their lenders to use one agency's score and not the others for consistency. For the most part, the scores and narrative reports that accompany the score would typically be relatively close to one another and move in a strong correlated pattern as much of the information is the same or very similar.

Your score will be based on several factors such as payment history, outstanding balances, length of credit history, types of credit accounts, and new credit applications made. With your score and report, if the score is over 670 or so, it indicates good credit and should enable access to capital, though it would be preferred to be at 740 or greater indicating very good credit. Anything above 800 indicates exceptional credit, and if you have that, then this section is likely providing little benefit as you would already have established good credit history, don't miss payments, and would otherwise already be aware of and exercising good personal financial habits that got you to that point.

If your score is not so good, the ideal time to repair it is before you need credit. But in my experience, it seems more common that those with poor credit realize the hard way the price they pay for having poor credit right when they need credit. This leaves them with much fewer desirable forms of credit like loan sharks and payday loans. Correcting your credit can be an arduous process. There are many operators out there that promise to help fix your credit and renegotiate debt and do all sorts of magical stuff for a fee. Some of them may be worth it, but in any case, the tools and techniques are out there for everyone to access.

The first step is getting the report and seeing what can be done. If there are discrepancies or issues you disagree with, then file a complaint or dispute with the credit reporting agency. They typically have a limited amount of time to address. Work with the lenders and creditors that have filed items on your report and see how to restore good standing with them so that it starts reporting positively on your report, etc. The moral of the story is that there is no bad time to start owning your credit score and report; address the issues and take steps to improve and maintain a good credit score, even if you don't plan to use it. That way, it's there for you if/when you do.

> Even those that have been good, responsible financial citizens for years can be plagued by bad credit. I have clients who have been good about managing their debt, making payments, being current on taxes, and so forth for several years, but when the time came to expand the business and they needed additional working capital, the banks said no thanks because there was a tax lien that will stay on their report until the debt is paid in full. So even though they were making payments and being current on everything for years, certain items can stain your ability to access capital for many years.

Business Credit

Yes, a business can have a credit rating! Sure, large businesses are able to borrow billions of dollars with just their reputation (in addition to reputable third parties that report on their credit worthiness). For a small business though, it can take a good amount of time and good financial behavior to have enough credit not to have to personally guarantee unsecured debt for your business. Initially, most unsecured, uncollateralized, and unguaranteed finances would be through vendors, if at all. This would come from ordering supplies and materials, inventory, engaging contractors for work performance, etc. As for loans and debt, banks and financial institutions are quite guarded and conservative when it comes to lending. I haven't seen an unsecured note underwritten to a small business without a personal guarantee on it. More common is the additional requirement to also have life insurance and liens and other aspects that provide recourse to their non-collateralized debt. For debt with collateral, like in real estate, vehicles, or equipment, there is a bit more flexibility, but again, the banks have actuaries that do the math and require a good starting amount of equity in the asset and an amortization schedule that approximates a greater principal payment than the expected depreciation in value. So if worse comes to worst, they are more likely than not to recover their position through the calculation and mitigation of the risk they are undertaking in their underwriting.

That being said, the business credit scoring and reporting is out there and does have some value. Even though banks do most lending, markets are continuously changing and trending into more decentralized and P2P (peer-to-peer) lending mechanisms, which would likely rely upon third-party data sources in order to provide a risk and appropriate rate to apply as a cost of capital being deployed to an entity without personal guarantee. Also, the banks and SBA incorporate business credit scores into their decision-making process, even if they are demanding a personal guarantee from the owner. There are different agencies out there. Which ones are the most important are difficult to determine as different lenders may use different agencies or none at all in their decision. When you open a credit card, line of credit, note, or other loan, you should inquire which, if any, agencies they report to.

Dun and Bradstreet

www.dandb.com

You can register for your free D-U-N-S number and self-report on certain aspects. They collect data from different sources and generate a paydex score. Their scoring is based primarily on payment history, so paying on time, or better yet early, is what will give you a better score, but you'd want to ensure with the lender they are reporting to the credit reporting agencies.

Experian

www.experian.com/small-business/services.jsp

They use data points from various sources to compile a profile and score about your business. They also incorporate personal credit info into a blended scoring metric that may include multiple business owners' personal credit information into how they calculate.

Equifax

www.equifax.com/business/

Equifax uses information from public sources, in addition to consolidated reporting from the SBFE (Small Business Financial Exchange) to develop their metric and reporting on business credit worthiness. They have several grades and scores that indicate a business' risk and likelihood of payment default, etc.

FICO

www.fico.com/en/products/fico-small-business-scoring-service

The FICO business score, which also incorporates owner's personal credit into its algorithm to determine business credit score, has seen use by the SBA in particular as a qualifier tool in credit decisions. Though it may not negate the requirement to have a personal guarantee on an SBA note, it could prequalify or speed up the time it takes to underwrite and close on such a valuable source of capital for a small business.

SALES

I'd be remiss if I didn't discuss sales. Some people love sales, others find the whole process abhorrent. Unfortunately, we all have to sell to a certain extent. You may think that as an engineer or cook you don't have to sell anything, but even as employees or contractors, we have to sell our most valuable asset: our time. In that sense, we all are bound to the task of selling. They didn't teach sales in accounting school, and it isn't on the curriculum for many disciplines, but is a critical component of being successful as an entrepreneur.

At least as employees, there is a certain degree of continuity and stability in one's earnings. Some self-employed may also enjoy a certain level of certainty depending on how they entered into their contract position with respect to previously established rapport or relationships that guarantee a duration and volume of compensation. For most, we have to sell products or services and participate in the great marketplace that is our capitalistic economy.

Sales is a process, which can encompass a wide array of activities and an even more diverse set of definitions and interpretations. Generally, the process of "sales" involves just about everything that happens before that handshake signaling the deal has been made; before actual work begins. The lines can get blurry, especially with respect to services in which the bidding and work can overlap, or where one has to exert a considerable amount of effort in just obtaining the job. Additionally, with aspects like existing customers or clients, remarketing, upselling, and referral opportunities encompass sales, but can typically be done seamlessly alongside normal work if incorporated into the natural process of delivering services.

I don't like the concept of "selling" to someone; I like how Jeffrey Gitomer, who wrote the "Little Red Book of Selling," puts it: people hate to be sold, but love to buy. I know I certainly don't like pushy sales people trying to sell me (gross), but when I am looking for a product or service, and the company or sales rep addresses my concerns in a trustworthy manner and meets my expectations, then I am excited to buy.

We can be really good at what we do, from accounting to apothecary manufacturing, but if we don't have people buying, it doesn't matter how good we are. Ever wonder why there are scam artists, fraudsters, liars, and just plain crap out there? You'd think people wouldn't fall for tricks and traps. Nope. If you are good at sales, you can sell just about anything, including nothing. Snake oil peddlers can be a good thing. I know nobody wants their grandma getting duped into throwing her money away, but for every victim and crook, there is the opportunity to be a champion. Not of the Super Bowl, but of whatever it is you're in the business of providing. Simply by being good at what you do, honest, and transparent... booya! You too can sell. The hard part is just getting that phone to ring—the rest is just describing what you are an expert at, and that shouldn't be too hard, right?

Know Your Product

Selling products may sound simple, but a customer's purchasing decision isn't always about price. Look at Amazon—they don't always have the lowest price, but they have created a marketplace like no other, and their distribution system is so efficient and dependable that many choose to trust Amazon. Amazon also has created a massive marketplace in which sellers compete with one another to reach those customers, so customers get the best of both worlds: the guarantees, ease of use, trustworthiness, and reliability of the platform combined with a highly competitive pricing marketplace that ensures the customer (and Jeff Bezos) end up the winner.

Retail can be a tough business to be in because of the Amazons of the world. It used to be the big box stores snuffing out the little mom and pop storefronts. Now even some of the big box retailers have to evolve their business models to square off with Amazon and others. Amazon is so good at what they do that for many products, you can order it and receive it in less time than it would take for you to go to the store and pick it up.

Don't throw rocks at a tank. What I mean is that as a little guy, one doesn't have the same economies of scale and supply and distribution channels as the big guys. So, selling the exact same thing as a larger, more efficient competitor is not likely to yield positive results. Like trying to sell corn that costs you more to bring to market than your neighbor—they can always have a lower price and higher profit margin than you.

There is hope, and if you are selling products and intend to sell on Amazon, I would recommend curating your strategy for just that. There are good resources available including books, blogs, and other content that are specifically targeted towards the Amazon business. Otherwise, specialization or differentiation is essential. If you are different and/or unique to what is available elsewhere, then the customer is not comparing apples to apples. But being different isn't enough—you have to be able to communicate why different is better than the alternative. Being able to showcase how you are different and better can enable success, even if you're not offering the lowest cost.

It used to be that people would go to a retail establishment, try things out, price the items, and then buy on Amazon. Now we are seeing some of the opposite, where people do their research online first, then go to a store and if the price is within a reasonable range from the Amazons of the world, then the purchase is made in person. In any case, selling products and being in retail can be a tough business, but one can be successful as long as they understand the marketplace and competition and carve out their place with deliberate execution of a strategy.

Services as Products

Being a service provider myself, I can tell you, I was very skeptical and resistant to the idea of productization of service offerings. My initial reaction was that it would only lead to commoditization, which is in a sense the opposite of differentiation, and in the world of the small service provider, being identical to larger, more optimized competitors sounds like a recipe for disaster. But it actually ends up being quite the opposite in many cases, which is counterintuitive. Even if service offerings are very similar to larger companies, as a smaller firm with less overhead and operating costs, one can be nimbler and successfully compete. although, many of the larger service providers can often leverage their size and economies of scale and add auxiliary functions and support capabilities to put icing on the cake for the core services, which may be difficult to match. But with the ever-expanding technology and decentralization of our economy, even the most centralized functions can be available to increasingly smaller and smaller operators.

What productization does is provide a description of the scope of services included in a particular service, and as the scope is clearly defined, the price as well can be clearly stated. Since the service provider can control the costs associated with the scope of work, this leads to greater standardization of service delivery, greater efficiencies, and scalability of the business itself. It becomes much easier to charge for out-of-scope work, since the scope is clearly defined. It can also broaden the spectrum of potential clients that the business can serve as one can more precisely match work with billings.

For example, as an accountant, typical "products" might be something like monthly accounting for a standard-sized small business, and the scope would be limited to X number of transactions, X number of checks written, or a number of other variables, and the price for this standard product would be $XXX per month. When I moved to a productized service menu, it provided more of a modularized scope building exercise. Some clients need corporate tax returns, some are self-employed, etc., so now I can tailor the engagement to meet their needs while still being profitable, because every product is clearly defined, and I know exactly what my cost input is for delivering such services. Though there will always be the tire kickers or the prospects that want you to do things a certain way, by defining what you do and for how much, you eliminate the negotiation—you are either a fit or you are not a fit. If they're a good fitting client, then the client gets great service at reasonable prices that provide the firm with a good profit margin on the relationship. If they are not a good fit, then you don't take on the prospect; it's that simple.

> When I started my accounting firm, and being hungry for new business, I would take on just about any project that came my way. It took a while to get to a stable client base and regular cash flow to have the confidence to turn down prospects. Cash flow, and the amount of time one has to achieve it, are essential. If you are looking at less than three months of cash available for your business that is running a deficit, it puts you in a state of duress in which decisions are made out of the perception of necessity rather than what is the best course of action for the business. Having enough cash is essential so that you can build the business you envision and not grow sideways just to keep from drowning. Though this is more of a finance aspect, the conversation around productization can be difficult if you need any client you can get your hands on. Now I only work with clients that fit the mold that my firm is designed to serve, but it took a while to get to that point.

Service productization further creates incentives to drive innovation and efficiencies. With the end result and the price determined, the aspects in between the handshake and service completion can change over time, such as utilizing software to automate certain tasks, outsourcing aspects that can be done by lower cost labor resources, and so on. It is akin to fixed fee or value-based billing. This, in a sense, is aligning your pricing with clients' perception of value, the client is paying for the result not the effort. So rather than billing by the hour which incentivizes more effort, billing by the result incentivizes efficiency and creates a win-win.

It's not always possible to productize or use value-based billing. Sometimes the variables are too great—like with a mechanic shop, replacing one component may have a good amount of predictability, but there could be other things that become apparent as the job progresses. Many in the legal profession may not be able to know how many hours they will have to exert in order to resolve a client's case and have to bill by the hour. But even if most of the services can't be productized, sometimes there will be certain items that can and have a fixed and determined price that is published, such as an oil change, or an estate planning initial consultation. Such services (products), though limited, would also serve as a potential foundation to building a larger relationship with more services delivered.

Know Your Customer

Knowing your customer is an important skill. Who is your ideal customer? It can be a difficult question to answer—though we know our own experience and interpretations, we can't really get into the mind of others. Thankfully, there is a considerable amount of information that is available to the public to answer that question. But experience can be the best teacher. As in, those who have considerable experience in the field or profession that their business will operate may already have an idea of who that customer is, what their expectations are, etc.

Why must one know who their customer is? Because it can be difficult to be successful if you are not selling the right products and services at the right price and so on. A helpful exercise is to imagine you are the customer, and from the customer's point of view, define the product or service that the customer is looking for. How old is your ideal customer? What stage of life or affluence does this person have? Where are they located from your business? When do they make the decision to buy? Is it after work, in their mid-career, in retirement, before they attend grad school, etc.? What specific attributes is your customer looking for from your product or service?

Once you are able to identify your customer, you can then use that information to create advertising campaigns targeted towards this person. It also helps refine yourself and business to better meet this person's needs and wants. Your preferred customer can change as other aspects change, like what products or services your business is optimized to deliver to the economy, changes in customers' preferences or needs, etc. Understanding your customer, much like many aspects, is not a fixed description, but one of many moving parts that come together to enable success as an entrepreneur.

Know Yourself

Equally important is to understand what we are capable of. What products or services are you designed to deliver to the market? What are you good at, and what should you avoid? Conducting a SWOT analysis (strengths, weaknesses, opportunities, and threats) is a good place to start when evaluating what we can and should be engaging in. Taking a hard look at yourself and the business you are building is a great exercise. Sometimes one can get tunnel vision, and without deliberate tasks like conducting a SWOT analysis, things can get missed. A SWOT analysis isn't a one-and-done exercise; one can do it periodically and ideally see changes and continue to strive for improvement. A SWOT analysis is sort of like a performance review for your business—you as the owner are reviewing your employee (the business) in order to identify the various aspects, highlight and accentuate the strengths, address weaknesses, mitigate threats, and seize on opportunities.

Strengths would encompass advantages that your business has. What you are able to do better, faster, or at a lower cost than others? A particular process, product, or unique service offering that potential customers can't get elsewhere would be excellent to accentuate. Weaknesses are what cause you to lose a sale—it could be price, it could be experience in a particular service area, etc. Sometimes weaknesses can also serve as opportunities in the sense that improving upon a weakness can create strengths. Opportunities can come from external factors like trends in the marketplace, lifestyle patterns, technology, social behavior, changes in purchasing preferences, etc. Threats can come from competition, obstacles, financial stress (cash flow), changes in the business environment, etc. For example, if new machinery that you can't afford is making a process you employ obsolete, that might be considered a threat.

After you've gone through your analysis and identified your strengths, weaknesses, opportunities, and threats, this would potentially lead toward the creation of a unique selling proposition (or USP). A USP is like it sounds: something unique about your business, products, or services that are somewhat exclusive to you. There are worksheets and other tools available online (most are even free) that can help with the exercise; for the most part, you'd be evaluating various aspects of your products or services, ideally from a customer's value perception. Identifying what makes your business unique can give you a competitive edge to leverage into greater sales and profitability. Considerations like speed of delivery, price, quality, reliability, etc. would receive a quantitative grade, and a comparison to your competition would determine aspects that need improvement to help your business stand out. Of course, you will need to know who your competition is before you can make comparisons.

Competition, the (In)visible Hand

Understanding who you are competing with is vital. Fortunately, with the advent of the internet and the information revolution, knowing what is out there is much easier than it used to be. Even aspects like your competition's pricing and quality can be available through crowd-sourced data sets that are on Google, Yelp, social media, lead generation marketplaces, and others. A quick Google search for your particular product or service in your geographic area can show you a few options, and taking a gander at their websites can tell you a lot about who they are.

How do you stack up? Are they cheaper, faster, have a broader selection of offerings, etc.? Experience, again, can be the best teacher. Ever wonder why whenever you go anywhere, call Comcast, message Sprint, or interact with just about any business that isn't small, you get inundated with requests for feedback? The "would you recommend us to a friend" question is a big one—someone somewhere determined that by answering that question, it will lead to a better potential of actually getting a referral. Such information is invaluable to a business, instantaneously receiving data from customers pertaining to the value perception or lack thereof from their customers.

You too can check the pulse of your business. Simply asking for candid feedback, expressing a genuine desire to improve satisfaction can get even better information than the big guys get from their automated surveys. Plus, as a small and nimbler operator, you can evolve more rapidly to the changing preferences and demands of the customers. You can also employ software and deploy robots just like the big guys, but be sure that such engagement fits with the kind of customer relationships you are striving to build.

Who is your real competition? Just because two businesses are in the same industry or profession doesn't mean they are in direct competition with one another. As a CPA firm, I am not necessarily competing with every other CPA firm out there. Some focus solely on individual tax return clients, some do auditing, etc. It isn't just businesses that have a similar profession or license, but more so businesses that provide the same or similar products or services to the same or similar customer that you target.

After a few years in business, it can be easier to pinpoint some of the more direct competition, either through customer acquisitions or attrition, by finding out where the customer came from in the case of an acquisition and where they went to for attrition. Even better information is to find out why they left or why they came, was it price, quality, etc.? With that info, it wouldn't be a guessing game as to what your customers' value perception is—you can potentially have access to your customers' value reality.

Like many things, competition changes over time. Businesses evolve and adjust their products and services along with their target audience and preferred customer. Being cognizant of the competition along with having a relevant product or service that meets the needs and demands of the customer/client are essential in staying on top of the constantly changing business environment.

Know Your Market and Price Accordingly

Marketing is a process that strives to achieve customer satisfaction and alignment of a business's actions towards that objective. In layman's terms, it's to figure out what the customer wants and make sure that we are selling what they are buying. Marketing can get incredibly complex, which is why there are professions and advanced degree disciplines in the subject area.

With an understanding of your products or services, your customer, your competition, and your costs or inputs, you can then strive to determine what the best medium is for engaging your customer and the appropriate price points for your products and services. This is critical, as trying to deploy a product or service at a price that is inconsistent with customer expectation may not provide the results you are hoping for. Just because your cost to deliver a product or service is X, doesn't mean that the customer is willing to pay X + 1; market forces determine prices.

Price can be somewhat subjective, especially with respect to services as it is not as homogeneous as products tend to be. Differentiating your products and services can also help provide additional wiggle room in the price, providing you can articulate and incorporate into the customer's value perception. In any case, price is a major factor and should not be applied arbitrarily. An evaluation of your market, competition, and customer preferences collide to determine reasonable prices. If the prices are too high, you won't have as many sales; too low and you could lose money or be perceived as being the "cheap guy," which most prefer not to be the cheap operator.

Before I productized my services, there was always an expectation of negotiation, which I am not a big fan of. I'd have to add an extra 10-20% to my initial proposal just so I could give it back to sweeten the pot and close the deal. But now that my services are modular and productized, there is no negotiation.

Nobody goes to a restaurant and says, "I'll take the hamburger, that looks good, but I'll only pay you 80% of what you want." The price is the price, take it or leave it. That doesn't mean I can charge whatever I want—the prices are within a reasonable range of the market. With price being in the expected range that a customer had in mind, providing the other components they are looking for are present, then there is no need to negotiate—a good value exists for both parties.

Your market also includes consideration as to how you will deliver your product or service. Will it be online or in person? Will you have a storefront or commercial space that customers can visit, like an office for service provides, or a showroom, etc.? The "place," as it is referred to in the four Ps concept of marketing, is the very medium in which commerce is engaged.

Expect the Unexpected

We are not always good about predicting the future, but one can develop reasonable anticipations about the future by paying attention to what is going on in the world. The overall economy may be growing, or it could be contracting—how would that change the decisions you anticipate about the business? Many of us by default project in more or less a linear fashion. For instance, if you have been growing the business by about 2% per month over the previous year or so on average, it would seem logical to expect a continuation of such trend. However, life isn't always that simple. Seasonality, contingency, chance, or other factors can contribute to a trend, which may or may not continue. Extrapolation of a trend can be a reasonable assumption, but it could also lead to false indicators and reliance upon resources that don't materialize.

Climate change and severe weather can alter the consumer's demands, preferences, and timing of purchases. Though some products and services can recover from temporary alterations in sales, others are not so resilient. I think of burritos, an example used on a news report after a massive snow storm seized Boston; the analyst explained how people who were going to buy shoes still need shoes, so there may be pent up demand for some things, but not for others—like burritos. People are not going to buy two burritos to make up for the burrito they didn't buy on the day the storm hit. Having contingency plans and exploring scenarios that could impact your business can help you be prepared for such occurrences and limit the negative impact that may be felt. Some things will be more visible with experience—a little rain may not impact sales, but if you rely upon people dining at your rooftop restaurant, it just might.

International trade and government regulations can also create some headaches. Not just for those in the import-export businesses either. Changing costs for supply chains can impact decisions up and down the economy, regardless of industry, though certain industries would feel the pinch much more directly. For instance, a tariff on agricultural products would cause farmers to potentially reduce their outlook as far as profitability in the future. As a result, they may decide to extend the use on some equipment, delaying major purchases, and/or reducing consulting and other service providers' scope of work provided to them. Government regulations, whether for environmental, financial, safety, or other aspects, can create additional burdens and compliance costs on businesses and affiliated industries. Getting some regular news from reliable sources can help provide some of the warning signs to offset regulatory and trade risk through preparedness of potential changes, along with having some diversification in your revenue sources.

Own Your Brand

A brand is your business's personality—it is what you are known for. Having consistency with respect to language, imagery, and other items help contribute to a brand. A professionally designed logo provides a nice polished look. Fortunately, with the ever-expanding sharing and gig economy, there are marketplaces out there like 99designs. This site allows you to create a competition among designers around the world, and after a few rounds of filtering out the designers you don't fancy, you can get a decent logo, optimized for web, social media, print, and other aspects, all for less than a thousand bucks typically. Alternatively, you could go to a local designer or advertising firm to help. The costs would be much higher, but the results can be much better tailored to your desires. Your logo is just part of your brand. No, you don't need a logo, and in many instances, like real estate, your picture is sort of your logo.

A decent website is a must. Even if most prospects don't find you online, having a presentable website is like a resume and provides assurance to a prospect that you are professional and legitimate. Many industries and professions do rely to a certain extent upon web and search traffic to generate leads. As such, a well-optimized site is important to actually generate leads through your website. Optimized, which is short for search engine optimized or SEO, means that the site is designed and curated in a way that is better suited to match with internet searches. Google and other search engines are continuously improving and changing their algorithms to align the end user's desired and expected outcome with results. As such, much of the tricks of the trade change rapidly. We can't just put a bunch of keywords or zip codes in the footer of a site and hope for traffic—you actually have to have relevant, recent, and organic content. Not too much, not too little, not too young, not too old, and so on. There are entire books and blog series on the subject, so if you are going to do it yourself, getting some more specific and dedicated knowledge in the subject would be advisable.

As for site building, that too has become much easier than in the past. One doesn't need to buy a URL (web address) from one broker, subscribe to a hosting site from another company to actually publish your site, and manage the site through yet another application. It can be done all in one through one of the website building sites like Wordpress, Squarespace, Weebly, Wix, and others. Some have greater flexibility in the design elements, but most include cookie-cutter, drag-and-drop style editors. Squarespace (and possibly others) goes a step further where you can get a Gmail account set up alongside the website. I generally would prefer to see email addresses match with the websites for the businesses I engage with. If your email is johndoeconstruction8573@gmail.com, it doesn't have the same impact as a more professional looking john@doeconstruciton.com would have.

There are many elements that go into a brand. Website and logo are big ones, but many smaller aspects add up to the larger impression and perception of what your brand is. Get decent business cards—unless you plan to give out 10,000 cards before you get one phone call, it is worth the extra ten cents per card for higher quality print and stock. I like moo.com for business cards but Vistaprint, among others, can also provide a good product at reasonable rates. Your letterhead, if you use one, doesn't have to be super fancy or expensive; you can even download some professional looking templates for Microsoft Word or a Google Docs, and when combined with printing on something other than standard copier paper, it takes it to a whole new level. Choice of font can be a big decision. Some advocate for having a font for digital content and a font for print, or a pair of fonts for each that mesh well. In any case, having the consistency of language, tone, font, imagery, and other elements is important for building and maintaining a brand; if you are not telling the same story, it becomes difficult for people to associate your brand with a particular story. Don't forget that as the entrepreneur, you are the star of the story; big businesses are faceless. If you don't advocate for the individual that puts the face on the business, then a prospect is choosing between a big business with a more reputable brand and credibility versus a small and less established entity. People do business with people.

Advertising

Advertising is a means of communicating with your intended audience. It is how people become aware that your business and products or services even exist. There is a lot that goes into advertising. Back in the day, one would hang a shingle outside their storefront, put their listing in the Yellow Pages, and send out fliers or mailers, among other methodologies. Today there is a plethora of ways to get the attention of your intended customer. The mechanics continue to change, as does the appetite the customer has for being subjected to advertising.

Advertising can encompass images and videos to help capture attention and motivate action. Some try to be funny, or serious, or play on emotional responses like fear. For instance, an elder care law firm may put out copy (as in ad copy, or copywriting material) that might have a tagline of, "Dying without a will or estate plan kills your legacy." The goal being to spark action, so that someone who is advanced in age (ideally with enough assets to worry about an estate plan) sees the ad and remembers that they don't have a plan and might contact that firm to have a conversation.

There are all sorts of companies and freelance individuals that can help with some or all aspects of advertising. Additionally, there are many titles available on specific channels (like Google, Facebook, etc.) for those who wish to do it themselves. Even if you intend to outsource the advertising component, a certain degree of ownership in the process should be expected. You can't just hire someone that will be able to read your mind and know what your vision or intended message and brand is for the business you are trying to build. They would be there for the technical aspects, like taking your message, tone, etc., and translating it into actionable items that can be deployed into the space more efficiently than if you were to fumble through your AdWords account on your own.

The primary purpose of advertising—why we spend money on something that isn't part of our core operations—is to grow the business. I know there could be other aspects to advertising like maintaining a positive public image or instilling trust in a brand, communicating a positive message about this and that, but at the end of the day, most would agree that you engage in advertising to generate new business.

How can you tell if advertising is performing well? By the fact that you have more business as a direct result of advertising. Though there are many variables and indicators of interaction with your intended audience, much of the pipeline starts from a lead being generated, which can also be called a conversion. A conversion means that a person saw your ad, interacted with it, and completed the desired action by filling out a "contact me" button or initiated a phone call to set up a meeting, bought products from your e-commerce site, added items to their cart but didn't complete the order, etc. There are conversion tracking capabilities that can tell you how many conversions and from what referral source the conversion originated (organic, paid search advertising, direct link from another site, etc.).

Lead Generation

Lead generation is the name of the game, or at least that is the main purpose for spending so much money on advertising. If not for generating leads, we'd just be wasting money creating a bunch of noise. There are all sorts of channels, mediums, and strategies in which the generation of leads occurs. Some dabble in many different areas, others focus on just one or two. Not all will produce the best results for a particular business. Some prospects respond better or worse with various methodologies. Plus, as a small business, we only have so much time to devote to the various channels to generate those leads, not to mention that advertising isn't free, so selecting the right channels and focusing efforts can yield better results than just pouring resources into the universe and hoping to catch a shooting star. Working with an outside consultant to act as your chief marketing officer would likely help you develop a plan of attack and select the appropriate channels that fit your strategy.

Some of the major channels for lead generation include, but would certainly not be limited to, the following:

PPC & SEO – You built a decent website… if only that's all it took to get people's eyeballs on all your hard work. Unfortunately, a good website isn't enough until there is sufficient traffic for Google and other search engines to rank your site on the first page or two of listings. As mentioned previously, SEO is search engine optimization, which is sort of like playing a matching game to get the content of your site (along with the title, description, tags, and other elements) to naturally align with prospective visitor's search so that they find your site. Optimizing your site enhances the organic search results, which is like when we do a search and find what we are looking for without selecting ads.

Many of the website building applications have cookie cutter templates to make it easy to add tags, highlights, site description, images with proper formatting and references, etc. Not that just putting in some of those elements is all it takes to be "optimized," Google will want to see descriptions and titles with less than X amount of characters, tags and keywords matching with the actual content within the site, and so on. However, it is easier today for the layperson to manipulate and correct their website without advanced programming knowledge.

Pay-Per-Click or PPC generally refers to search advertising and is as it sounds: you pay every time someone clicks on your ad. Though it can be built around different concepts like cost per one thousand impressions or cost per conversion, the PPC concept is still the most widely understood and synonymous with search marketing, regardless of how Google and others collect their pound of flesh. An impression is your ad that is placed and potentially seen by a user conducting a search. A conversion can have different criteria, but would generally result from a user that interacts with an ad, and then initiates contact via the "contact us" button, or "call now." Conversion tracking tags can be placed on different pages to count. A conversion is, in a sense, a lead, what we're fishing for in the first place.

There is a lot that goes into search theory and search marketing campaigns. One should not try to fumble around and shoot from the hip or you'll end up spending a lot of money competing with the wrong competition for the wrong sets of eyeballs, only to receive negative ranking as a result from things like poor click-through rate (CTR) or a high bounce rate. CTR is the proportion of impressions that result in successfully hooking the user to interact with your ad and get them to click to your site. A bounce rate is when a user goes to your site and immediately leaves, which tells Google that the user was not looking for what you were selling, and as such, the keywords that were used to find your site may not be the best ones to be competing on. Other aspects like quality play a big role too, where if you are competing for certain keywords and Google's analysis of your site seems to indicate a poor correlation to the keywords you are fighting for, you pay more to get those clicks.

Google has become the 8,000-pound gorilla that you cannot ignore. Not only does Google control a majority of the core search traffic already, but also much of the avenues well beyond it. Ever visit a site for say shoes, then later you're checking on a blog or whatever else and there are those shoes you looked at? That's remarketing, which is to target users that have visited a site already, combined with Google's partner network. AdSense is Google's program that incentivizes websites to put in a plug-in expanding the empire. That plug-in is where those shoes get displayed on a totally unrelated site. If you click on it, the site owner will get part of the PPC that Google collects from the shoe company that put the ad there for you.

Like it or not, we have to conform to the rules of the game that Google makes. If Google says your site is not well optimized for mobile, you change it; if it loads too slowly, you speed it up... You build your site for Google searches; you put your store location on Google maps. Is it a good thing or a bad thing? It's tough to say. It is good to have protocols and standards, but should a single enterprise be in command of what the collective standards are? Good thing we are not in a philosophy class—we'll just move on and not worry about the big questions of the universe.

Keywords are the foundation of search. What words do your potential customers use to search for your business? In PPC campaigns, you are paying to get traffic for your site based on keywords that users are putting in searches. It is a constantly evolving marketplace with endless combinations of possibilities for strategy, placement, etc. PPC campaigns generate inorganic search results, which is traffic to your site but comes from the ads that are at the top and along the side of a search result. Getting traffic, especially if it is good traffic that results in the customer finding what they are looking for, helps strengthen your organic search results. So, in time, effective campaigns with enough resources committed to the effort, combined with a well-optimized website containing good quality, relevant and recent content, and the heavy lifting of generating leads from search traffic, doesn't have to all be paid; you will start seeing free traffic from organic searches as well.

To set up and run PPC campaigns, the big toolset is of course with Google. By now you may already have a Google business account set up, and with the admin of that account, it ties into all the other Google apps and products. AdWords is the Google product where you manage your PPC campaigns. Google Analytics is the toolset that you'd use to evaluate your site's performance. Though the web builder sites do incorporate a certain amount of analytics as well, Google's is superior and is included in their suite of apps for just being a Google business user. Even if you don't use Gmail, for a nominal fee per month, you do get quite a lot of resources for your money.

There are numerous books, blogs, videos, and other content available for managing your AdWords campaigns. You can do it yourself—there is a lot to it, but if you like the challenge, there's nothing stopping you from advertising on your own. Alternatively, you could outsource all or some of the function. Either way, if you want your site to get ranked on the first page of Google, an AdWords campaign will likely be needed to get your well-optimized website generating leads from search traffic.

Content Deployment – Content deployment encompasses blog posts, newsletters, YouTube channels, Medium series and publications, and much more. There continue to be more and more channels for deploying content into the universe. Why would someone generate content? For many reasons; it conveys a degree of expertise and competence in your particular business area, strengthens your community engagement with current and prospective customers, enhances your brand and reputation, and so on. Content deployment can be a good source to generate leads. When someone is doing a search online to answer a question or solve a problem, your content may be the answer they are looking for. When they find that you have the answers and can solve problems, they may decide to reach out and engage your products or services.

In general, good organic content gets a priority or premium for search results. Organic content means that you created it—it originated with you. Yes, there are lots of purchased content that you can regurgitate into the world, but will your branded copy of the same exact content that 100 other similar businesses get to the top of the search results? When google and other search engines determine that certain content is not organic or is just a copy of a copy it doesn't rank as high as an organic piece that has similar or greater relevance.

Technology is moving very fast and the robots are already scanning videos and pictures to map the taxonomy, description, and appropriate tags (keywords and synonyms) so that, even though a searcher enters in text, the written word will not be the only result in the top. Often video and pictures have greater engagement and can result in preferred results. Though depending on your area of expertise, a well-written article may be a better format than a how-to YouTube video.

Some employ multiple formats for the same content, like a short snippet and a link to your blog on LinkedIn, the full-length article with pictures on Facebook, and a video presentation of the same content on the YouTube channel. There is more than one way to get the content out there, and there is no "one size fits all" approach, especially with a constantly changing environment and economy.

Mailchimp, Constant Contact, and other platforms provide a centralized hub for deploying content to many people without having email groups, spreadsheets, or manually drafting emails. It also would generally enable recipients to manage the subscriptions on their end, so you wouldn't need to be bothered by someone who doesn't want to receive emails from you anymore. They click the link on the bottom and unsubscribe. The applications can also automatically add contacts into their mailing list without you having to manually decide who is worthy of your content. It can add any new email interaction as an additional contact to the list, and you've got an ever-expanding population of people seeing your content. Even if they don't read it, if it is good content that may potentially have relevance to them sometime in the future, they probably won't unsubscribe. The big benefit is remaining top of mind, so that when they need a financial planner, a real estate agent, etc., they just remembered from that email they received three weeks ago the first person they thought to reach out to.

Camera shy? Don't know what to write? You can still generate organic content if you have a strong understanding of the business you are in. You can engage freelancers like ghostwriters to write the content or other independent contractors to craft videos like whiteboard animation presentations (that's the videos where a hand is writing on a whiteboard while there is talking and/or music), which can be much better than a static power point presentation.

Social Media – Social Media is an excellent source to generate leads. After all, Facebook alone has over two billion users and many spend a reasonable amount of time on the platform every single day. It is where many go to keep in touch, consume their news and information, get recommendations from their friends on products and services, and much more. There are several platforms besides Facebook, and each platform will have its own advertising function.

With social media marketing, it isn't as simple as PPC advertising. At least with PPC advertising, there is a user conducting a search for particular keywords that may line up with your product or service, so they are looking for what you may be selling. Social media marketing can involve much more nuanced and complex strategies. One can be soliciting a particular product or service, building your brand and reputation, fostering a community with audience engagement, and so much more beyond simply just delivering an ad to a person. There is a good deal of specialized content with respect to social media advertising, and it would be a good idea to dive deeper into such content rather than winging it. Each platform (Facebook, LinkedIn, etc.) will have their own unique characteristics that alter the who, what, where, when, and why; once you've decided on a particular social media outlet, consider also doing the appropriate research and reading on the particular toolset or possibly outsource the function.

As for the actions themselves, there are the commonplace ones like generating traffic to your social media page or to your website. This would be an ad designed to entice people to click on the ad and jump to your page or website; the goal being that once they are on your page or website, they may want to reach out and take the next step. There is generally the ability to promote or boost a posting or your page, with the idea being that because audience builds audience, getting more people to see your content, like your page, and so on (especially with a good amount of engagement) will lead to more people organically seeing your content and generating more leads down the road without having to pay so much to be noticed.

Social media is a great source, as most people are on it. But I do want to urge caution and advocate for greater learning before just spending money on Facebook ads. If not done with some intent, there could be adverse effects from the advertising. For instance, if you simply promote your page and don't filter the target audience, you'll still get people that like your page, but if those people are not engaged listeners, it can influence the algorithms that display your content to the right people. Also, for getting traffic to your site, without specific targeting, you'll still get clicks, but if they just leave right away, it may tell Google and others that the site isn't as relevant since the bounce rate is high. The big takeaway is to learn the platforms and have a plan before executing so you are reaching the right audience.

Networking and Referrals – What is better than getting found on Google? That's right, a referral. Referrals are one of the best sources for lead generation. Do you know why? Because when you get a referral, it bypasses much of the frustrations and challenges inherent with advertising. A referral is a recommendation, a stellar review, and a warm introduction all in one. But how do you get referrals? By building a network. You didn't think you could just get referrals without having friends, did you? Not that you need to dump all your friends or that you have to be actual friends with your network, but to a certain extent, you do need to build a level of trust, rapport, and confidence in order for people to feel comfortable sending people they influence your way. A big hesitation to making a referral is that if you don't actually know much about the person or company you are sending your friend, colleague, client, etc. to, it could come back on you that you led them astray and did them a disservice. This is why you need to have good relations with those you consider to be in your network.

There are several networking organizations that have local chapters, like BNI (Business Network International). The objective remains the same: to generate new business through referrals. With networking groups, you have your team of salespeople who can send new prospects your way. In a typical group, there would only be one person from any particular profession, so just one real estate agent, one chiropractor, one bookkeeper, etc., which helps to ensure that referrals for that particular service would ideally go to you. Just because you are in a group and are the only person in that industry doesn't mean they will or have to send you the referrals; you still have to work at it. Networking is like dating—you go on coffee dates, learn about each other, you give them a referral, and ideally, they reciprocate with referrals in turn. Networking groups allow you to have an assembly of people for your network without you having to call a random banker to ask out on a coffee date—everyone in the group understands the principles and objective to get referrals by giving referrals.

Networking can be time consuming and take up a lot of emotional and social capital. But don't worry, you don't need a massive rolodex to have a good pipeline going. Ideally, just a few people with good collaborative and cross-referral opportunities and it can feed off itself; particularly with not too dissimilar industries. A real estate agent and a mortgage broker would likely be a good pair to pass referrals to each other. But a real estate agent and big data analytics firm, not so much.

> When I started out, I joined a networking group. It was a big-time commitment, but as I was just starting out, I had some time available that I wanted to fill with new client work. As an accountant serving small business clients, I learned to devote more time on the network members that have the greatest potential to refer clients, such as lawyers that do business-related law, a small business banker, the ADP payroll rep,

and so on. It works well, so long as you keep up with your breakfast club.

Some of the best referrals come from your existing clients. If you provide good service and have a solid rapport with your clients, then asking for a referral is not being too pushy or foreword. The best time is usually soon after you take on a new client and solve a problem or make your first deliverable—the telltale sign would be the client saying something like, "Wow, this is great, thank you, such fast turnaround." That would be your cue to reply with, "I'm happy you are pleased. If you know anyone else that might need an (accountant, lawyer, etc.), I'd love an introduction." The big thing to remember is that referrals, regardless if they come from a friend, a client, a networking group, etc., are great and often produce far superior leads than the potential random tire kickers you might get from the universe through other means.

Public Speaking – This can be a tough sell as it is one of the top fears for many. But if you can get over your fears, public speaking has tremendous benefits. When you are on stage or behind a podium giving a presentation about your industry, profession, business, etc., you have everyone's attention. You are instantly seen as an expert in your field, even if you aren't, since the audience thinks that you wouldn't be up there if you weren't. Imagine you go to meet a prospect at a coffee shop to discuss business and pitch your services. It can go great and you can get a new client, or they could hem and haw and not pull the trigger, meaning you've wasted your time. With public speaking, you are sort of going on 50 coffee dates at once—if you are in front of the right audience and talk about the right subject areas, people will naturally come up to you afterwards and ask additional questions or get your business card and set up a time to learn more about what you can do for them.

There are all sorts of potential avenues for public speaking opportunities, such as the chambers of commerce, rotary clubs and other organizations, classes and courses on similar topics, and more. Your particular industry and where your ideal customer is lurking will help drive what kind of engagements might be the best to seek. Networking groups like BNI can give you the experience and confidence to take it to the next level since every week you have to stand up and talk about yourself and your business for at least a minute, which is great practice. It may not be a good fit for your business or industry, or there could be limited opportunities or a lack of appetite to get up on that stage, but if you've got the guts and can put together a 5-15-minute presentation about something you are already passionate about, then the juice is worth the squeeze.

Lead Generation Marketplaces – Lead generation marketplaces seem to have exploded over the last few years. They have names like Thumbtack, Bark, Thervo, and others. Even sites like TripAdvisor can fit into this category. What they are is an online platform in which prospects tell the universe (Google) they are looking for something (accountant, painter, hotel, etc.) and one or more of these sites gets their attention—they fill out a simple form and presto, a lead is born. That lead, which is what we are all hunting for, is valuable property; as such, these sites typically charge you to get access to them. They can be good leads or could be people that are really just curious about how much things cost or what capabilities a typical professional in an industry has, but isn't ready or willing to actually buy anything. Usually, some details are included with the lead that you can see before deciding to pay to contact them, and with some experience, you should be able to discern who is serious and who is just doing research.

I have used some of these marketplaces before. If you are trying to build a business that is based on quality and not price, it can be a challenge to compete in some of these marketplaces since there will always be the "cheap guy" that charges far less and likely cuts corners somewhere. It seems that this guy will be placed right beside the listing for your business, and sometimes it appears the prospect only has price to compare service providers on. So, if you are able to get a phone call or consultation out of the marketplace and communicate the value, it can be a good source for leads. But if you end up slugging it out in a price war with fly-by-night operators, it can be very frustrating and expensive to pay for leads that you don't win business out of.

Qualification

Qualification can save a ton of time, and as already mentioned, time is money. Qualification is the process of filtering out leads into prospects. Since not every lead is a good lead, they need to be qualified. Sometimes it can be a timing issue, as in maybe in six months they will be in a better position to buy that house or whatever. Sometimes they are just browsing and want to check prices. A good practice is to develop a system or process to qualify them as quickly as possible. You don't want to spend a bunch of time and possibly money if you are buying them dinner to find out they aren't actually in the market.

Communicate with your network. This is essential if you rely upon networking and referrals. If they don't know what kind of client you are looking for, they won't be much help. Let them know the specifics so that they can pre-qualify leads and save everyone time before they refer to you. Plus, it can put you in something of a tight spot if your friend sent you their grandma as a potential client and she isn't a good fit; you don't want them to stop sending referrals, but maybe grandma isn't your kind of client. Do you take grandma as a client, even though it is outside of your wheelhouse, try to refer her to the right resource, or just decline and have your friend potentially offended?

Your website and other marketing material can help communicate what you are looking for. I try to be clear that I am looking for small business clients built around a recurring monthly billed subscription type of engagement that encompasses the monthly accounting, year-end taxes, tax planning, and most other accounting-related aspects in between, but the foundation of the relationship is the monthly accounting work. What I don't put on my website is that I am a tax guy; in fact, I say that I am "Not Your Dad's Tax Guy" to try and be clear. Sure, it's possible that some people who may have been a fit don't call, but for the most part, people who are looking for what I am selling appreciate the transparency. I don't need to waste time answering the phone, listening for several minutes to discern that someone is just looking for a tax return and wants to pay a lower price than what H&R Block charges. No thanks.

Move to Close!

There's no business like new business, right? Making that sale is a great feeling. It validates that what you are doing is the right path. When do you get them to sign on the dotted line? That can be difficult in some cases; sometimes a person is ready to buy today, sometimes they are evaluating their options, etc. What helps take the process from prospect to client/customer is a solid understanding of your own products and services, along with what the prospect is looking for. If you can say with confidence that the solution to their problem will have X price and they are in agreement, then they will sign on the spot. But if you need to figure out how much you are going to charge them after they are gone and then send them a proposal, it can give them time to cool off and re-evaluate. Not that you need to rely upon impulsivity, but when they are in the room or on the phone, you've got a good rapport going, and they are ready to take their wallet out, it's kind of a buzzkill to end the conversation and two days later send them something to sign. When that happens, you have a whole new process of following up and re-touching-base conversations and possibly having to go through the entire pitch again, just to get that signature. So, in general, if you are at the price part of the conversation, you should be ready to hand them the pen (or collect the e-signature).

Starting off with price can put you in a tight spot if the customer is not comparing apples to apples, since your oranges may cost more than the apples they're being compared to. As such, you will have ideally been able to communicate the value of your oranges and how they are better than the apples so that when you get to price, they understand that they are not buying apples anymore because they really want oranges.

Closing on a sale is the completion of the sales process and the beginning of the operations process where onboarding or other aspects will take place. Just because you've already closed on this customer doesn't mean you can't sell to them again and again or employ remarketing and other strategies to get referrals, upsells, or other additional potential from the relationship. Managing relationships is the core of a good system to manage your sales pipeline.

Pipeline Management and Software

All these people and conversations going on through many different mediums can be a nightmare to manage with a spreadsheet or just using your reminders in your calendar or email system. This is why they have CRM software. There are many out there—the big player in the field is Sales Force, which has all sorts of products and solutions. CRM software helps manage your pipeline, which is the flow of contacts from being totally non-existent to making the sale or being engaged by a client.

Depending on your size and the number of potential prospects and leads, certain solutions like a robust CRM software may be overkill. But, if you are working with 10+ new conversations a month and the pipeline process can span over a month, it can be quite a noisy process to just manage while still trying to run a business.

Whatever you use to manage your pipeline, you should have some regimentation or structure. It could even be a whiteboard where you write people's names on it and move their name to the "qualified" column when they get to the next phase, etc. Without a system, things can get lost or eat up way more time than they should. You don't need to be wasting time on prospects who are not prospects. So, having structure forces the conversation with a prospect or lead to be focused and streamlined; if they are not a good fit, then send them down the road and remove the distraction, but if they are a good fit, let's move to close. You are not running a charity providing free advice to random people. Time is money, and if you let people steal your time, they are in actuality taking food out of your kid's mouth—that's how you should look at it.

How Much is Enough?

Good question. Creating a budget for your sales pipeline can be like creating a budget for other aspects in the business—start from the bottom and work up. Every business is unique and has its own challenges and needs to contend with, but even simply writing out and doing the math can provide the framework for action. Knowing how many new customers or clients you need over a certain period of time is the first step. If you want to grow to a certain size, how many customers over the next month do you need to reach that target?

Let's do some math now. We'll take as an example a small business and say they are in the professional services area. They want to grow—they currently have the capacity to serve 20 new clients, in addition to the 20 clients they already have, and would like to have 40 clients by the end of 12 months. Churn rate, which is a calculation of the amount of client losses, can be calculated in many different ways. For simplicity, we'll say that this small business will experience 40% loss of clients over the course of a year. So, for the 20 clients, eight will fall off within 12 months. It is important to incorporate attrition into such models or we may be too generous with our expectations.

Some additional numbers to add to our model: let's say their close rate is 33% of prospects, their lead qualification rate is 33% that will become prospects, they are confident they can generate nine new leads a month from networking, referrals, public speaking and other avenues per month, and they will have a conversion rate of 10% of the clicks from social media and PPC campaigns that will cost $2.50 per click.

So, now that we went through all that mumbo jumbo, let's break it down. If they have 20 clients, will lose eight and need a total of 40 in 12 months, that means they need 28 new clients in the next year. Divided by 12 gives us 2.3 new client acquisitions per month.

- 2.3 new clients divided by .33 (close rate) tells us they need seven new prospects per month.
- Seven new prospects divided by .33 (qualification rate) means they need 21 new leads.
- Since nine leads come from networking, referrals, and public speaking, they are 12 leads short.

- Twelve new leads from PPC and social media advertising divided by 10% conversion rate means they need 120 clicks per month.
- And at $2.50 per click, the budget for Facebook, Google, and other advertising should be about $300 per month to achieve the 2.3 new client acquisitions per month.

It can get much more complicated and involved to manage and budget for a sales pipeline. The principals should remain the same regardless of how involved or complicated the calculations and algorithms. The main point is that sales is an unavoidable part of being an entrepreneur or self-employed individual. Understanding your business and what it takes to generate more of that business are valuable skills in being successful.

TERMINATION

As much as we all like to think positive, there is no sense in denying the inevitable. The terminal point of a small business doesn't get as much attention as does starting a small business. Let's face it, most small businesses will end. That doesn't mean everyone will go belly-up, but aside from inheritance, even the sale of a business typically results in the termination of the entity and all that goes with it. This means the vast majority of small business owners and self-employed individuals will outlive their entities. As such, there are actions that need to be done in order to shut it down properly and have it stay down.

If the business is to be sold intact, transferred to heirs, or otherwise will remain as a going concern entity, then it is not really the same as being terminated and one should work with attorneys and accountants to ensure a complete transition. This would be where the signature authority on bank accounts, personal guarantees, and other aspects will be transferred to new individuals, but the business itself will remain and continue to own assets, owe liabilities. and do all the other things it was doing the day before any transition took place. This chapter is not for such circumstances since it isn't really a termination of the business. Now that we've gone through our disclaimers, let's move on.

Winding Down Business

First things first: shut the doors and stop future transactions. Every business will have different things going on and there typically wouldn't be any main switch or shutoff valve, so you'll have to go through and make a list of the various parties and relationships that need to be notified.

Assets – There may be assets such as vehicles, buildings, or other equipment that is in the company's name. In the process of selling or distributing the assets, the titles will be transferred to new owners. Often with vehicles I see the titles in the owner's name, even if used 100% for business, because it is simpler to do, and the insurance is typically less. Even if not titled in the business's name, one would still need to account for it if it correctly. If the economic reality was that you used something for business and wrote the cost off or depreciated it, you'd want to take it off the books correctly and transparently so you are not giving the IRS any reason to take a second look at your books or tax filings. The last thing you'd want to deal with after you have terminated a small business is anything to do with that small business three years later.

Lease Obligations – When a business is shutting down, that doesn't always mean the landlord won't want to collect on the remainder of the lease, if there is one. Ideally, there will either not be a lease, or the business closure will correspond with the ending of such a lease so that there isn't the headache to deal with. If there is significant time remaining on the lease, especially if there is a personal guarantee on it that will come to haunt you, try and work with your landlord to either sublet, have him/her get a new tenant, or see about forgiveness of the remaining lease. Landlords are humans too, and if you are going out of business, sometimes people do have a heart and don't want to kick you when you're down. If there is a security deposit that you are due, you'd want to get that back, along with, of course, vacating the space when you are supposed to and make arrangements for whatever furniture, equipment, files, etc., that are in the space by putting in storage, selling, giving away, etc.

Vendors, Suppliers, and Subcontractors – Close out your accounts with vendors and suppliers, cancel any pending future obligations, and settle any balances, if any. Getting a full reckoning of what the business owes is important so that it can be accounted for and closed out. Plus, if you've made promises to pay and don't, those people may be upset. If you can't pay because of insolvency or will be going through bankruptcy, then a bankruptcy lawyer would be better suited to advise on the entire process of shutting down the business.

Software and Subscriptions – Nowadays, just about everything, especially with software, is on a subscription basis. Many times, we also get discounts for paying for an entire year's subscription. So, we may only see a transaction from Dropbox, Microsoft, and others on an annual basis, which makes it really easy to forget that they still have our credit card info and authorization to continue billing. This would also be a good time to consider taking down the website and possibly social media pages that may have been set up for the business.

Document retention may be an issue if you have data in certain proprietary software formats. Usually you should be able to extract into more universal formats to store elsewhere as an archive. The IRS may want to examine your returns or books up to several years after the business is closed. As you cancel software and subscriptions, consider what needs to be retained and extracted prior to decommissioning.

Insurance Policies – Canceling policies before the end of the coverage term can potentially provide a refund. There may be policies that are paid contemporaneously, like worker's compensation insurance, which may require additional payment to cover things like an expense constant or other fixed charges that were supposed to be collected over the remainder of the policy. Some coverage you may want to convert or keep in place like professional liability insurance, just in case there is a claim after the fact. Health insurance, if in the business's name, can create some frustrations since you wouldn't want to have a lapse in coverage, so evaluate options carefully. Create an inventory of all policies for the business; with that, you can go through the list and decide which policies to cancel, which to extend, which to try transferring the responsible party or billing information, etc.

Permits and Licenses – In the process of winding down, you may have professional licenses or permits. If you will continue to use your license, you may need to transfer it from one organization to another. There could be notification procedures with the state's board of whatever that handles the permits and licenses for your particular industry; as such, much like getting licensed had a process, de-licensing may also come with a process. Not only licenses managed at the state level, but there could also be local permits from the department of health or other organizations that may need to be notified and terminated.

Customers – What to tell your customers and the community that you've built? You don't really have to tell everyone in the world that the business is going away, but a bulk email just letting them know that the business is being shut down wouldn't hurt. You may have gift cards, retainers, or unfilled service obligations to satisfy as well, so making arrangements to close the books on customer accounts is a good idea. Additionally, some customers may still owe you money and you should continue to go through the process of collecting such money if it is collectable rather than writing it off.

Employees – Seems like employees are some of the last to find out about the end. When a large business closes a division or relocates operations, they have transition plans, severance payments, and other aspects that ensure they can complete the task. A small business that is being shut down doesn't always have additional resources for termination. I can understand the motivation for secrecy—if you tell people the ship is sinking, who will be left to man the ship as she goes down? It's a tough call, there is no right or wrong answer.

When you have employees, there may be other aspects that were set up in conjunction with payroll that may also need to be terminated or shut down. This includes flex spending accounts, health savings accounts, parking reimbursement arrangements, and others. Some may be on a recurring schedule, some could auto renew like software. You'll need to review the various obligations and ensure they are funded and closed out.

Retirement Plans – Defined benefit plans are very rare for small businesses, which could create some really large headaches in order to have the IRS approve your release from responsibility. The main plans nowadays being defined contribution plans are much simpler but would nonetheless need to be fully funded in accordance with the plan adoption agreements and terminated in accordance with procedures, laws, and regulations. Depending on what kind of plan and who you are using for administration and custodial functions, there could be significant fees in the process to terminate the plan, which you'd want to account for before closing the books.

Lenders and Note Holders – Many banks and lenders require a personal guarantee, meaning that if the business is to close with debts, the debts don't die with the business. As such, arrangements will likely need to be made for all debts. Occasionally, when this occurs, it may be coupled with bankruptcy proceedings. If not going through bankruptcy and you don't want to destroy your credit, then get in touch with the various lenders and set up installment agreements, renegotiate a substitution of the debtor, or make other arrangements for after the business is closed. This is important since they certainly won't forget that there is a debt that exists.

Bank and Credit Accounts – Though it is tempting to close all accounts as a precaution, it may be better to keep some money in the account for a couple months just in case. Without any money or ability to resolve issues that arise after the fact, it then requires the owners to flip the bill, which not only can be burdensome, but also create some frustrations in closing the books and ensuring all transactions are recorded.

Close the Books

After going through the various parties that may be affiliated with or impacted by the business termination, it's time to get a full accounting. Beyond the basic bookkeeping would be the added transactions to account for the additional costs of dissolution from retirement plan termination fees to uncollectible accounts receivables. Generally, the books for the business may include the entire year, even if the business shuts down mid-year. That way, one can incorporate the transactions that occur or are settled after the business officially closed the doors like with loan forgiveness, asset sales, partner distributions, and other items that may not be readily available at the time of business closure. The final impact and the closing of the books for good would typically happen in conjunction with the final tax return of the entity.

The Taxman Cometh

Before jumping right into the final income tax return for the entity, it's important to close out other relationships you might have with the government, especially if you had payroll. These would include, but are certainly not limited to, the following: quarterly 941 federal payroll tax returns, quarterly state withholding tax returns, quarterly state unemployment tax returns, annual federal unemployment tax returns, W-2 and W-3 forms, annual reconciliation and state filings for payroll related compliance tasks, Employer's Annual Information Return of Tip Income and Allocated Tips (if applicable), 1099 forms, etc. Also, if you had a 401k plan or other retirement plan that requires the filing of an annual 5500 series filing, in conjunction with terminating the plan, the filing of the final return would be required or they will be demanding it and assessing penalties for not filing. Fortunately, most payroll and retirement plans are done through third parties that have tools, procedures, and other resources for the termination of payroll compliance aspects. The big thing is to make sure that it is final returns and indicates that there will be no more returns after that date—some agencies may require a process other than just the filing to terminate the account, and others will have a checkbox saying "final return" which makes it easier.

Different states and local jurisdictions have taxes as well, like sales tax among others. The list of potential tax types can be exhaustive—I'd like to think at the point of termination one will know what tax types they have been paying (or should have been paying) and can contact that agency to file final returns and terminate that compliance requirement. Additionally, for corporations, the IRS would like you to file Form 966 Corporate Dissolution or Liquidation within 30 days after the resolution or plan is adopted to dissolve the corporation or liquidate any of its stock.

Final Income Tax Return

To get ready for the preparation of the final income tax return, we need to account for the assets. The ones being sold are easy enough to account for and most tax software allows you to select the appropriate asset that was being depreciated and indicate that it was sold or disposed of, enter the sales price and any costs of the sale like commissions, along with applicable dates, and it'll populate the appropriate form for you.

Many times, when a business shuts down, there are assets that get converted to personal use. Remember that SUV that created all those nice benefits a couple years ago? Well, it may not be so beneficial on the way out. When you convert assets from business use to personal use, it is like a sale, and like a sale, there is the calculation of gain or loss. When you have an asset like a vehicle that was fully depreciated and still has value, the difference may need to be reported as depreciation recapture, which is taxable.

With the balance sheet cleared out and the profit and loss having all the relevant information for the final year's tax return, we can prepare the tax return. For sole proprietorships, this would be on the Schedule C, which is an attachment to the 1040. There isn't a checkbox on the schedule itself to indicate a final return. The other main tax return forms (1120, 1120s, and 1065) do have a checkbox to mark it as a final return, which should be checked. The final tax return that encapsulates the results of the business, not only the income and expenses but also in the gains, losses, and distribution and allocation of assets and liabilities, is the biggest and most important item in the termination process. We want to make sure we get everything accounted for and on that return because there won't be any more returns to report anything on.

Depending on circumstances, there could be considerable gain from termination resulting in taxes due. Alternatively, there could be considerable losses that can create a net operating loss for the owner to carry forward if there isn't enough income from other sources to absorb it. Also, for the businesses that were passive activities that carried losses forward, the termination of the activity frees up such losses to now be utilized by the owner on their personal tax return.

Entity Dissolution

With the books closed, all the taxes and compliance tasks sorted out, the assets, liabilities and other aspects transferred, sold or disposed of appropriately, and bank and credit accounts closed, the final task is to dissolve the entity. Much like setting up the entity, you'd go to the secretary of state's website for the state(s) the business has an entity set up in to file the entity dissolution (which may have different names like Statement of Dissolution or Statement of Termination). There may be some differences between a dissolution and a termination based sometimes on the voluntary nature of the action, but otherwise should have a similar result. Some states may require a filing fee; others are free. Once filed, you may even get a certified copy of dissolution for your records. Finally, the last thing to do is to retain the records, just in case.

APPENDIX

When you have a small business or are self-employed, you will have to report your business income/loss by filing taxes. What goes on which tax form can be quite complex to say the least. This appendix is meant to be a guide to help showcase the main methods by which we report business income and the related consequences associated with the various tax returns. We start with a profit and loss statement and a balance sheet statement for our hypothetical business "Entrepreneur LLC" for the year 2018. With that we outline the four main Tax Returns that could be filed for our hypothetical business, which are: Sole proprietorship, S Corporation, Partnership, or C Corporation and the corresponding individual returns to show the total tax impact as well as a practical example of what information goes where on a particular tax return.

For simplicity and comparability a few notes:

1. Employment taxes – All the scenarios will have employment tax related items to the owner (wages, officer compensation, guaranteed payments, etc.) as self-employment earnings reported on the individual return for comparability even though wages are generally reported differently in actuality. This will help provide a "total tax" perspective that is easier to compare between the scenarios. Additionally for our scenarios, the owner pay is $60,000.

2. As buying equipment and depreciating it is very common, we have our business doing the same thing; as such, the business bought an SUV for $44,000 and wrote the whole thing off through accelerated depreciation means using $25,000 of Section 179 depreciation and $19,000 of Bonus Depreciation. As such, with all scenarios having the same amount for depreciation we will not

include the schedules and forms that pertain to depreciation.

3.   We have not included the home office deduction for our scenarios but as mentioned in previous sections of the book the home office deduction can be made available regardless of entity type, since it would create confusion in comparability, none of the scenarios have the home office deduction.

4.   The diversity of different income and expense types was intentional to show how different items get reported differently in the tax return(s). Some items like charitable contributions would show up on Schedule A if the tax payer were to itemize deductions which our scenarios don't since the standard deduction is higher; some items are not deductible at all like officer life insurance, etc.

5.   Though partnerships require two partners, we show the partnership return with just one for comparability.

6.   Draws, Dividends, distributions, etc. – Our hypothetical business owner has decided to take $31,992 from the business as draws, which brings the ending equity for the business to zero. This allows for a better depiction of the "total tax" picture since it incorporates the full side of the "double taxation" concept for the C Corporation scenario.

Spoiler Alert

From our scenarios using the same financial data, the total federal taxes associated with each scenario (Corporate and Personal as applicable) are as follows:

Sole Proprietor	$23,897
S Corporation	$19,031
Partnership	$23,441
C Corporation	$25,838

Appendix Schedule of Contents

Entrepreneur, LLC
Profit and Loss
January through December 2018

	Jan – Dec '18
Ordinary Income/Expense	
Income	
Services	260,000.00
Total Income	260,000.00
Expense	
Advertising and Promotion	5,200.00
Automobile Expense	5,400.00
Bad Debt Expense	8,500.00
Charitable Contributions	1,200.00
Depreciation Expense	44,000.00
Dues and Subscriptions	1,650.00
Insurance Expense	7,400.00
Interest Expense	4,400.00
Legal and Professional Expenses	6,000.00
Meals and Entertainment	1,400.00
Office Supplies	2,800.00
Payroll Taxes	4,100.00
Payroll Wages	36,000.00
Rent Expense	10,200.00
SEP Contribution	10,000.00
Sub Contractor	10,000.00
Supplies and Materials	2,000.00
Telephone Expense	1,500.00
Travel Expense	2,800.00
Utilities	3,100.00
Total Expense	167,650.00
Net Ordinary Income	92,350.00
Other Income/Expense	
Other Income	
Interest Income	242.00
Total Other Income	242.00
Other Expense	
Officer Life Insurance	600.00
Owner Pay	60,000.00
Total Other Expense	60,600.00
Net Other Income	-60,358.00
Net Income	31,992.00

Entrepreneur, LLC
Balance Sheet
As of December 31, 2018

	Dec 31, '18
ASSETS	
Current Assets	
Checking/Savings	
Checking	24,000.00
Total Checking/Savings	24,000.00
Accounts Receivable	
Accounts Receivable	12,000.00
Total Accounts Receivable	12,000.00
Total Current Assets	36,000.00
Fixed Assets	
Vehicles	44,000.00
Accumulated Depreciation	-44,000.00
Total Fixed Assets	0.00
TOTAL ASSETS	36,000.00
LIABILITIES & EQUITY	
Liabilities	
Long Term Liabilities	
Car Loan	36,000.00
Total Long Term Liabilities	36,000.00
Total Liabilities	36,000.00
Equity	
Dividends Paid	-31,992.00
Net Income	31,992.00
Total Equity	0.00
TOTAL LIABILITIES & EQUITY	36,000.00

Sole Proprietorship Tax Return (No Separate Entity Filing)

Form 1040 Department of the Treasury — Internal Revenue Service (99)
U.S. Individual Income Tax Return **2018** OMB No. 1545-0074 IRS Use Only — Do not write or staple in this space.

Filing status: [X] Single [ ] Married filing jointly [ ] Married filing separately [ ] Head of household [ ] Qualifying widow(er)

Your first name and initial: **John Doe** Last name:

Your social security number: **111-22-3333**

Your standard deduction: [ ] Someone can claim you as a dependent [ ] You were born before January 2, 1954 [ ] You are blind

If joint return, spouse's first name and initial: Last name:

Spouse's social security number:

Spouse standard deduction: [ ] Someone can claim your spouse as a dependent [ ] Spouse was born before January 2, 1954 [X] Full-year health care coverage or exempt (see inst.)
[ ] Spouse is blind [ ] Spouse itemizes on a separate return or you were dual-status alien

Home address (number and street). If you have a P.O. box, see instructions: **123 Main Street** Apt. no.

Presidential Election Campaign (see inst.) [ ] You [ ] Spouse

City, town or post office, state, and ZIP code. If you have a foreign address, attach Schedule 6: **Saint Paul, MN 55101**

If more than four dependents, see inst. and ✓ here ► [ ]

Dependents (see instructions):
(1) First name Last name	(2) Social security number	(3) Relationship to you	(4) ✓ if qualifies for (see inst.): Child tax credit / Credit for other dependents

Sign Here
Joint return? See instructions.
Keep a copy for your records.

Under penalties of perjury, I declare that I have examined this return and accompanying schedules and statements, and to the best of my knowledge and belief, they are true, correct, and complete. Declaration of preparer (other than taxpayer) is based on all information of which preparer has any knowledge.

Your signature | Date | Your occupation | If the IRS sent you an Identity Protection PIN, enter it here (see inst.)

Spouse's signature. If a joint return, both must sign. | Date | Spouse's occupation | If the IRS sent you an Identity Protection PIN, enter it here (see inst.)

Paid Preparer Use Only
Preparer's name | Preparer's signature **Self-Prepared** | PTIN | Firm's EIN | Check if: [ ] 3rd Party Designee [ ] Self-employed
Firm's name ►
Firm's address ►

BAA For Disclosure, Privacy Act, and Paperwork Reduction Act Notice, see separate instructions. Form 1040 (2018)

Form 1040 (2018) John Doe 111-22-3333 Page 2

Attach Form(s) W-2. Also attach Form(s) W-2G and 1099-R if tax was withheld.

1 Wages, salaries, tips, etc. Attach Form(s) W-2		1	
2a Tax-exempt interest	2a	b Taxable interest 2b	242.
3a Qualified dividends	3a	b Ordinary dividends 3b	
4a IRAs, pensions, and annuities	4a	b Taxable amount 4b	
5a Social security benefits	5a	b Taxable amount 5b	
6 Total income. Add lines 1 through 5. Add any amount from Schedule 1, line 22	104,250.	6	104,492.
7 Adjusted gross income. If you have no adjustments to income, enter the amount from line 6; otherwise, subtract Schedule 1, line 36, from line 6.		7	87,127.
8 Standard deduction or itemized deductions (from Schedule A)		8	12,000.
9 Qualified business income deduction (see instructions)		9	15,025.
10 Taxable income. Subtract lines 8 and 9 from line 7. If zero or less, enter -0-		10	60,102.
11 a Tax (see inst.) 9,167. (check if any from: 1 [ ] Form(s) 8814 2 [ ] Form 4972 3 [ ])			9,167.
b Add any amount from Schedule 2 and check here ► [ ]		11	9,167.
12 a Child tax credit/credit for other dependents b Add any amount from Schedule 3 and check here ► [ ]		12	
13 Subtract line 12 from line 11. If zero or less, enter -0-		13	9,167.
14 Other taxes. Attach Schedule 4		14	14,730.
15 Total tax. Add lines 13 and 14		15	23,897.
16 Federal income tax withheld from Forms W-2 and 1099		16	
17 Refundable credits: a EIC (see inst.) b Sch. 8812 c Form 8863 Add any amount from Schedule 5		17	
18 Add lines 16 and 17. These are your total payments		18	0.

Standard Deduction for —
• Single or married filing separately, $12,000.
• Married filing jointly or Qualifying widow(er), $24,000.
• Head of household, $18,000.
• If you checked any box under Standard deduction, see instructions.

Refund
| 19 If line 18 is more than line 15, subtract line 15 from line 18. This is the amount you overpaid | 19 | |
| 20a Amount of line 19 you want refunded to you. If Form 8888 is attached, check here ► [ ] | 20a | |

Direct deposit? See instructions.
► b Routing number | ► c Type [ ] Checking [ ] Savings
► d Account number

21 Amount of line 19 you want applied to your 2019 estimated tax ► | 21 |

Amount You Owe
| 22 Amount you owe. Subtract line 18 from line 15. For details on how to pay, see instructions ► | 22 | 23,897. |
| 23 Estimated tax penalty (see instructions) | 23 | |

Go to www.irs.gov/Form1040 for instructions and the latest information. Form 1040 (2018)

SCHEDULE 1
(Form 1040)

Department of the Treasury
Internal Revenue Service

Additional Income and Adjustments to Income

▶ Attach to Form 1040.
▶ Go to *www.irs.gov/Form1040* for instructions and the latest information.

OMB No. 1545-0074

2018

Attachment
Sequence No. 01

Name(s) shown on Form 1040
John Doe

Your social security number
111-22-3333

Additional Income	1–9b	Reserved	1–9b	
	10	Taxable refunds, credits, or offsets of state and local income taxes	10	
	11	Alimony received	11	
	12	Business income or (loss). Attach Schedule C or C-EZ	12	104,250.
	13	Capital gain or (loss). Attach Schedule D if required. If not required, check here ▶ ☐	13	
	14	Other gains or (losses). Attach Form 4797	14	
	15a	Reserved	15b	
	16a	Reserved	16b	
	17	Rental real estate, royalties, partnerships, S corporations, trusts, etc. Attach Schedule E	17	
	18	Farm income or (loss). Attach Schedule F	18	
	19	Unemployment compensation	19	
	20a	Reserved	20b	
	21	Other income. List type and amount _____	21	
	22	Combine the amounts in the far right column. If you don't have any adjustments to income, enter here and include on Form 1040, line 6. Otherwise, go to line 23	22	104,250.

Adjustments to Income	23	Educator expenses	23		
	24	Certain business expenses of reservists, performing artists, and fee-basis government officials. Attach Form 2106	24		
	25	Health savings account deduction. Attach Form 8889	25		
	26	Moving expenses for members of the Armed Forces. Attach Form 3903	26		
	27	Deductible part of self-employment tax. Attach Schedule SE	27	7,365.	
	28	Self-employed SEP, SIMPLE, and qualified plans	28	10,000.	
	29	Self-employed health insurance deduction	29		
	30	Penalty on early withdrawal of savings	30		
	31a	Alimony paid b Recipient's SSN ▶	31a		
	32	IRA deduction	32		
	33	Student loan interest deduction	33		
	34	Reserved	34		
	35	Reserved	35		
	36	Add lines 23 through 35	36	17,365.	

BAA For Paperwork Reduction Act Notice, see your tax return instructions.   Schedule 1 (Form 1040) 2018

SCHEDULE 4
(Form 1040)

Department of the Treasury
Internal Revenue Service

Other Taxes

▶ Attach to Form 1040.
▶ Go to *www.irs.gov/Form1040* for instructions and the latest information.

OMB No. 1545-0074

2018

Attachment
Sequence No. 04

Name(s) shown on Form 1040
John Doe

Your social security number
111-22-3333

Other Taxes	57	Self-employment tax. Attach Schedule SE	57	14,730.
	58	Unreported social security and Medicare tax from: Form a ☐ 4137 b ☐ 8919	58	
	59	Additional tax on IRAs, other qualified retirement plans, and other tax-favored accounts. Attach Form 5329 if required	59	
	60a	Household employment taxes. Attach Schedule H	60a	
	b	Repayment of first-time homebuyer credit from Form 5405. Attach Form 5405 if required	60b	
	61	Health care: individual responsibility (see instructions)	61	
	62	Taxes from: a ☐ Form 8959 b ☐ Form 8960 c ☐ Instructions; enter code(s) _____	62	
	63	Section 965 net tax liability installment from Form 965-A	63	
	64	Add the amounts in the far right column. These are your total other taxes. Enter here and on Form 1040, line 14	64	14,730.

BAA For Paperwork Reduction Act Notice, see your tax return instructions.   Schedule 4 (Form 1040) 2018

SCHEDULE C
(Form 1040)

Department of the Treasury
Internal Revenue Service (99)

Profit or Loss From Business
(Sole Proprietorship)

► Go to *www.irs.gov/ScheduleC* for instructions and the latest information.
► Attach to Form 1040, 1040NR, or 1041; partnerships generally must file Form 1065.

OMB No. 1545-0074

2018

Attachment
Sequence No. **09**

Name of proprietor
John Doe

Social security number (SSN)
111-22-3333

A Principal business or profession, including product or service (see instructions)
Consulting

B Enter code from instructions
► 541600

C Business name. If no separate business name, leave blank.
Entrepreneur, LLC

D Employer ID number (EIN) (see instr.)
99-1234567

E Business address (including suite or room no.) ►

City, town or post office, state, and ZIP code

F Accounting method: (1) ☐ Cash (2) ☒ Accrual (3) ☐ Other (specify) ►

G Did you 'materially participate' in the operation of this business during 2018? If 'No,' see instructions for limit on losses . ☒ Yes ☐ No

H If you started or acquired this business during 2018, check here . . . . ► ☐

I Did you make any payments in 2018 that would require you to file Form(s) 1099? (see instructions) . . . . ☐ Yes ☒ No

J If 'Yes,' did you or will you file required Forms 1099? . . . . ☐ Yes ☐ No

Part I Income

1	Gross receipts or sales. See instructions for line 1 and check the box if this income was reported to you on Form W-2 and the 'Statutory employee' box on that form was checked . . . . ► ☐	**1** 260,000.
2	Returns and allowances	**2**
3	Subtract line 2 from line 1	**3** 260,000.
4	Cost of goods sold (from line 42)	**4**
5	**Gross profit.** Subtract line 4 from line 3	**5** 260,000.
6	Other income, including federal and state gasoline or fuel tax credit or refund (see instructions)	**6**
7	**Gross income.** Add lines 5 and 6 . . . . ►	**7** 260,000.

Part II Expenses. Enter expenses for business use of your home **only** on line 30.

8	Advertising	**8** 5,200.	18	Office expense (see instructions)	**18** 2,800.
9	Car and truck expenses (see instructions)	**9** 5,400.	19	Pension and profit-sharing plans	**19**
10	Commissions and fees	**10**	20	Rent or lease (see instructions):	
11	Contract labor (see instructions)	**11** 10,000.		a Vehicles, machinery, and equipment . . .	**20a**
12	Depletion	**12**		b Other business property	**20b** 10,200.
13	Depreciation and section 179 expense deduction (not included in Part III) (see instructions)	**13** 44,000.	21	Repairs and maintenance	**21**
			22	Supplies (not included in Part III)	**22** 2,000.
			23	Taxes and licenses	**23** 4,100.
14	Employee benefit programs (other than on line 19)	**14**	24	Travel and meals:	
				a Travel	**24a** 2,800.
15	Insurance (other than health) . .	**15** 7,400.		b Deductible meals (see instructions)	**24b** 700.
16	Interest (see instr.):		25	Utilities	**25** 3,100.
	a Mortgage (paid to banks, etc.)	**16a** 4,400.	26	Wages (less employment credits)	**26** 36,000.
	b Other	**16b**	27a	Other expenses (from line 48)	**27a** 11,650.
17	Legal and professional services	**17** 6,000.	b	Reserved for future use	**27b**

28	**Total expenses** before expenses for business use of home. Add lines 8 through 27a . . . . ►	**28** 155,750.
29	Tentative profit or (loss). Subtract line 28 from line 7	**29** 104,250.
30	Expenses for business use of your home. Do not report these expenses elsewhere. Attach Form 8829 unless using the simplified method (see instructions). **Simplified method filers only:** enter the total square footage of: (a) your home: _____ and (b) the part of your home used for business: _____ . Use the Simplified Method Worksheet in the instructions to figure the amount to enter on line 30	**30**
31	**Net profit or (loss).** Subtract line 30 from line 29. ● If a profit, enter on both **Schedule 1 (Form 1040), line 12** (or **Form 1040NR, line 13**) and on **Schedule SE, line 2.** (If you checked the box on line 1, see instructions). Estates and trusts, enter on **Form 1041, line 3.** ● If a loss, **you must** go to line 32.	**31** 104,250.
32	If you have a loss, check the box that describes your investment in this activity (see instructions). ● If you checked 32a, enter the loss on both **Schedule 1 (Form 1040), line 12** (or **Form 1040NR, line 12**) and on **Schedule SE, line 2.** (If you checked the box on line 1, see the line 31 instructions). Estates and trusts, enter on **Form 1041, line 3.** ● If you checked 32b, you **must** attach **Form 6198.** Your loss may be limited.	32a ☐ All investment is at risk. 32b ☐ Some investment is not at risk.

BAA For Paperwork Reduction Act Notice, see the separate instructions.   FDIZ0112L 09/24/18   Schedule C (Form 1040) 2018

Schedule C (Form 1040) 2018 John Doe   111-22-3333   Page 2

Part III Cost of Goods Sold (see instructions)

33 Method(s) used to value closing inventory: a ☐ Cost   b ☐ Lower of cost or market   c ☐ Other (attach explanation)

34 Was there any change in determining quantities, costs, or valuations between opening and closing inventory?
    If 'Yes,' attach explanation.. ☐ Yes ☐ No

35 Inventory at beginning of year. If different from last year's closing inventory, attach explanation	35	
36 Purchases less cost of items withdrawn for personal use	36	
37 Cost of labor. Do not include any amounts paid to yourself	37	
38 Materials and supplies	38	
39 Other costs	39	
40 Add lines 35 through 39	40	
41 Inventory at end of year	41	
42 Cost of goods sold. Subtract line 41 from line 40. Enter the result here and on line 4	42	

Part IV Information on Your Vehicle. Complete this part **only** if you are claiming car or truck expenses on line 9 and are not required to file Form 4562 for this business. See the instructions for line 13 to find out if you must file Form 4562.

43 When did you place your vehicle in service for business purposes? (month, day, year) ▸ _____

44 Of the total number of miles you drove your vehicle during 2018, enter the number of miles you used your vehicle for:

   a Business _____   b Commuting (see instructions) _____   c Other _____

45 Was your vehicle available for personal use during off-duty hours?................................. ☐ Yes ☐ No

46 Do you (or your spouse) have another vehicle available for personal use?........................ ☐ Yes ☐ No

47 a Do you have evidence to support your deduction?... ☐ Yes ☐ No

   b If 'Yes,' is the evidence written?.. ☐ Yes ☐ No

Part V Other Expenses. List below business expenses not included on lines 8-26 or line 30.

Bad Debts from Sales or Service	8,500.
Dues and Subscriptions	1,650.
Telephone	1,500.
48 Total other expenses. Enter here and on line 27a	48 11,650.

Schedule C (Form 1040) 2018

S Corporation and Corresponding Individual Return

Form **1120S**		**U.S. Income Tax Return for an S Corporation**			OMB No. 1545-0123
Department of the Treasury Internal Revenue Service		► Do not file this form unless the corporation has filed or is attaching Form 2553 to elect to be an S corporation. ► Go to *www.irs.gov/Form1120S* for instructions and the latest information.			**2018**

For calendar year 2018 or tax year beginning _____ 2018, ending _____

A S election effective date 1/01/2018	**TYPE** **OR** **PRINT**	Entrepreneur, LLC 123 Main Street Saint Paul, MN 55101		**D** Employer identification number 99-1234567	
B Business activity code number (see instructions) 541600				**E** Date incorporated 1/01/2018	
C Check if Schedule M-3 attached ☐				**F** Total assets (see instructions) $ 36,000.	

G Is the corporation electing to be an S corporation beginning with this tax year? ☐ Yes ☒ No If 'Yes,' attach Form 2553 if not already filed

H Check if: **(1)** ☐ Final return **(2)** ☐ Name change **(3)** ☐ Address change **(4)** ☐ Amended return **(5)** ☐ S election termination or revocation

I Enter the number of shareholders who were shareholders during any part of the tax year .... ► 1

Caution: Include only trade or business income and expenses on lines 1a through 21. See the instructions for more information.

I N C O M E	**1a** Gross receipts or sales..........................	**1a**	260,000.		
	b Returns and allowances..........................	**1b**			
	c Balance. Subtract line 1b from line 1a...........................			**1c**	260,000.
	2 Cost of goods sold (attach Form 1125-A)...........................			**2**	
	3 Gross profit. Subtract line 2 from line 1c...........................			**3**	260,000.
	4 Net gain (loss) from Form 4797, line 17 (attach Form 4797)..........			**4**	
	5 Other income (loss) (see instrs — att statement).........................			**5**	
	6 Total income (loss). Add lines 3 through 5.......................... ►			**6**	260,000.
D E D U C T I O N S *(SEE INSTRS)*	**7** Compensation of officers (see instructions - attach Form 1125-E).....			**7**	60,000.
	8 Salaries and wages (less employment credits)........................			**8**	36,000.
	9 Repairs and maintenance..........................			**9**	
	10 Bad debts..........................			**10**	
	11 Rents..........................			**11**	8,500.
	12 Taxes and licenses..........................			**12**	10,200.
	13 Interest (see instructions)..........................			**13**	4,100.
	14 Depreciation not claimed on Form 1125-A or elsewhere on return (attach Form 4562).....			**14**	4,400.
	15 Depletion (Do not deduct oil and gas depletion.)..................			**15**	19,000.
	16 Advertising..........................			**16**	
	17 Pension, profit-sharing, etc., plans..........................			**17**	5,200.
	18 Employee benefit programs..........................			**18**	10,000.
	19 Other deductions (attach statement).......... See Statement 1			**19**	
	20 Total deductions. Add lines 7 through 19.......................... ►			**20**	43,350.
	21 Ordinary business income (loss). Subtract line 20 from line 6..........			**21**	200,750.
T A X A N D P A Y M E N T S	**22a** Excess net passive income or LIFO recapture tax (see instructions).............	**22a**			59,250.
	b Tax from Schedule D (Form 1120S).............	**22b**			
	c Add lines 22a and 22b (see instructions for additional taxes)........			**22c**	
	23a 2018 estimated tax payments and 2017 overpayment credited to 2018....	**23a**			
	b Tax deposited with Form 7004...........	**23b**			
	c Credit for federal tax paid on fuels (attach Form 4136)...........	**23c**			
	d Refundable credit from Form 8827, line 8c...........	**23d**			
	e Add lines 23a through 23d..........................			**23e**	
	24 Estimated tax penalty (see instructions). Check if Form 2220 is attached........ ► ☐			**24**	
	25 Amount owed. If line 23e is smaller than the total of lines 22c and 24, enter amount owed......			**25**	
	26 Overpayment. If line 23e is larger than the total of lines 22c and 24, enter amount overpaid.....			**26**	0.
	27 Enter amount from line 26: Credited to 2019 estimated tax ► _____ Refunded ►			**27**	

Sign Here	Under penalties of perjury, I declare that I have examined this return, including accompanying schedules and statements, and to the best of my knowledge and belief, it is true, correct, and complete. Declaration of preparer (other than taxpayer) is based on all information of which preparer has any knowledge. ► _____ Signature of officer Date ► _____ Title May the IRS discuss this return with the preparer shown below (see instructions)? ☐ Yes ☐ No

Paid Preparer Use Only	Print/Type preparer's name	Preparer's signature Self-Prepared	Date	Check ☒ if self-employed	PTIN
	Firm's name ►			Firm's EIN ►	
	Firm's address ►			Phone no.	

BAA For Paperwork Reduction Act Notice, see separate instructions.   SPSA0112L 08/23/18   Form **1120S** (2018)

Form 1120S (2018) Entrepreneur, LLC   99-1234567   Page 2

Schedule B	Other Information (see instructions)		Yes	No

1 Check accounting method: **a** ☐ Cash   **b** ☒ Accrual   **c** ☐ Other (specify) ▶ _ _ _ _ _ _ _ _ _ _ _

2 See the instructions and enter the:
   a Business activity ▶ Service _ _ _ _ _ _ _ _ _ _ _   **b** Product or service... ▶ Consulting _ _ _ _ _ _ _ _ _ _

3 At any time during the tax year, was any shareholder of the corporation a disregarded entity, a trust, an estate, or a
   nominee or similar person? If "Yes," attach Schedule B-1, Information on Certain Shareholders of an S Corporation . . . . . | | X

4 At the end of the tax year, did the corporation:
   a Own directly 20% or more, or own, directly or indirectly, 50% or more of the total stock issued and outstanding of
   any foreign or domestic corporation? For rules of constructive ownership, see instructions. If "Yes," complete (i)
   through (v) below. . . . . | | X

(i) Name of Corporation	(ii) Employer Identification Number (if any)	(iii) Country of Incorporation	(iv) Percentage of Stock Owned	(v) If Percentage in (iv) is 100%, Enter the Date (if any) a Qualified Subchapter S Subsidiary Election Was Made

b Own directly an interest of 20% or more, or own, directly or indirectly, an interest of 50% or more in the profit, loss, or
   capital in any foreign or domestic partnership (including an entity treated as a partnership) or in the beneficial interest
   of a trust? For rules of constructive ownership, see instructions. If "Yes," complete (i) through (v) below. | | X

(i) Name of Entity	(ii) Employer Identification Number (if any)	(iii) Type of Entity	(iv) Country of Organization	(v) Maximum % Owned in Profit, Loss, or Capital

5a At the end of the tax year, did the corporation have any outstanding shares of restricted stock? . . . . | | X
   If "Yes," complete lines (i) and (ii) below.
   (i) Total shares of restricted stock . . . . ▶ _ _ _ _ _ _ _ _ _ _ _
   (ii) Total shares of non-restricted stock . . . . ▶ _ _ _ _ _ _ _ _ _ _ _

b At the end of the tax year, did the corporation have any outstanding stock options, warrants, or similar instruments? . . . . . | | X
   If "Yes," complete lines (i) and (ii) below.
   (i) Total shares of stock outstanding at the end of the tax year . . . . ▶ _ _ _ _ _ _ _ _ _ _ _
   (ii) Total shares of stock outstanding if all instruments were executed . . . . ▶ _ _ _ _ _ _ _ _ _ _ _

6 Has this corporation filed, or is it required to file, **Form 8918**, Material Advisor Disclosure Statement, to provide
   information on any reportable transaction? . . . . ▶ ☐ | | X

7 Check this box if the corporation issued publicly offered debt instruments with original issue discount . . . . ▶ ☐
   If checked, the corporation may have to file **Form 8281**, Information Return for Publicly Offered Original Issue Discount
   Instruments.

8 If the corporation **(a)** was a C corporation before it elected to be an S corporation **or** the corporation acquired an
   asset with a basis determined by reference to the basis of the asset (or the basis of any other property) in
   the hands of a C corporation **and (b)** has net unrealized built-in gain in excess of the net recognized built-in gain
   from prior years, enter the net unrealized built-in gain reduced by net recognized built-in gain from prior years (see
   instructions) . . . . ▶ $ _ _ _ _ _ _ _

9 Did the corporation have an election under section 163(j) for any real property trade or business or any farming business
   in effect during the tax year? See instructions . . . . | | X

10 Does the corporation satisfy one of the following conditions and the corporation doesn't own a pass-through entity with
   current year, or prior year carryover, excess business interest expense? See instructions. . . . . | X |
   a The corporation's aggregate average annual gross receipts (determined under section 448(c)) for the 3 tax years
   preceding the current tax year don't exceed $25 million, and the corporation isn't a tax shelter; or
   b The corporation only has business interest expense from (1) an electing real property trade or business, (2) an electing
   farming business, or (3) certain utility businesses under section 163(j)(7).
   If "No," complete and attach Form 8990.

11 Does the corporation satisfy **both** of the following conditions?
   a The corporation's total receipts (see instructions) for the tax year were less than $250,000 . . . . | | X
   b The corporation's total assets at the end of the tax year were less than $250,000 . . . .
   If "Yes," the corporation is not required to complete Schedules L and M-1.

SPSA0112L 08/23/18   Form **1120S** (2018)

Form 1120S (2018)	Entrepreneur, LLC		99-1234567		Page 3

Schedule B	**Other Information** (see instructions) *(continued)*		Yes	No
12	During the tax year, did the corporation have any non-shareholder debt that was canceled, was forgiven, or had the terms modified so as to reduce the principal amount of the debt?			X
	If "Yes," enter the amount of principal reduction.......................... ▶ $			
13	During the tax year, was a qualified subchapter S subsidiary election terminated or revoked? If "Yes," see instructions.....			X
14a	Did the corporation make any payments in 2018 that would require it to file Form(s) 1099?			X
b	If "Yes," did the corporation file or will it file required Forms 1099?			
15	Is the corporation attaching Form 8996 to certify as a Qualified Opportunity Fund?			X
	If "Yes," enter the amount from Form 8996, line 13 ▶ $			

Schedule K		**Shareholders' Pro Rata Share Items**			Total amount
Income (Loss)	1	Ordinary business income (loss) (page 1, line 21)	1		59,250.
	2	Net rental real estate income (loss) (attach Form 8825)	2		
	3 a	Other gross rental income (loss)	3 a		
	b	Expenses from other rental activities (attach statement)	3 b		
	c	Other net rental income (loss). Subtract line 3b from line 3a	3 c		
	4	Interest income	4		242.
	5	Dividends: a Ordinary dividends	5 a		
		b Qualified dividends	5 b		
	6	Royalties	6		
	7	Net short-term capital gain (loss) (attach Schedule D (Form 1120S))	7		
	8 a	Net long-term capital gain (loss) (attach Schedule D (Form 1120S))	8 a		
	b	Collectibles (28%) gain (loss)	8 b		
	c	Unrecaptured section 1250 gain (attach statement)	8 c		
	9	Net section 1231 gain (loss) (attach Form 4797)	9		
	10	Other income (loss) (see instructions) Type ▶	10		
Deductions	11	Section 179 deduction (attach Form 4562)	11		25,000.
	12a	Charitable contributions See Statement 2	12a		1,200.
	b	Investment interest expense	12b		
	c	Section 59(e)(2) expenditures (1) Type ▶ _____ (2) Amount ▶	12c (2)		
	d	Other deductions (see instructions) Type ▶	12d		
Credits	13a	Low-income housing credit (section 42(j)(5))	13a		
	b	Low-income housing credit (other)	13b		
	c	Qualified rehabilitation expenditures (rental real estate) (attach Form 3468, if applicable)	13c		
	d	Other rental real estate credits (see instrs) Type ▶	13d		
	e	Other rental credits (see instrs) Type ▶	13e		
	f	Biofuel producer credit (attach Form 6478)	13f		
	g	Other credits (see instructions) Type ▶	13g		
Foreign Trans-actions	14a	Name of country or U.S. possession ▶			
	b	Gross income from all sources	14b		
	c	Gross income sourced at shareholder level	14c		
		Foreign gross income sourced at corporate level			
	d	Section 951A category	14d		
	e	Foreign branch category	14e		
	f	Passive category	14f		
	g	General category	14g		
	h	Other (attach statement)	14h		
		Deductions allocated and apportioned at shareholder level			
	i	Interest expense	14i		
	j	Other	14j		
		Deductions allocated and apportioned at corporate level to foreign source income			
	k	Section 951A category	14k		
	l	Foreign branch category	14l		
	m	Passive category	14m		
	n	General category	14n		
	o	Other (attach statement)	14o		
		Other information			
	p	Total foreign taxes (check one). ▶ ☐ Paid ☐ Accrued	14p		
	q	Reduction in taxes available for credit (attach statement)	14q		
	r	Other foreign tax information (attach statement)			

BAA   SPSA0134L 08/23/18   Form **1120S** (2018)

Form 1120S (2018) Entrepreneur, LLC   99-1234567   Page **4**

Schedule K	Shareholders' Pro Rata Share Items (continued)		Total amount

Alternative Minimum Tax (AMT) Items	15a Post-1986 depreciation adjustment	15a	
	b Adjusted gain or loss	15b	
	c Depletion (other than oil and gas)	15c	
	d Oil, gas, and geothermal properties — gross income	15d	
	e Oil, gas, and geothermal properties — deductions	15e	
	f Other AMT items (attach statement)	15f	
Items Affecting Shareholder Basis	16a Tax-exempt interest income	16a	
	b Other tax-exempt income	16b	
	c Nondeductible expenses	16c	1,300.
	d Distributions (attach stmt if required) (see instrs)	16d	31,992.
	e Repayment of loans from shareholders	16e	
Other Information	17a Investment income	17a	242.
	b Investment expenses	17b	
	c Dividend distributions paid from accumulated earnings and profits	17c	
	d Other items and amounts (attach statement) See Statement 3		
Reconciliation	18 Income/loss reconciliation. Combine the amounts on lines 1 through 10 in the far right column. From the result, subtract the sum of the amounts on lines 11 through 12d and 14p	18	33,292.

Schedule L	Balance Sheets per Books	Beginning of tax year		End of tax year	
	Assets	(a)	(b)	(c)	(d)
1	Cash				24,000.
2a	Trade notes and accounts receivable			12,000.	
b	Less allowance for bad debts				12,000.
3	Inventories				
4	U.S. government obligations				
5	Tax-exempt securities (see instructions)				
6	Other current assets (attach stmt)				
7	Loans to shareholders				
8	Mortgage and real estate loans				
9	Other investments (attach statement)				
10a	Buildings and other depreciable assets			44,000.	
b	Less accumulated depreciation			44,000.	
11a	Depletable assets				
b	Less accumulated depletion				
12	Land (net of any amortization)				
13a	Intangible assets (amortizable only)				
b	Less accumulated amortization				
14	Other assets (attach stmt)				
15	Total assets		0.		36,000.
	Liabilities and Shareholders' Equity				
16	Accounts payable				
17	Mortgages, notes, bonds payable in less than 1 year				
18	Other current liabilities (attach stmt)				
19	Loans from shareholders				
20	Mortgages, notes, bonds payable in 1 year or more				36,000.
21	Other liabilities (attach statement)				
22	Capital stock				
23	Additional paid-in capital				
24	Retained earnings				
25	Adjustments to shareholders' equity (att stmt)				
26	Less cost of treasury stock				
27	Total liabilities and shareholders' equity		0.		36,000.

SPSA0134L 09/23/18   Form **1120S** (2018)

Form **1120S** (2018) Entrepreneur, LLC   99-1234567   Page **5**

Schedule M-1 Reconciliation of Income (Loss) per Books With Income (Loss) per Return

Note: The corporation may be required to file Schedule M-3 (see instructions)

1	Net income (loss) per books.	31,992.	5	Income recorded on books this year not included on Schedule K, lines 1 through 10 (itemize)	
2	Income included on Schedule K, lines 1, 2, 3c, 4, 5a, 6, 7, 8a, 9, and 10, not recorded on books this year (itemize):			a Tax-exempt interest $ _____	
3	Expenses recorded on books this year not included on Schedule K, lines 1 through 12 and 14p (itemize):		6	Deductions included on Schedule K, lines 1 through 12 and 14p, not charged against book income this year (itemize):	
a	Depreciation. $ _____			a Depreciation ... $ _____	
b	Travel and entertainment. $ ____700.				
	See Statement 4 ____600.	1,300.	7	Add lines 5 and 6	0.
4	Add lines 1 through 3	33,292.	8	Income (loss) (Schedule K, line 18). Line 4 less line 7	33,292.

Schedule M-2 Analysis of Accumulated Adjustments Account, Shareholders' Undistributed Taxable Income Previously Taxed, Accumulated Earnings and Profits, and Other Adjustments Account

(see instructions)

		(a) Accumulated adjustments account	(b) Shareholders' undistributed taxable income previously taxed	(c) Accumulated earnings and profits	(d) Other adjustments account
1	Balance at beginning of tax year.	0.			
2	Ordinary income from page 1, line 21	59,250.			
3	Other additions See Statement 5	242.			
4	Loss from page 1, line 21				
5	Other reductions See Statement 6	(27,500.)			
6	Combine lines 1 through 5	31,992.			
7	Distributions	31,992.			
8	Balance at end of tax year. Subtract line 7 from line 6	0.			

SPSA0134L 06/03/18   Form **1120S** (2018)

C.S. THOMAS, CPA

OMB No. 1545-0123

☐ Final K-1	☐ Amended K-1

Schedule K-1
(Form 1120S)
Department of the Treasury
Internal Revenue Service

For calendar year 2018, or tax year

2018

beginning __/__/__ ending __/__/__

Shareholder's Share of Income, Deductions, Credits, etc. ► See page 2 of form and separate instructions.

Part I	Information About the Corporation

A Corporation's employer identification number
99-1234567

B Corporation's name, address, city, state, and ZIP code
Entrepreneur, LLC
123 Main Street
Saint Paul, MN 55101

C IRS Center where corporation filed return
e-file

Part II	Information About the Shareholder

D Shareholder's identifying number
111-22-3333

E Shareholder's name, address, city, state, and ZIP code
John Doe
123 Main Street
Saint Paul, MN 55101

F Shareholder's percentage of stock
ownership for tax year.................... 100 %

Part III	Shareholder's Share of Current Year Income, Deductions, Credits, and Other Items
1 Ordinary business income (loss) 59,250.	13 Credits
2 Net rental real estate income (loss)	
3 Other net rental income (loss)	
4 Interest income 242.	
5a Ordinary dividends	
5b Qualified dividends	14 Foreign transactions
6 Royalties	
7 Net short-term capital gain (loss)	
8a Net long-term capital gain (loss)	
8b Collectibles (28%) gain (loss)	
8c Unrecaptured section 1250 gain	
9 Net section 1231 gain (loss)	
10 Other income (loss)	15 Alternative minimum tax (AMT) items
11 Section 179 deduction 25,000.	16 Items affecting shareholder basis C 1,300.
12 Other deductions A 1,200.	D 31,992.
	17 Other information A 242.
	V 59,250.
	W 96,000.
	X 44,000.

*See attached statement for additional information.

BAA For Paperwork Reduction Act Notice, see the Instructions for Form 1120S.

Schedule K-1 (Form 1120S) 2018

Shareholder 1

252

2018	Federal Statements	Page 1
	Entrepreneur, LLC	99-1234567

Statement 1
Form 1120S, Line 19
Other Deductions

Auto and Truck Expense	$	5,400.
Dues and Subscriptions		1,650.
Insurance		7,400.
Legal and Professional		6,000.
Meals		700.
Office Expense		2,800.
Outside Services		10,000.
Supplies		2,000.
Telephone		1,500.
Travel		2,800.
Utilities		3,100.
Total	$	43,350.

Statement 2
Form 1120S, Schedule K, Line 12a
Charitable Contributions

Cash Contributions - 60% Limitation	$	1,200.
Total	$	1,200.

Statement 3
Form 1120S, Schedule K, Line 17d
Other Items and Amounts

Section 199A Qualified Business Income	$	59,250.
Section 199A W-2 Wages	$	96,000.
Section 199A Unadjusted Basis	$	44,000.

Statement 4
Form 1120S, Schedule M-1, Line 3
Expenses On Books Not On Schedule K

Officers Life Insurance Premiums	$	600.
Total	$	600.

Statement 5
Form 1120S, Schedule M-2, Column A, Line 3
Other Additions

Interest Income	$	242.
Total	$	242.

2018	Federal Statements	Page 2
	Entrepreneur, LLC	99-1234567

Statement 6
Form 1120S, Schedule M-2, Column A, Line 5
Other Reductions

Contributions	$	1,200.
Disallowed Meals and Entertainment		700.
Officers Life Insurance Premiums		600.
Section 179 Expense		25,000.
	Total $	27,500.

Form 1040 Department of the Treasury — Internal Revenue Service (99) **U.S. Individual Income Tax Return** **2018** OMB No. 1545-0074 IRS Use Only — Do not write or staple in this space.

Filing status: ☒ Single ☐ Married filing jointly ☐ Married filing separately ☐ Head of household ☐ Qualifying widow(er)

Your first name and initial: **John** Last name: **Doe**

Your standard deduction: ☐ Someone can claim you as a dependent ☐ You were born before January 2, 1954 ☐ You are blind

Your social security number: **111-22-3333**

If joint return, spouse's first name and initial: _____ Last name: _____

Spouse's social security number: _____

Spouse standard deduction: ☐ Someone can claim your spouse as a dependent ☐ Spouse was born before January 2, 1954 ☐ Spouse itemizes on a separate return or you were dual-status alien ☒ Full-year health care coverage or exempt (see inst.)

Home address (number and street). If you have a P.O. box, see instructions. **123 Main Street** Apt. no. _____

City, town or post office, state, and ZIP code. If you have a foreign address, attach Schedule 6. **Saint Paul, MN 55101**

Presidential Election Campaign (see inst.) ☐ You ☐ Spouse

If more than four dependents, see inst. and ✓ here ► ☐

Dependents (see instructions):

(1) First name Last name	(2) Social security number	(3) Relationship to you	(4) ✓ if qualifies for (see inst.): Child tax credit / Credit for other dependents

Sign Here
Joint return? See instructions.
Keep a copy for your records.

Under penalties of perjury, I declare that I have examined this return and accompanying schedules and statements, and to the best of my knowledge and belief, they are true, correct, and complete. Declaration of preparer (other than taxpayer) is based on all information of which preparer has any knowledge.

Your signature _____ Date _____ Your occupation **Entrepreneur** If the IRS sent you an Identity Protection PIN, enter it here (see inst.)

Spouse's signature. If a joint return, both must sign. _____ Date _____ Spouse's occupation _____ If the IRS sent you an Identity Protection PIN, enter it here (see inst.)

Paid Preparer Use Only
Preparer's name _____ Preparer's signature **Self-Prepared** PTIN _____ Firm's EIN _____ Check if: ☐ 3rd Party Designee ☐ Self-employed
Firm's name ► _____ Phone no. _____
Firm's address ► _____

BAA **For Disclosure, Privacy Act, and Paperwork Reduction Act Notice, see separate instructions.** FDIA0112L 01/08/19 Form **1040** (2018)

Form 1040 (2018) Page 2

Attach Form(s) W-2. Also attach Form(s) W-2G and 1099-R if tax was withheld.

1	Wages, salaries, tips, etc. Attach Form(s) W-2	**1**	60,000.
2a	Tax-exempt interest **2a**	b Taxable interest . . . **2b**	242.
3a	Qualified dividends **3a**	b Ordinary dividends . . **3b**	
4a	IRAs, pensions, and annuities . . **4a**	b Taxable amount . . . **4b**	
5a	Social security benefits **5a**	b Taxable amount . . . **5b**	
6	Total income. Add lines 1 through 5. Add any amount from Schedule 1, line 22 **34,250.**	**6**	94,492.
7	Adjusted gross income. If you have no adjustments to income, enter the amount from line 6; otherwise, subtract Schedule 1, line 36, from line 6	**7**	90,253.

Standard Deduction for —
* Single or married filing separately, $12,000
* Married filing jointly or Qualifying widow(er), $24,000
* Head of household, $18,000
* If you checked any box under Standard deduction, see instructions.

8	Standard deduction or itemized deductions (from Schedule A)	**8**	12,000.
9	Qualified business income deduction (see instructions)	**9**	11,850.
10	Taxable income. Subtract lines 8 and 9 from line 7. If zero or less, enter –0– . . .	**10**	66,403.
11	a Tax (see inst.) **10,553.** (check if any from: 1 ☐ Form(s) 8814 2 ☐ Form 4972 3 ☐ _____) b Add any amount from Schedule 2 and check here . . . . ► ☐	**11**	10,553.
12	a Child tax credit/credit for other dependents _____ b Add any amount from Schedule 3 and check here . . . . ► ☐	**12**	
13	Subtract line 12 from line 11. If zero or less, enter -0-	**13**	10,553.
14	Other taxes. Attach Schedule 4	**14**	8,478.
15	Total tax. Add lines 13 and 14	**15**	19,031.
16	Federal income tax withheld from Forms W-2 and 1099	**16**	
17	Refundable credits: a EIC (see inst.) _____ b Sch. 8812 _____ c Form 8863 _____ Add any amount from Schedule 5	**17**	
18	Add lines 16 and 17. These are your total payments	**18**	0.

Refund
Direct deposit? See instructions.

19	If line 18 is more than line 15, subtract line 15 from line 18. This is the amount you **overpaid**	**19**	
20a	Amount of line 19 you want **refunded to you.** If Form 8888 is attached, check here ► ☐	**20a**	
	► b Routing number _____ ► c Type: ☐ Checking ☐ Savings ► d Account number _____		
21	Amount of line 19 you want applied to your 2019 estimated tax . . ► **21**		

Amount You Owe

22	Amount you owe. Subtract line 18 from line 15. For details on how to pay, see instructions . . . ►	**22**	19,031.
23	Estimated tax penalty (see instructions) . . . . ► **23**		

Go to *www.irs.gov/Form1040* for instructions and the latest information.

Form **1040** (2018)

SCHEDULE 1
(Form 1040)

Department of the Treasury
Internal Revenue Service

Additional Income and Adjustments to Income

▶ Attach to Form 1040.
▶ Go to *www.irs.gov/Form1040* for instructions and the latest information.

OMB No. 1545-0074

2018

Attachment
Sequence No. **01**

Name(s) shown on Form 1040
John Doe

Your social security number
111-22-3333

Additional Income	1–9b	Reserved	1–9b	
	10	Taxable refunds, credits, or offsets of state and local income taxes	10	
	11	Alimony received	11	
	12	Business income or (loss). Attach Schedule C or C-EZ	12	
	13	Capital gain or (loss). Attach Schedule D if required. If not required, check here ▶ ☐	13	
	14	Other gains or (losses). Attach Form 4797	14	
	15a	Reserved	15b	
	16a	Reserved	16b	
	17	Rental real estate, royalties, partnerships, S corporations, trusts, etc. Attach Schedule E	17	34,250.
	18	Farm income or (loss). Attach Schedule F	18	
	19	Unemployment compensation	19	
	20a	Reserved	20b	
	21	Other income. List type and amount _ _ _ _ _ _ _ _ _ _ _ _	21	
	22	Combine the amounts in the far right column. If you don't have any adjustments to income, enter here and include on Form 1040, line 6. Otherwise, go to line 23	22	34,250.
Adjustments to Income	23	Educator expenses	23	
	24	Certain business expenses of reservists, performing artists, and fee-basis government officials. Attach Form 2106	24	
	25	Health savings account deduction. Attach Form 8889	25	
	26	Moving expenses for members of the Armed Forces. Attach Form 3903	26	
	27	Deductible part of self-employment tax. Attach Schedule SE	27	4,239.
	28	Self-employed SEP, SIMPLE, and qualified plans	28	
	29	Self-employed health insurance deduction	29	
	30	Penalty on early withdrawal of savings	30	
	31a	Alimony paid b Recipient's SSN ▶	31a	
	32	IRA deduction	32	
	33	Student loan interest deduction	33	
	34	Reserved	34	
	35	Reserved	35	
	36	Add lines 23 through 35	36	4,239.

BAA For Paperwork Reduction Act Notice, see your tax return instructions.

Schedule 1 (Form 1040) 2018

SCHEDULE 4
(Form 1040)

Department of the Treasury
Internal Revenue Service

Other Taxes

▶ Attach to Form 1040.
▶ Go to *www.irs.gov/Form1040* for instructions and the latest information.

OMB No. 1545-0074

2018

Attachment
Sequence No. **04**

Name(s) shown on Form 1040
John Doe

Your social security number
111-22-3333

Other Taxes	57	Self-employment tax. Attach Schedule SE	57	8,478.
	58	Unreported social security and Medicare tax from: Form a ☐ 4137		
		b ☐ 8919	58	
	59	Additional tax on IRAs, other qualified retirement plans, and other tax-favored accounts. Attach Form 5329 if required	59	
	60a	Household employment taxes. Attach Schedule H	60a	
	b	Repayment of first-time homebuyer credit from Form 5405. Attach Form 5405 if required	60b	
	61	Health care: individual responsibility (see instructions)	61	
	62	Taxes from: a ☐ Form 8959 b ☐ Form 8960 c ☐ Instructions; enter code(s) _ _ _ _ _ _ _ _ _ _	62	
	63	Section 965 net tax liability installment from Form 965-A	63	
	64	Add the amounts in the far right column. These are your **total other taxes**. Enter here and on Form 1040, line 14	64	8,478.

BAA For Paperwork Reduction Act Notice, see your tax return instructions.

Schedule 4 (Form 1040) 2018

Schedule E (Form 1040) 2018   Attachment Sequence No. **13**   Page **2**

Name(s) shown on return. Do not enter name and social security number if shown on Page 1.

	Your social security number
John Doe	111-22-3333

Caution: The IRS compares amounts reported on your tax return with amounts shown on Schedule(s) K-1.

Part II   Income or Loss From Partnerships and S Corporations

Note: If you report a loss, receive a distribution, dispose of stock, or receive a loan repayment from an S corporation, you **must** check the box in column **(e)** on line 28 and attach the required basis computation. If you report a loss from an at-risk activity for which **any** amount is **not** at risk, you **must** check the box in column **(f)** on line 28 and attach **Form 6198** (see instructions).

27   Are you reporting any loss not allowed in a prior year due to the at-risk, excess farm loss, or basis limitations, a prior year unallowed loss from a passive activity (if that loss was not reported on Form 8582), or unreimbursed partnership expenses? If you answered "Yes," see instructions before completing this section ....   ☐ Yes   ☒ No

28	(a) Name	(b) Enter P for partnership; S for S corporation	(c) Check if foreign partnership	(d) Employer identification number	(e) Check if basis computation is required	(f) Check if any amount is not at risk
A	Entrepreneur, LLC	S		99-1234567	X	
B						
C						
D						

	Passive Income and Loss			Nonpassive Income and Loss		
	(g) Passive loss allowed (attach Form 8582 if required)	(h) Passive income from Schedule K-1	(i) Nonpassive loss from Schedule K-1	(j) Section 179 expense deduction from Form 4562	(k) Nonpassive income from Schedule K-1	
A				25,000.	59,250.	
B						
C						
D						
29 a Totals					59,250.	
b Totals				25,000.		
30	Add columns (h) and (k) of line 29a				30	59,250.
31	Add columns (g), (i), and (j) of line 29b				31	-25,000.
32	Total partnership and S corporation income or (loss). Combine lines 30 and 31				32	34,250.

Part III   Income or Loss From Estates and Trusts

33	(a) Name	(b) Employer ID no.
A		
B		

	Passive Income and Loss		Nonpassive Income and Loss		
	(c) Passive deduction or loss allowed (attach Form 8582 if required)	(d) Passive income from Schedule K-1	(e) Deduction or loss from Schedule K-1	(f) Other income from Schedule K-1	
A					
B					
34 a Totals					
b Totals					
35	Add columns (d) and (f) of line 34a		35	
36	Add columns (c) and (e) of line 34b		36	
37	Total estate and trust income or (loss). Combine lines 35 and 36		37	

Part IV   Income or Loss From Real Estate Mortgage Investment Conduits (REMICs) — Residual Holder

38	(a) Name	(b) Employer identification number	(c) Excess inclusion from Schedules Q, line 2c (see instructions)	(d) Taxable income (net loss) from Schedules Q, line 1b	(e) Income from Schedules Q, line 3b

39	Combine columns (d) and (e) only. Enter the result here and include in the total on line 41 below	39	

Part V   Summary

40	Net farm rental income or (loss) from Form 4835. Also, complete line 42 below.	40	
41	Total income or (loss). Combine lines 26, 32, 37, 39, and 40. Enter the result here and on Schedule 1 (Form 1040), line 17, or Form 1040NR, line 18. . . . . ►	41	34,250.
42	Reconciliation of farming and fishing income. Enter your gross farming and fishing income reported on Form 4835, line 7; Schedule K-1 (Form 1065), box 14, code B; Schedule K-1 (Form 1120S), box 17, code AC; and Schedule K-1 (Form 1041), box 14, code F (see instructions)	42	
43	Reconciliation for real estate professionals. If you were a real estate professional (see instructions), enter the net income or (loss) you reported anywhere on Form 1040 or Form 1040NR from all rental real estate activities in which you materially participated under the passive activity loss rules.	43	

BAA   FDIZ2302L 02/15/19   Schedule E (Form 1040) 2018

2018	Federal Worksheets	Page 1
	John Doe	111-22-3333

Wage Schedule

Taxpayer - Employer	Wages	Federal W/H	FICA	Medi-care	State W/H	Local W/H
Entrepreneur, LLC	60,000.					
Grand Total	60,000.	0.	0.	0.	0.	0.

Form 1040, Line 2b
Interest Income

Entrepreneur, LLC	242.
Total	242.

Qualified Business Income

Trade or business name:	Entrepreneur, LLC
Taxpayer identification number:	99-1234567
Business income	59,250.
Qualified Business Income	59,250.

Qualified Business Income Deduction - Simplified Worksheet
(Form 1040, line 9)

1. (a) Trade or business name	(b) EIN/SSN	(c) Qual bus. inc or loss
Entrepreneur, LLC	99-1234567 $	59,250.
2. Total qualified business income or (loss)	59,250.	
3. Qualified business loss carryforward	0.	
4. Total qualified business income. Combine lines 2 and 3 If zero or less, enter 0	59,250.	
5. Qualified business income component. Multiply line 4 by 20%		11,850.
6. Qualified REIT dividends and PTP income or loss	0.	
7. Qualified REIT and PTP loss carryforward	0.	
8. Total qualified REIT and PTP income. Add lines 6 and 7. If zero or less, enter 0	0.	
9. REIT and PTP component. Multiply line 8 by 20%		0.
10. Qualified business income deduction before the income limitation. Add lines 5 and 9		11,850.
11. Income before qualified business income deduction	78,253.	
12. Net capital gains	0.	
13. Subtract line 12 from line 11. If zero or less, enter 0	78,253.	
14. Income limitation. Multiply line 13 by 20%		15,651.
15. Qualified business income deduction. Enter the smaller of line 10 or line 14		11,850.
16. Total qualified business loss carryforward. Add lines 2 and 3. If more than zero, enter 0		0.
17. Total qualified REIT income and PTP loss carryforward. Add lines 6 and 7. If more than zero, enter 0		0.

Partnership and Corresponding Individual Return

Form **1065**	**U.S. Return of Partnership Income**		OMB No. 1545-0123
Department of the Treasury Internal Revenue Service	For calendar year 2018, or tax year beginning _____, 2018. ending _____ , 20 _____ . ▶ Go to *www.irs.gov/Form1065* for instructions and the latest information.		**2018**

A Principal business activity			D Employer identification no.
Service			99-1234567
B Principal product or service	Type or Print	Entrepreneur, LLC 123 Main Street Saint Paul, MN 55101	E Date business started
Consulting			1/01/2018
C Business code number			F Total assets (see instructions)
541600			$ 36,000.

G Check applicable boxes: (1) ☐ Initial return (2) ☐ Final return (3) ☐ Name change (4) ☐ Address change (5) ☐ Amended return

H Check accounting method: (1) ☐ Cash (2) ☒ Accrual (3) ☐ Other (specify) ▶

I Number of Schedules K-1. Attach one for each person who was a partner at any time during the tax year. ▶ 1

J Check if Schedules C and M-3 are attached ▶ ☐

Caution: Include only trade or business income and expenses on lines 1a through 22 below. See the instructions for more information.

INCOME	1 a Gross receipts or sales	1a	260,000.
	b Returns and allowances	1b	
	c Balance. Subtract line 1b from line 1a	1c	260,000.
	2 Cost of goods sold (attach Form 1125-A)	2	
	3 Gross profit. Subtract line 2 from line 1c	3	260,000.
	4 Ordinary income (loss) from other partnerships, estates, and trusts (attach statement)	4	
	5 Net farm profit (loss) (attach Schedule F (Form 1040))	5	
	6 Net gain (loss) from Form 4797, Part II, line 17 (attach Form 4797)	6	
	7 Other income (loss) (attach statement)	7	
	8 Total income (loss). Combine lines 3 through 7	8	260,000.
DEDUCTIONS (SEE INSTRUCTIONS FOR LIMITATIONS)	9 Salaries and wages (other than to partners) (less employment credits)	9	36,000.
	10 Guaranteed payments to partners	10	60,000.
	11 Repairs and maintenance	11	
	12 Bad debts	12	8,500.
	13 Rent	13	10,200.
	14 Taxes and licenses	14	4,100.
	15 Interest (see instructions)	15	4,400.
	16 a Depreciation (if required, attach Form 4562)	16a	19,000.
	b Less depreciation reported on Form 1125-A and elsewhere on return	16b	
		16c	19,000.
	17 Depletion (**Do not deduct oil and gas depletion.**)	17	
	18 Retirement plans, etc.	18	10,000.
	19 Employee benefit programs	19	
	20 Other deductions (att stmt) ....See Statement 1	20	48,550.
	21 Total deductions. Add the amounts shown in the far right column for lines 9 through 20	21	200,750.
	22 Ordinary business income (loss). Subtract line 21 from line 8	22	59,250.
TAX AND PAYMENT	23 Interest due under the look-back method — completed long-term contracts (attach Form 8697)	23	
	24 Interest due under the look-back method — income forecast method (attach Form 8866)	24	
	25 BBA AAR imputed underpayment (see instructions)	25	
	26 Other taxes (see instructions)	26	
	27 Total balance due. Add lines 23 through 26	27	
	28 Payment (see instructions)	28	
	29 Amount owed. If line 28 is smaller than line 27, enter amount owed	29	
	30 Overpayment. If line 28 is larger than line 27, enter overpayment	30	

Sign Here

Under penalties of perjury, I declare that I have examined this return, including accompanying schedules and statements, and to the best of my knowledge and belief, it is true, correct, and complete. Declaration of preparer (other than partner or limited liability company member) is based on all information of which preparer has any knowledge.

▶ _____ Signature of partner or limited liability company member

▶ _____ Date

May the IRS discuss this return with the preparer shown below? See instructions. ☐ Yes ☐ No

Paid Preparer Use Only	Print/Type preparer's name	Preparer's signature Self-Prepared	Date	Check ☐ if self-employed	PTIN
	Firm's name ▶			Firm's EIN ▶	
	Firm's address ▶			Phone no.	

BAA For Paperwork Reduction Act Notice, see separate instructions.   PTPA0105L 09/10/18   Form **1065** (2018)

Form 1065 (2018) Entrepreneur, LLC 99-1234567 Page **2**

Schedule B	**Other Information**		

		Yes	No
1	What type of entity is filing this return? Check the applicable box:		

a ☐ Domestic general partnership b ☐ Domestic limited partnership

c ☒ Domestic limited liability company d ☐ Domestic limited liability partnership

e ☐ Foreign partnership f ☐ Other ►

			Yes	No
2	At the end of the tax year:			
a	Did any foreign or domestic corporation, partnership (including any entity treated as a partnership), trust, or tax-exempt organization, or any foreign government own, directly or indirectly, an interest of 50% or more in the profit, loss, or capital of the partnership? For rules of constructive ownership, see instructions. If "Yes," attach Schedule B-1, Information on Partners Owning 50% or More of the Partnership			X
b	Did any individual or estate own, directly or indirectly, an interest of 50% or more in the profit, loss, or capital of the partnership? For rules of constructive ownership, see instructions. If "Yes," attach Schedule B-1, Information on Partners Owning 50% or More of the Partnership		X	
3	At the end of the tax year, did the partnership:			
a	Own directly 20% or more, or own, directly or indirectly, 50% or more of the total voting power of all classes of stock entitled to vote of any foreign or domestic corporation? For rules of constructive ownership, see instructions. If "Yes," complete (i) through (iv) below.			X

(i) Name of Corporation	(ii) Employer Identification Number (if any)	(iii) Country of Incorporation	(iv) Percentage Owned in Voting Stock

b Own directly an interest of 20% or more, or own, directly or indirectly, an interest of 50% or more in the profit, loss, or capital in any foreign or domestic partnership (including an entity treated as a partnership) or in the beneficial interest of a trust? For rules of constructive ownership, see instructions. If "Yes," complete (i) through (v) below.   X

(i) Name of Entity	(ii) Employer Identification Number (if any)	(iii) Type of Entity	(iv) Country of Organization	(v) Maximum Percentage Owned in Profit, Loss, or Capital

		Yes	No
4	Does the partnership satisfy **all four** of the following conditions?		
a	The partnership's total receipts for the tax year were less than $250,000.		
b	The partnership's total assets at the end of the tax year were less than $1 million.		
c	Schedules K-1 are filed with the return and furnished to the partners on or before the due date (including extensions) for the partnership return.		
d	The partnership is not filing and is not required to file Schedule M-3		X
	If "Yes," the partnership is not required to complete Schedules L, M-1, and M-2; item F on page 1 of Form 1065; or item L on Schedule K-1.		
5	Is this partnership a publicly traded partnership as defined in section 469(k)(2)?		X
6	During the tax year, did the partnership have any debt that was canceled, was forgiven, or had the terms modified so as to reduce the principal amount of the debt?		X
7	Has this partnership filed, or is it required to file, Form 8918, Material Advisor Disclosure Statement, to provide information on any reportable transaction?		X
8	At any time during calendar year 2018, did the partnership have an interest in or a signature or other authority over a financial account in a foreign country (such as a bank account, securities account, or other financial account)? See the instructions for exceptions and filing requirements for FinCEN Form 114, Report of Foreign Bank and Financial Accounts (FBAR). If "Yes," enter the name of the foreign country. ►		X
9	At any time during the tax year, did the partnership receive a distribution from, or was it the grantor of, or transferor to, a foreign trust? If "Yes," the partnership may have to file Form 3520, Annual Return To Report Transactions With Foreign Trusts and Receipt of Certain Foreign Gifts. See instructions		X
10 a	Is the partnership making, or had it previously made (and not revoked), a section 754 election?		X
	See instructions for details regarding a section 754 election.		
b	Did the partnership make for this tax year an optional basis adjustment under section 743(b) or 734(b)? If "Yes," attach a statement showing the computation and allocation of the basis adjustment. See instructions		X

BAA   PTPA0112L 09/04/18   Form **1065** (2018)

	Yes	No

Form 1065 (2018) Entrepreneur, LLC   99-1234567   Page 3

Schedule B   Other Information (continued)

c Is the partnership required to adjust the basis of partnership assets under section 743(b) or 734(b) because of a substantial built-in loss (as defined under section 743(d)) or substantial basis reduction (as defined under section 734(d))? If "Yes," attach a statement showing the computation and allocation of the basis adjustment. See instructions — No: X

11 Check this box if, during the current or prior tax year, the partnership distributed any property received in a like-kind exchange or contributed such property to another entity (other than disregarded entities wholly owned by the partnership throughout the tax year) ▶ ☐

12 At any time during the tax year, did the partnership distribute to any partner a tenancy-in-common or other undivided interest in partnership property? — No: X

13 If the partnership is required to file Form 8858, Information Return of U.S. Persons With Respect To Foreign Disregarded Entities (FDEs) and Foreign Branches (FBs), enter the number of Forms 8858 attached. See instructions ▶

14 Does the partnership have any foreign partners? If "Yes," enter the number of Forms 8805, Foreign Partner's Information Statement of Section 1446 Withholding Tax, filed for this partnership. ▶ — No: X

15 Enter the number of Forms 8865, Return of U.S. Persons With Respect to Certain Foreign Partnerships, attached to this return. ▶

16a Did you make any payments in 2018 that would require you to file Form(s) 1099? See instructions — No: X
 b If "Yes," did you or will you file required Form(s) 1099?

17 Enter the number of Form(s) 5471, Information Return of U.S. Persons With Respect To Certain Foreign Corporations, attached to this return. ▶

18 Enter the number of partners that are foreign governments under section 892. ▶ 0

19 During the partnership's tax year, did the partnership make any payments that would require it to file Form 1042 and 1042-S under chapter 3 (sections 1441 through 1464) or chapter 4 (sections 1471 through 1474)? — No: X

20 Was the partnership a specified domestic entity required to file Form 8938 for the tax year? See the Instructions for Form 8938 — No: X

21 Is the partnership a section 721(c) partnership, as defined in Treasury Regulations section 1.721(c)-1T(b)(14)? — No: X

22 During the tax year, did the partnership pay or accrue any interest or royalty for which the deduction is not allowed under section 267A? See instructions. If "Yes," enter the total amount of the disallowed deductions. ▶ $

23 Did the partnership have an election under section 163(j) for any real property trade or business or any farming business in effect during the tax year? See instructions — No: X

24 Does the partnership satisfy one of the following conditions and the partnership does not own a pass-through entity with current year, or prior year, carryover excess business interest expense? See instructions. — Yes: X
 a The partnership's aggregate average annual gross receipts (determined under section 448(c)) for the 3 tax years preceding the current tax year do not exceed $25 million, and the partnership is not a tax shelter, or
 b The partnership only has business interest expense from (1) an electing real property trade or business, (2) an electing farming business, or (3) certain utility businesses under section 163(j)(7).
 If "No," complete and attach Form 8990.

25 Is the partnership electing out of the centralized partnership audit regime under section 6221(b)? See instructions. If "Yes," the partnership must complete Schedule B-2 (Form 1065). Enter the total from Schedule B-2, Part III, line 3 ▶ — No: X
 If "No," complete Designation of Partnership Representative below.

Designation of Partnership Representative (see instructions)
Enter below the information for the partnership representative (PR) for the tax year covered by this return.

Name of PR ▶ John Doe   U.S. taxpayer identification number of PR ▶ 111-22-3333

U.S. address of PR ▶ 123 Main Street Saint Paul, MN 55101   U.S. phone number of PR ▶

If the PR is an entity, name of the designated individual for the PR ▶   U.S. taxpayer identification number of the designated individual ▶

U.S. address of designated individual ▶   U.S. phone number of designated individual ▶

26 Is the partnership attaching Form 8996 to certify as a Qualified Opportunity Fund? — No: X
 If "Yes," enter the amount from Form 8996, line 13. ▶ $

BAA   PTPA0112L 12/21/18   Form 1065 (2018)

Form 1065 (2018) Entrepreneur, LLC   99-1234567   Page 4

Schedule K	Partners' Distributive Share Items		Total amount

			Total amount
Income (Loss)	1 Ordinary business income (loss) (page 1, line 22)	1	59,250.
	2 Net rental real estate income (loss) (attach Form 8825)	2	
	3a Other gross rental income (loss)	3a	
	b Expenses from other rental activities (attach stmt)	3b	
	c Other net rental income (loss). Subtract line 3b from line 3a	3c	
	4 Guaranteed payments	4	60,000.
	5 Interest income	5	242.
	6 Dividends and dividend equivalents: a Ordinary dividends	6a	
	b Qualified dividends	6b	
	c Dividend equivalents	6c	
	7 Royalties	7	
	8 Net short-term capital gain (loss) (attach Schedule D (Form 1065))	8	
	9a Net long-term capital gain (loss) (attach Schedule D (Form 1065))	9a	
	b Collectibles (28%) gain (loss)	9b	
	c Unrecaptured section 1250 gain (attach statement)	9c	
	10 Net section 1231 gain (loss) (attach Form 4797)	10	
	11 Other income (loss) (see instructions) Type ►	11	
Deductions	12 Section 179 deduction (attach Form 4562)	12	25,000.
	13a Contributions . . . See Statement 2	13a	1,200.
	b Investment interest expense	13b	
	c Section 59(e)(2) expenditures: (1) Type ► _____ (2) Amount ►	13c(2)	
	d Other deductions (see instructions) Type ►	13d	
Self-Employment	14a Net earnings (loss) from self-employment	14a	119,250.
	b Gross farming or fishing income	14b	
	c Gross nonfarm income	14c	
Credits	15a Low-income housing credit (section 42(j)(5))	15a	
	b Low-income housing credit (other)	15b	
	c Qualified rehabilitation expenditures (rental real estate) (attach Form 3468, if applicable)	15c	
	d Other rental real estate credits (see instructions) Type ►	15d	
	e Other rental credits (see instructions) Type ►	15e	
	f Other credits (see instructions) Type ►	15f	
Foreign Transactions	16a Name of country or U.S. possession . . . ►		
	b Gross income from all sources	16b	
	c Gross income sourced at partner level	16c	
	Foreign gross income sourced at partnership level		
	d Section 951A category ► _____ e Foreign branch category ► _____	16e	
	f Passive category ► _____ g General category ► _____ h Other (att. stmt.)►	16h	
	Deductions allocated and apportioned at partner level		
	i Interest expense ► _____ j Other	16j	
	Deductions allocated and apportioned at partnership level to foreign source income		
	k Section 951A category ► _____ l Foreign branch category ► _____	16l	
	m Passive category ► _____ n General category ► _____ o Other (att. stmt.)►	16o	
	p Total foreign taxes (check one). ► Paid ☐ Accrued ☐	16p	
	q Reduction in taxes available for credit (attach statement)	16q	
	r Other foreign tax information (attach statement)		
Alternative Minimum Tax (AMT) Items	17a Post-1986 depreciation adjustment	17a	
	b Adjusted gain or loss	17b	
	c Depletion (other than oil and gas)	17c	
	d Oil, gas, and geothermal properties – gross income	17d	
	e Oil, gas, and geothermal properties – deductions	17e	
	f Other AMT items (attach stmt)	17f	
Other Information	18a Tax-exempt interest income	18a	
	b Other tax-exempt income	18b	
	c Nondeductible expenses	18c	1,300.
	19a Distributions of cash and marketable securities	19a	31,992.
	b Distributions of other property	19b	
	20a Investment income	20a	242.
	b Investment expenses	20b	
	c Other items and amounts (attach stmt) See Statement 3		

BAA   PTPA0134L 09/04/18   Form **1065** (2018)

Form 1065 (2018) Entrepreneur, LLC   99-1234567   Page 5

Analysis of Net Income (Loss)

1	Net income (loss). Combine Schedule K, lines 1 through 11. From the result, subtract the sum of Schedule K, lines 12 through 13d, and 16p					**1** 93,292.

2 Analysis by partner type:	(i) Corporate	(ii) Individual (active)	(iii) Individual (passive)	(iv) Partnership	(v) Exempt Organization	(vi) Nominee/Other
a General partners		93,292.				
b Limited partners						

Schedule L — Balance Sheets per Books

	Assets	Beginning of tax year (a)	(b)	End of tax year (c)	(d)
1	Cash				24,000.
2 a	Trade notes and accounts receivable			12,000.	
b	Less allowance for bad debts				12,000.
3	Inventories				
4	U.S. government obligations				
5	Tax-exempt securities				
6	Other current assets (attach stmt)				
7 a	Loans to partners (or persons related to partners)				
b	Mortgage and real estate loans				
8	Other investments (attach stmt)				
9 a	Buildings and other depreciable assets			44,000.	
b	Less accumulated depreciation			44,000.	
10 a	Depletable assets				
b	Less accumulated depletion				
11	Land (net of any amortization)				
12 a	Intangible assets (amortizable only)				
b	Less accumulated amortization				
13	Other assets (attach stmt)				
14	Total assets				36,000.
	Liabilities and Capital				
15	Accounts payable				
16	Mortgages, notes, bonds payable in less than 1 year				
17	Other current liabilities (attach stmt)				
18	All nonrecourse loans				
19 a	Loans from partners (or persons related to partners)				
b	Mortgages, notes, bonds payable in 1 year or more				36,000.
20	Other liabilities (attach stmt)				
21	Partners' capital accounts				0.
22	Total liabilities and capital				36,000.

Schedule M-1 — Reconciliation of Income (Loss) per Books With Income (Loss) per Return

Note: The partnership may be required to file Schedule M-3. See instructions.

1	Net income (loss) per books	31,992.	6	Income recorded on books this year not included on Schedule K, lines 1 through 11 (itemize):	
2	Income included on Schedule K, lines 1, 2, 3c, 5, 6a, 7, 8, 9a, 10, and 11, not recorded on books this year (itemize):			a Tax-exempt interest .. $	
3	Guaranteed payments (other than health insurance)	60,000.	7	Deductions included on Schedule K, lines 1 through 13d, and 16p, not charged against book income this year (itemize):	
4	Expenses recorded on books this year not included on Schedule K, lines 1 through 13d and 16p (itemize):			a Depreciation ..... $	
	a Depreciation ..... $				
	b Travel and entertainment ..... $ 700.		8	Add lines 6 and 7	
	Statement 4 600.	1,300.	9	Income (loss) (Analysis of Net Income (Loss), line 1) Subtract line 8 from line 5	
5	Add lines 1 through 4	93,292.			93,292.

Schedule M-2 — Analysis of Partners' Capital Accounts

1	Balance at beginning of year	0.	6	Distributions: a Cash	31,992.
2	Capital contributed: a Cash			b Property	
	b Property		7	Other decreases (itemize):	
3	Net income (loss) per books	31,992.			
4	Other increases (itemize):				
			8	Add lines 6 and 7	31,992.
5	Add lines 1 through 4	31,992.	9	Balance at end of year. Subtract line 8 from line 5	0.

BAA   PTPA0134L 09/04/18   Form 1065 (2018)

C.S. THOMAS, CPA

Information on Partners Owning 50% or More of the Partnership
► Attach to Form 1065.
► Go to *www.irs.gov/Form1065* for the latest information.

OMB No. 1545-0123

Name of partnership	Employer identification number (EIN)
Entrepreneur, LLC	99-1234567

Part I Entities Owning 50% or More of the Partnership (Form 1065, Schedule B, Question 3a)

Complete columns (i) through (v) below for any foreign or domestic corporation, partnership (including any entity treated as a partnership), trust, tax-exempt organization, or any foreign government that owns, directly or indirectly, an interest of 50% or more in the profit, loss, or capital of the partnership (see instructions).

(i) Name of Entity	(ii) Employer Identification Number (if any)	(iii) Type of Entity	(iv) Country of Organization	(v) Maximum Percentage Owned in Profit, Loss, or Capital

Part II Individuals or Estates Owning 50% or More of the Partnership (Form 1065, Schedule B, Question 3b)

Complete columns (i) through (iv) below for any individual or estate that owns, directly or indirectly, an interest of 50% or more in the profit, loss, or capital of the partnership (see instructions).

(i) Name of Individual or Estate	(ii) Identifying Number (if any)	(iii) Country of Citizenship (see instructions)	(iv) Maximum Percentage Owned in Profit, Loss, or Capital
John Doe	111-22-3333	United States	100.000

BAA For Paperwork Reduction Act Notice, see the Instructions for Form 1065.

Schedule **B-1** (Form 1065) (Rev. 9-2017)

Schedule K-1
(Form 1065)
Department of the Treasury
Internal Revenue Service

2018
For calendar year 2018, or tax year

beginning ___ / ___ / 2018 ending ___ / ___ / ___

☐ Final K-1   ☐ Amended K-1

651118
OMB No. 1545-0123

Partner's Share of Income, Deductions, Credits, etc.
▶ See separate instructions.

Part I	Information About the Partnership

A Partnership's employer identification number
99-1234567

B Partnership's name, address, city, state, and ZIP code

Entrepreneur, LLC
123 Main Street
Saint Paul, MN 55101

C IRS Center where partnership filed return
e-file

D ☐ Check if this is a publicly traded partnership (PTP)

Part II	Information About the Partner

E Partner's identifying number
111-22-3333

F Partner's name, address, city, state, and ZIP code

John Doe
123 Main Street
Saint Paul, MN 55101

G ☒ General partner or LLC member-manager   ☐ Limited partner or other LLC member

H ☒ Domestic partner   ☐ Foreign partner

I1 What type of entity is this partner?   Individual

I2 If this partner is a retirement plan (IRA/SEP/Keogh/etc.), check here ☐

J Partner's share of profit, loss, and capital (see instructions)

	Beginning	Ending
Profit	100 %	100 %
Loss	100 %	100 %
Capital	100 %	100 %

K Partner's share of liabilities:

	Beginning	Ending
Nonrecourse	$	$
Qualified nonrecourse financing	$	$
Recourse	$	$ 36,000.

L Partner's capital account analysis:

Beginning capital account	$ 0.
Capital contributed during the year	$
Current year increase (decrease)	$ 31,992.
Withdrawals & distributions	$ (31,992.)
Ending capital account	$ 0.

☒ Tax basis   ☐ GAAP   ☐ Section 704(b) book
☐ Other (explain)

M Did the partner contribute property with a built-in gain or loss?
☐ Yes   ☒ No
If "Yes," attach statement (see instructions)

Part III	Partner's Share of Current Year Income, Deductions, Credits, and Other Items

1	Ordinary business income (loss) 59,250.	15	Credits
2	Net rental real estate income (loss)		
3	Other net rental income (loss)	16	Foreign transactions
4	Guaranteed payments 60,000.		
5	Interest income 242.		
6a	Ordinary dividends		
6b	Qualified dividends		
6c	Dividend equivalents		
7	Royalties		
8	Net short-term capital gain (loss)	17	Alternative minimum tax (AMT) items
9a	Net long-term capital gain (loss)		
9b	Collectibles (28%) gain (loss)		
9c	Unrecaptured section 1250 gain	18	Tax-exempt income and nondeductible expenses
10	Net section 1231 gain (loss)	C	1,300.
11	Other income (loss)		
		19	Distributions
		A	31,992.
12	Section 179 deduction 25,000.		
13	Other deductions A 1,200.	20	Other information A 242.
		AA	36,000.
		AB	44,000.
14	Self-employment earnings (loss) A 119,250.	Z	34,250.

*See attached statement for additional information.

BAA For Paperwork Reduction Act Notice, see Instructions for Form 1065.

Schedule K-1 (Form 1065) 2018

Partner 1

PTPA0312L 08/31/18

2018	Federal Statements	Page 1
	Entrepreneur, LLC	99-1234567

Statement 1
Form 1065, Line 20
Other Deductions

Advertising	$	5,200.
Auto and Truck Expense		5,400.
Dues and Subscriptions		1,650.
Insurance		7,400.
Legal and Professional		6,000.
Meals		700.
Office Expense		2,800.
Outside Services		10,000.
Supplies		2,000.
Telephone		1,500.
Travel		2,800.
Utilities		3,100.
Total	$	48,550.

Statement 2
Form 1065, Schedule K, Line 13a
Charitable Contributions

Cash Contributions - 60% Limitation	$	1,200.
Total	$	1,200.

Statement 3
Form 1065, Schedule K, Line 20c
Other Reportable Items

Section 199A Qualified Business Income	$	59,250.
Section 199A W-2 Wages		36,000.
Section 199A Unadjusted Basis		44,000.
Gross Receipts for Section 59A(e)		260,242.

Statement 4
Form 1065, Schedule M-1, Line 4
Expenses on Books Not on Schedule K

Officer Life Ins	$	600.
Total	$	600.

Form **1040** | Department of the Treasury — Internal Revenue Service (99)
U.S. Individual Income Tax Return | **2018** | OMB No. 1545-0074 | IRS Use Only — Do not write or staple in this space.

Filing status: ☒ Single ☐ Married filing jointly ☐ Married filing separately ☐ Head of household ☐ Qualifying widow(er)

Your first name and initial: **John Doe**   Last name

Your social security number: **111-22-3333**

Your standard deduction: ☐ Someone can claim you as a dependent ☐ You were born before January 2, 1954 ☐ You are blind

If joint return, spouse's first name and initial   Last name

Spouse's social security number

Spouse standard deduction: ☐ Someone can claim your spouse as a dependent ☐ Spouse was born before January 2, 1954
☐ Spouse is blind ☐ Spouse itemizes on a separate return or you were dual-status alien

☒ Full-year health care coverage or exempt (see inst.)

Home address (number and street). If you have a P.O. box, see instructions.   Apt. no.
123 Main Street

Presidential Election Campaign (see inst.) ☐ You ☐ Spouse

City, town or post office, state, and ZIP code. If you have a foreign address, attach Schedule 6.
Saint Paul, MN 55101

If more than four dependents, see inst. and ✓ here ► ☐

Dependents (see instructions):
(1) First name Last name	(2) Social security number	(3) Relationship to you	(4) ✓ if qualifies for (see inst.): Child tax credit / Credit for other dependents

Sign Here
Joint return? See instructions.
Keep a copy for your records.

Under penalties of perjury, I declare that I have examined this return and accompanying schedules and statements, and to the best of my knowledge and belief, they are true, correct, and complete. Declaration of preparer (other than taxpayer) is based on all information of which preparer has any knowledge.

Your signature   Date   Your occupation: **Entrepreneur**   If the IRS sent you an Identity Protection PIN, enter it here (see inst.)

Spouse's signature. If a joint return, **both** must sign.   Date   Spouse's occupation   If the IRS sent you an Identity Protection PIN, enter it here (see inst.)

Paid Preparer Use Only
Preparer's name   Preparer's signature: **Self-Prepared**   PTIN   Firm's EIN   Check if: ☐ 3rd Party Designee ☐ Self-employed
Firm's name ►
Firm's address ►   Phone no.

BAA For Disclosure, Privacy Act, and Paperwork Reduction Act Notice, see separate instructions.   FDIA0112L 01/08/19   Form **1040** (2018)

Form 1040 (2018)   Page **2**

		Amount
Attach Form(s) W-2. Also attach Form(s) W-2G and 1099-R if tax was withheld.	1 Wages, salaries, tips, etc. Attach Form(s) W-2	**1**
	2a Tax-exempt interest ... 2a **b** Taxable interest ... **2b**	242.
	3a Qualified dividends ... 3a **b** Ordinary dividends ... **3b**	
	4a IRAs, pensions, and annuities ... 4a **b** Taxable amount ... **4b**	
	5a Social security benefits ... 5a **b** Taxable amount ... **5b**	
	6 Total income. Add lines 1 through 5. Add any amount from Schedule 1, line 22 94,250. **6**	94,492.
Standard Deduction for — • Single or married filing separately, $12,000 • Married filing jointly or Qualifying widow(er), $24,000 • Head of household, $18,000 • If you checked any box under Standard deduction, see instructions.	7 Adjusted gross income. If you have no adjustments to income, enter the amount from line 6; otherwise, subtract Schedule 1, line 36, from line 6 ... **7**	87,833.
	8 Standard deduction or itemized deductions (from Schedule A) ... **8**	12,000.
	9 Qualified business income deduction (see instructions) ... **9**	11,366.
	10 Taxable income. Subtract lines 8 and 9 from line 7. If zero or less, enter -0- ... **10**	64,467.
	11 a Tax (see inst.) 10,124. (check if any from: 1 ☐ Form(s) 8814 2 ☐ Form 4972 3 ☐) **b** Add any amount from Schedule 2 and check here ... ► ☐ **11**	10,124.
	12 a Child tax credit/credit for other dependents **b** Add any amount from Schedule 3 and check here ... ► ☐ **12**	
	13 Subtract line 12 from line 11. If zero or less, enter -0- ... **13**	10,124.
	14 Other taxes. Attach Schedule 4 ... **14**	13,317.
	15 Total tax. Add lines 13 and 14 ... **15**	23,441.
	16 Federal income tax withheld from Forms W-2 and 1099 ... **16**	
	17 Refundable credits: **a** EIC (see inst.) **b** Sch. 8812 **c** Form 8863 Add any amount from Schedule 5 ... **17**	
	18 Add lines 16 and 17. These are your total payments ... **18**	0.
Refund Direct deposit? See instructions.	19 If line 18 is more than line 15, subtract line 15 from line 18. This is the amount you **overpaid** ... **19**	
	20 a Amount of line 19 you want **refunded to you.** If Form 8888 is attached, check here ► ☐ **20a**	
	► **b** Routing number ... ► **c** Type ☐ Checking ☐ Savings ► **d** Account number ...	
	21 Amount of line 19 you want **applied to your 2019 estimated tax** ► 21	
Amount You Owe	22 **Amount you owe.** Subtract line 18 from line 15. For details on how to pay, see instructions ► **22**	23,441.
	23 Estimated tax penalty (see instructions) ► 23	

Go to *www.irs.gov/Form1040* for instructions and the latest information.   Form **1040** (2018)

SCHEDULE 1 (Form 1040)	Additional Income and Adjustments to Income	OMB No. 1545-0074 2018
Department of the Treasury Internal Revenue Service	▶ Attach to Form 1040. ▶ Go to www.irs.gov/Form1040 for instructions and the latest information.	Attachment Sequence No. 01

Name(s) shown on Form 1040: John Doe

Your social security number: 111-22-3333

Additional Income

1–9b	Reserved	1–9b	
10	Taxable refunds, credits, or offsets of state and local income taxes	10	
11	Alimony received	11	
12	Business income or (loss). Attach Schedule C or C-EZ	12	
13	Capital gain or (loss). Attach Schedule D if required. If not required, check here ▶ ☐	13	
14	Other gains or (losses). Attach Form 4797	14	
15a	Reserved	15b	
16a	Reserved	16b	
17	Rental real estate, royalties, partnerships, S corporations, trusts, etc. Attach Schedule E	17	94,250.
18	Farm income or (loss). Attach Schedule F	18	
19	Unemployment compensation	19	
20a	Reserved	20b	
21	Other income. List type and amount	21	
22	Combine the amounts in the far right column. If you don't have any adjustments to income, enter here and include on Form 1040, line 6. Otherwise, go to line 23	22	94,250.

Adjustments to Income

23	Educator expenses	23	
24	Certain business expenses of reservists, performing artists, and fee-basis government officials. Attach Form 2106	24	
25	Health savings account deduction. Attach Form 8889	25	
26	Moving expenses for members of the Armed Forces. Attach Form 3903	26	
27	Deductible part of self-employment tax. Attach Schedule SE	27	6,659.
28	Self-employed SEP, SIMPLE, and qualified plans	28	
29	Self-employed health insurance deduction	29	
30	Penalty on early withdrawal of savings	30	
31a	Alimony paid b Recipient's SSN ▶	31a	
32	IRA deduction	32	
33	Student loan interest deduction	33	
34	Reserved	34	
35	Reserved	35	
36	Add lines 23 through 35	36	6,659.

BAA For Paperwork Reduction Act Notice, see your tax return instructions. Schedule 1 (Form 1040) 2018

SCHEDULE 4 (Form 1040)	Other Taxes	OMB No. 1545-0074 2018
Department of the Treasury Internal Revenue Service	▶ Attach to Form 1040. ▶ Go to www.irs.gov/Form1040 for instructions and the latest information.	Attachment Sequence No. 04

Name(s) shown on Form 1040: John Doe

Your social security number: 111-22-3333

Other Taxes

57	Self-employment tax. Attach Schedule SE	57	13,317.
58	Unreported social security and Medicare tax from: Form a ☐ 4137 b ☐ 8919	58	
59	Additional tax on IRAs, other qualified retirement plans, and other tax-favored accounts. Attach Form 5329 if required	59	
60a	Household employment taxes. Attach Schedule H	60a	
b	Repayment of first-time homebuyer credit from Form 5405. Attach Form 5405 if required	60b	
61	Health care: individual responsibility (see instructions)	61	
62	Taxes from: a ☐ Form 8959 b ☐ Form 8960 c ☐ Instructions; enter code(s)	62	
63	Section 965 net tax liability installment from Form 965-A 63		
64	Add the amounts in the far right column. These are your total other taxes. Enter here and on Form 1040, line 14	64	13,317.

BAA For Paperwork Reduction Act Notice, see your tax return instructions. Schedule 4 (Form 1040) 2018

Schedule E (Form 1040) 2018   Attachment Sequence No. 13   Page 2

Name(s) shown on return. Do not enter name and social security number if shown on Page 1.

John Doe

Your social security number: 111-22-3333

Caution: The IRS compares amounts reported on your tax return with amounts shown on Schedule(s) K-1.

Part II   Income or Loss From Partnerships and S Corporations

Note: If you report a loss, receive a distribution, dispose of stock, or receive a loan repayment from an S corporation, you must check the box in column **(e)** on line 28 and attach the required basis computation. If you report a loss from an at-risk activity for which **any** amount is **not** at risk, you **must** check the box in column **(f)** on line 28 and attach **Form 6198** (see instructions).

27   Are you reporting any loss not allowed in a prior year due to the at-risk, excess farm loss, or basis limitations, a prior year unallowed loss from a passive activity (if that loss was not reported on Form 8582), or unreimbursed partnership expenses? If you answered "Yes," see instructions before completing this section . . . . ☐ Yes   ☒ No

28	(a) Name	(b) Enter P for partnership; S for S corporation	(c) Check if foreign partnership	(d) Employer identification number	(e) Check if basis computation is required	(f) Check if any amount is not at risk
A	Entrepreneur, LLC	P		99-1234567		
B						
C						
D						

	Passive Income and Loss			Nonpassive Income and Loss		
	(g) Passive loss allowed (attach Form 8582 if required)	(h) Passive income from Schedule K-1	(i) Nonpassive loss from Schedule K-1	(j) Section 179 expense deduction from Form 4562	(k) Nonpassive income from Schedule K-1	
A				25,000.	119,250.	
B						
C						
D						

29 a Totals					119,250.	
b Totals				25,000.		
30	Add columns (h) and (k) of line 29a				30	119,250.
31	Add columns (g), (i), and (j) of line 29b				31	-25,000.
32	Total partnership and S corporation income or (loss). Combine lines 30 and 31				32	94,250.

Part III   Income or Loss From Estates and Trusts

33	(a) Name	(b) Employer ID no.
A		
B		

	Passive Income and Loss		Nonpassive Income and Loss	
	(c) Passive deduction or loss allowed (attach Form 8582 if required)	(d) Passive income from Schedule K-1	(e) Deduction or loss from Schedule K-1	(f) Other income from Schedule K-1
A				
B				

34 a Totals			
b Totals			
35	Add columns (d) and (f) of line 34a	35	
36	Add columns (c) and (e) of line 34b	36	
37	Total estate and trust income or (loss). Combine lines 35 and 36	37	

Part IV   Income or Loss From Real Estate Mortgage Investment Conduits (REMICs) — Residual Holder

38	(a) Name	(b) Employer identification number	(c) Excess inclusion from Schedules Q, line 2c (see instructions)	(d) Taxable income (net loss) from Schedules Q, line 1b	(e) Income from Schedules Q, line 3b

39	Combine columns (d) and (e) only. Enter the result here and include in the total on line 41 below	39	

Part V   Summary

40	Net farm rental income or (loss) from Form 4835. Also, complete line 42 below	40	
41	Total income or (loss). Combine lines 26, 32, 37, 39, and 40. Enter the result here and on Schedule 1 (Form 1040), line 17, or Form 1040NR, line 18 ►	41	94,250.
42	Reconciliation of farming and fishing income. Enter your gross farming and fishing income reported on Form 4835, line 7; Schedule K-1 (Form 1065), box 14, code B; Schedule K-1 (Form 1120S), box 17, code AC; and Schedule K-1 (Form 1041), box 14, code F (see instructions)	42	
43	Reconciliation for real estate professionals. If you were a real estate professional (see instructions), enter the net income or (loss) you reported anywhere on Form 1040 or Form 1040NR from all rental real estate activities in which you materially participated under the passive activity loss rules	43	

BAA   FDIZ2302L   02/15/19   Schedule E (Form 1040) 2018

2018	Federal Worksheets	Page 1
	John Doe	111-22-3333

Form 1040, Line 2b
Interest Income

Entrepreneur, LLC		242.
	Total	242.

Qualified Business Income

Trade or business name:	Entrepreneur, LLC
Taxpayer identification number:	99-1234567
Business income	59,250.
Allocated deduction for one-half of self-employment tax	-2,420.
Qualified Business Income	56,830.

Qualified Business Income Deduction - Simplified Worksheet
(Form 1040, line 9)

1. (a) Trade or business name	(b) EIN/SSN	(c) Qual bus. inc or loss
Entrepreneur, LLC	99-1234567 $	56,830.

2. Total qualified business income or (loss)	56,830.	
3. Qualified business loss carryforward	0.	
4. Total qualified business income. Combine lines 2 and 3 If zero or less, enter 0	56,830.	
5. Qualified business income component. Multiply line 4 by 20%		11,366.
6. Qualified REIT dividends and PTP income or loss	0.	
7. Qualified REIT and PTP loss carryforward	0.	
8. Total qualified REIT and PTP income. Add lines 6 and 7. If zero or less, enter 0	0.	
9. REIT and PTP component. Multiply line 8 by 20%		0.
10. Qualified business income deduction before the income limitation. Add lines 5 and 9		11,366.
11. Income before qualified business income deduction	75,833.	
12. Net capital gains	0.	
13. Subtract line 12 from line 11. If zero or less, enter 0	75,833.	
14. Income limitation. Multiply line 13 by 20%		15,167.
15. Qualified business income deduction. Enter the smaller of line 10 or line 14		11,366.
16. Total qualified business loss carryforward. Add lines 2 and 3. If more than zero, enter 0		0.
17. Total qualified REIT income and PTP loss carryforward. Add lines 6 and 7. If more than zero, enter 0		0.

C Corporation and Corresponding Individual Return

Form **1120**		**U.S. Corporation Income Tax Return**		OMB No. 1545-0123
Department of the Treasury Internal Revenue Service		For calendar year 2018 or tax year beginning _____ , 2018, ending _____ . ► Go to www.irs.gov/Form1120 for instructions and the latest information.		**2018**

A Check if:					**B** Employer identification number
1 a Consolidated return (attach Form 851) ☐		TYPE	Entrepreneur, LLC		99-1234567
b Life/nonlife consoli- dated return ☐		OR	123 Main Street		**C** Date incorporated
2 Personal holding co. (attach Sch. PH) ☐		PRINT	Saint Paul, MN 55101 US		1/01/2018
3 Personal service corp. (see instrs.) ☐					**D** Total assets (see instructions)
4 Schedule M-3 attached ☐					$ 41,990.

E Check if:	(1) ☐ Initial return	(2) ☐ Final return	(3) ☐ Name change	(4) ☐ Address change

I N C O M E	1a Gross receipts or sales	**1a** 260,000.	
	b Returns and allowances	**1b**	
	c Balance. Subtract line 1b from line 1a	**1c**	260,000.
	2 Cost of goods sold (attach Form 1125-A)	**2**	
	3 Gross profit. Subtract line 2 from line 1c	**3**	260,000.
	4 Dividends and inclusions (Schedule C, line 23, column (a))	**4**	
	5 Interest	**5**	242.
	6 Gross rents	**6**	
	7 Gross royalties	**7**	
	8 Capital gain net income (attach Schedule D (Form 1120))	**8**	
	9 Net gain or (loss) from Form 4797, Part II, line 17 (attach Form 4797)	**9**	
	10 Other income (see instructions — attach statement)	**10**	
	11 **Total income.** Add lines 3 through 10	**11**	260,242.
D E D U C T I O N S (see instructions for limitations on deductions)	12 Compensation of officers (see instructions — attach Form 1125-E)	**12**	60,000.
	13 Salaries and wages (less employment credits)	**13**	36,000.
	14 Repairs and maintenance	**14**	
	15 Bad debts	**15**	
	16 Rents	**16**	8,500.
	17 Taxes and licenses	**17**	10,200.
	18 Interest (see instructions)	**18**	4,100.
	19 Charitable contributions	**19**	4,400.
	20 Depreciation from Form 4562 not claimed on Form 1125-A or elsewhere on return (attach Form 4562)	**20**	1,200.
	21 Depletion	**21**	44,000.
	22 Advertising	**22**	
	23 Pension, profit-sharing, etc., plans	**23**	5,200.
	24 Employee benefit programs	**24**	10,000.
	25 Reserved for future use	**25**	
	26 Other deductions (attach statement) .... See Statement 1	**26**	43,350.
	27 **Total deductions.** Add lines 12 through 26	**27**	226,950.
	28 Taxable income before net operating loss deduction and special deductions. Subtract line 27 from line 11	**28**	33,292.
	29a Net operating loss deduction (see instructions)	**29a**	
	b Special deductions (Schedule C, line 24, column (c))	**29b**	
	c Add lines 29a and 29b	**29c**	
TAX, REFUNDABLE CREDITS, AND PAYMENTS	30 **Taxable income.** Subtract line 29c from line 28. See instructions	**30**	33,292.
	31 Total tax (Schedule J, Part I, line 11)	**31**	6,991.
	32 2018 net 965 tax liability paid (Schedule J, Part II, line 12)	**32**	
	33 Total payments, credits, and section 965 net tax liability (Schedule J, Part III, line 23)	**33**	0.
	34 Estimated tax penalty. See instructions. Check if Form 2220 is attached ► ☐	**34**	
	35 **Amount owed.** If line 33 is smaller than the total of lines 31, 32, and 34, enter amount owed	**35**	6,991.
	36 **Overpayment.** If line 33 is larger than the total of lines 31, 32, and 34, enter amount overpaid	**36**	
	37 Enter amount from line 36 you want: Credited to 2019 estimated tax ► _____ Refunded ►	**37**	

Sign Here	Under penalties of perjury, I declare that I have examined this return, including accompanying schedules and statements, and to the best of my knowledge and belief, it is true, correct, and complete. Declaration of preparer (other than taxpayer) is based on all information of which preparer has any knowledge.	May the IRS discuss this return with the preparer shown below? See instructions. ☐ Yes ☐ No
	► _____ _____ ► _____ Signature of officer — Date — Title	

Paid Preparer Use Only	Print/Type preparer's name	Preparer's signature Self-Prepared	Date	Check ☐ if self-employed	PTIN
	Firm's name ►			Firm's EIN ►	
	Firm's address ►			Phone no.	

BAA For Paperwork Reduction Act Notice, see separate instructions.   CPCA0212L 01/04/19   Form **1120** (2018)

Form 1120 (2018) Entrepreneur, LLC		99-1234567	Page 2

Schedule C	Dividends, Inclusions, and Special Deductions (see instructions)	(a) Dividends and inclusions	(b) Percentage	(c) Special deductions (a) x (b)
1	Dividends from less-than-20%-owned domestic corporations (other than debt-financed stock)		50	
2	Dividends from 20%-or-more-owned domestic corporations (other than debt-financed stock)		65	
3	Dividends on certain debt-financed stock of domestic and foreign corporations		see instructions	
4	Dividends on certain preferred stock of less-than-20%-owned public utilities		23.3	
5	Dividends on certain preferred stock of 20%-or-more-owned public utilities		26.7	
6	Dividends from less-than-20%-owned foreign corporations and certain FSCs		50	
7	Dividends from 20%-or-more-owned foreign corporations and certain FSCs		65	
8	Dividends from wholly owned foreign subsidiaries		100	
9	Subtotal. Add lines 1 through 8. See instructions for limitations		see instructions	
10	Dividends from domestic corporations received by a small business investment company operating under the Small Business Investment Act of 1958		100	
11	Dividends from affiliated group members		100	
12	Dividends from certain FSCs		100	
13	Foreign-source portion of dividends received from a specified 10%-owned foreign corporation (excluding hybrid dividends) (see instructions)		100	
14	Dividends from foreign corporations not included on line 3, 6, 7, 8, 11, 12, or 13 (including any hybrid dividends)			
15	Section 965(a) inclusion		see instructions	
16a	Subpart F inclusions derived from the sale by a controlled foreign corporation (CFC) of the stock of a lower-tier foreign corporation treated as a dividend (attach Form(s) 5471) (see instructions)		100	
b	Subpart F inclusions derived from hybrid dividends of tiered corporations (attach Form(s) 5471) (see instructions)			
c	Other inclusions from CFCs under subpart F not included on line 15, 16a, 16b, or 17 (attach Form(s) 5471) (see instructions)			
17	Global Intangible Low-Taxed Income (GILTI) (attach Form(s) 5471 and Form 8992)			
18	Gross-up for foreign taxes deemed paid			
19	IC-DISC and former DISC dividends not included on line 1, 2, or 3			
20	Other dividends			
21	Deduction for dividends paid on certain preferred stock of public utilities			
22	Section 250 deduction (attach Form 8993)			
23	Total dividends and inclusions. Add lines 9 through 20. Enter here and on page 1, line 4			
24	Total special deductions. Add lines 9 through 22, column (c). Enter here and on page 1, line 29b			

Form 1120 (2018)

272

Form 1120 (2018)   Entrepreneur, LLC   99-1234567   Page 3

Schedule J	**Tax Computation and Payment** (see instructions)		

Part I — Tax Computation

1	Check if the corporation is a member of a controlled group (attach Schedule O (Form 1120)). See instructions ▶ ☐		
2	Income tax. See instructions	2	6,991.
3	Base erosion minimum tax (attach Form 8991)	3	
4	Add lines 2 and 3	4	6,991.
5a	Foreign tax credit (attach Form 1118)	5a	
b	Credit from Form 8834 (see instructions)	5b	
c	General business credit (attach Form 3800)	5c	
d	Credit for prior year minimum tax (attach Form 8827)	5d	
e	Bond credits from Form 8912	5e	
6	Total credits. Add lines 5a through 5e	6	
7	Subtract line 6 from line 4	7	6,991.
8	Personal holding company tax (attach Schedule PH (Form 1120))	8	
9a	Recapture of investment credit (attach Form 4255)	9a	
b	Recapture of low-income housing credit (attach Form 8611)	9b	
c	Interest due under the look-back method — completed long-term contracts (attach Form 8697)	9c	
d	Interest due under the look-back method — income forecast method (attach Form 8866)	9d	
e	Alternative tax on qualifying shipping activities (attach Form 8902)	9e	
f	Other (see instructions — attach statement)	9f	
10	Total. Add lines 9a through 9f	10	
11	Total tax. Add lines 7, 8, and 10. Enter here and on page 1, line 31	11	6,991.

Part II — Section 965 Payments (see instructions)

12	2018 net 965 tax liability paid from Form 965-B, Part II, column (k), line 2. Enter here and on page 1, line 32	12	

Part III — Payments and Refundable Credits, and Section 965 Net Tax Liability

13	2017 overpayment credited to 2018	13	
14	2018 estimated tax payments	14	
15	2018 refund applied for on Form 4466	15	
16	Combine lines 13, 14, and 15	16	0.
17	Tax deposited with Form 7004	17	
18	Withholding (see instructions)	18	
19	Total payments. Add lines 16, 17, and 18	19	0.
20	Refundable credits from:		
a	Form 2439	20a	
b	Form 4136	20b	
c	Form 8827, line 8c	20c	
d	Other (attach statement — see instructions)	20d	
21	Total credits. Add lines 20a through 20d	21	
22	2018 net 965 tax liability from Form 965-B, Part I, column (d), line 2. See instructions	22	
23	Total payments, credits, and section 965 net tax liability. Add lines 19, 21, and 22. Enter here and on page 1, line 33	23	0.

CPCA0334L 08/21/18   Form 1120 (2018)

Form 1120 (2018)   Entrepreneur, LLC   99-1234567   Page **4**

Schedule K	**Other Information** (see instructions)		Yes	No

1 Check accounting method: a ☐ Cash b ☒ Accrual c ☐ Other (specify) ▶ _____

2 See the instructions and enter the:

a Business activity code no. ▶ 541600

b Business activity ▶ Consulting

c Product or service ▶ Management

3 Is the corporation a subsidiary in an affiliated group or a parent-subsidiary controlled group? .... | | | | X

If "Yes," enter name and EIN of the parent corporation ▶ _____

4 At the end of the tax year:

a Did any foreign or domestic corporation, partnership (including any entity treated as a partnership p), trust, or tax-exempt organization own directly 20% or more, or own, directly or indirectly, 50% or more of the total voting power of all classes of the corporation's stock entitled to vote? If "Yes," complete Part I of Schedule G (Form 1120) (attach Schedule G) ..... | | | | X

b Did any individual or estate own directly 20% or more, or own, directly or indirectly, 50% or more of the total voting power of all classes of the corporation's stock entitled to vote? If "Yes," complete Part II of Schedule G (Form 1120) (attach Schedule G) ...... | | | X |

5 At the end of the tax year, did the corporation:

a Own directly 20% or more, or own, directly or indirectly, 50% or more of the total voting power of all classes of stock entitled to vote of any foreign or domestic corporation not included on **Form 851**, Affiliations Schedule? For rules of constructive ownership, see instructions. ..... | | | | X

If "Yes," complete (i) through (iv) below.

(i) Name of Corporation	(ii) Employer Identification Number (if any)	(iii) Country of Incorporation	(iv) Percentage Owned in Voting Stock

b Own directly an interest of 20% or more, or own, directly or indirectly, an interest of 50% or more in any foreign or domestic partnership (including an entity treated as a partnership) or in the beneficial interest of a trust? For rules of constructive ownership, see instructions. ..... | | | | X

If "Yes," complete (i) through (iv) below.

(i) Name of Entity	(ii) Employer Identification Number (if any)	(iii) Country of Organization	(iv) Maximum Percentage Owned in Profit, Loss, or Capital

6 During this tax year, did the corporation pay dividends (other than stock dividends and distributions in exchange for stock) in excess of the corporation's current and accumulated earnings and profits? See sections 301 and 316 ..... | | | | X

If "Yes," file **Form 5452**, Corporate Report of Nondividend Distributions. See the instructions for Form 5452.

If this is a consolidated return, answer here for the parent corporation and on Form 851 for each subsidiary.

7 At any time during the tax year, did one foreign person own, directly or indirectly, at least 25% of the total voting power of all classes of the corporation's stock entitled to vote or at least 25% of the total value of all classes of the corporation's stock? For rules of attribution, see section 318. If "Yes," enter: | | | | X

(a) Percentage owned ▶ _____ and (b) Owner's country ▶ _____

(c) The corporation may have to file **Form 5472**, Information Return of a 25% Foreign-Owned U.S. Corporation or a Foreign Corporation Engaged in a U.S. Trade or Business. Enter the number of Forms 5472 attached ▶ _____

8 Check this box if the corporation issued publicly offered debt instruments with original issue discount ..... ▶ ☐

If checked, the corporation may have to file **Form 8281**, Information Return for Publicly Offered Original Issue Discount Instruments.

9 Enter the amount of tax-exempt interest received or accrued during the tax year ▶ $ None

10 Enter the number of shareholders at the end of the tax year (if 100 or fewer) ▶ 1

11 If the corporation has an NOL for the tax year and is electing to forego the carryback period, check here (see instructions) ..... ▶ ☐

If the corporation is filing a consolidated return, the statement required by Regulations section 1.1502-21(b)(3) must be attached or the election will not be valid.

12 Enter the available NOL carryover from prior tax years (do not reduce it by any deduction reported on page 1, line 29a.) ..... ▶ $ None

CPCA0234L 08/21/18   Form **1120** (2018)

UNTETHERED SUCCESS

Schedule K	Other Information *(continued from page 4)*	Yes	No

13 Are the corporation's total receipts (page 1, line 1a, plus lines 4 through 10) for the tax year and its total assets at the end of the tax year less than $250,000? — No: X

If "Yes," the corporation is not required to complete Schedules L, M-1, and M-2. Instead, enter the total amount of cash distributions and the book value of property distributions (other than cash) made during the tax year ▶ $

14 Is the corporation required to file Schedule UTP (Form 1120), Uncertain Tax Position Statement? See instructions — No: X
If "Yes," complete and attach Schedule UTP.

15a Did the corporation make any payments in 2018 that would require it to file Form(s) 1099? — No: X
  b If "Yes," did or will the corporation file required Forms 1099?

16 During this tax year, did the corporation have an 80% or more change in ownership, including a change due to redemption of its own stock? — No: X

17 During or subsequent to this tax year, but before the filing of this return, did the corporation dispose of more than 65% (by value) of its assets in a taxable, non-taxable, or tax deferred transaction? — No: X

18 Did the corporation receive assets in a section 351 transfer in which any of the transferred assets had a fair market basis or fair market value of more than $1 million? — No: X

19 During the corporation's tax year, did the corporation make any payments that would require it to file Forms 1042 and 1042-S under chapter 3 (sections 1441 through 1464) or chapter 4 (sections 1471 through 1474) of the Code? — No: X

20 Is the corporation operating on a cooperative basis? — No: X

21 During the tax year, did the corporation pay or accrue any interest or royalty for which the deduction is not allowed under section 267A? See instructions — No: X
If "Yes," enter the total amount of the disallowed deductions ▶ $

22 Does the corporation have gross receipts of at least $500 million in any of the 3 preceding tax years? (See sections 59A(e)(2) and (3)). — No: X
If "Yes," complete and attach Form 8991.

23 Did the corporation have an election under section 163(j) for any real property trade or business or any farming business in effect during the tax year? See instructions — No: X

24 Does the corporation satisfy one of the following conditions and the corporation does not own a pass-through entity with current year, or prior year carryover, excess business interest expense? See instructions. — Yes: X

  a The corporation's aggregate average annual gross receipts (determined under section 448(c)) for the 3 tax years preceding the current tax year do not exceed $25 million, and the corporation is not a tax shelter, or

  b The corporation only has business interest expense from (1) an electing real property trade or business, (2) an electing farming business, or (3) certain utility businesses under section 163(j)(7).
If "No," complete and attach Form 8990.

25 Is the corporation attaching Form 8996 to certify as a Qualified Opportunity Fund? — No: X
If "Yes," enter amount from Form 8996, line 13 ▶ $

Form 1120 (2018) Entrepreneur, LLC				99-1234567	Page 6

Schedule L	**Balance Sheets per Books**	Beginning of tax year		End of tax year	
	Assets	(a)	(b)	(c)	(d)
1	Cash				29,990.
2a	Trade notes and accounts receivable			12,000.	
b	Less allowance for bad debts				12,000.
3	Inventories				
4	U.S. government obligations				
5	Tax-exempt securities (see instructions)				
6	Other current assets (attach statement)				
7	Loans to shareholders				
8	Mortgage and real estate loans				
9	Other investments (attach statement)				
10a	Buildings and other depreciable assets			44,000.	
b	Less accumulated depreciation			44,000.	
11a	Depletable assets				
b	Less accumulated depletion				
12	Land (net of any amortization)				
13a	Intangible assets (amortizable only)				
b	Less accumulated amortization				
14	Other assets (attach statement)				
15	Total assets		0.		41,990.
	Liabilities and Shareholders' Equity				
16	Accounts payable				
17	Mortgages, notes, bonds payable in less than 1 year				
18	Other current liabilities (attach stmt)				
19	Loans from shareholders				
20	Mortgages, notes, bonds payable in 1 year or more				36,000.
21	Other liabilities (attach statement)				
22	Capital stock a Preferred stock				
	b Common stock				
23	Additional paid-in capital				
24	Retained earnings — Approp (att stmt)				
25	Retained earnings — Unappropriated				
26	Adjmt to shareholders' equity (att stmt)				
27	Less cost of treasury stock				
28	Total liabilities and shareholders' equity		0.		36,000.

Schedule M-1	**Reconciliation of Income (Loss) per Books With Income per Return**

Note: The corporation may be required to file Schedule M-3. See instructions.

1 Net income (loss) per books	31,992.	7 Income recorded on books this year not included on this return (itemize):	
2 Federal income tax per books		Tax-exempt interest $ _ _ _ _ _ _ _	
3 Excess of capital losses over capital gains		_ _ _ _ _ _ _ _ _ _ _ _ _ _ _	
4 Income subject to tax not recorded on books this year (itemize):			
		8 Deductions on this return not charged against book income this year (itemize):	
5 Expenses recorded on books this year not deducted on this return (itemize):		a Depreciation . . $ _ _ _ _ _	
a Depreciation . . . . . $ _ _ _ _		b Charitable contribns $ _ _ _ _	
b Charitable contributions . . $ _ _ _ _		_ _ _ _ _ _ _ _ _ _ _ _ _	
c Travel & entertainment . . $ _ _ _ 700.			
Statement 2 _ _ _ _ _ 600.			
	1,300.	9 Add lines 7 and 8	0.
6 Add lines 1 through 5	33,292.	10 Income (page 1, line 28) — line 6 less line 9	33,292.

Schedule M-2	**Analysis of Unappropriated Retained Earnings per Books (Line 25, Schedule L)**

1 Balance at beginning of year		5 Distributions a Cash	31,992.
2 Net income (loss) per books	31,992.	b Stock c Property	
3 Other increases (itemize):		6 Other decreases (itemize):	
_ _ _ _ _ _ _ _ _ _ _ _		7 Add lines 5 and 6	31,992.
4 Add lines 1, 2, and 3	31,992.	8 Balance at end of year (line 4 less line 7)	0.

CPCA0234L 08/21/18

Form 1120 (2018)

SCHEDULE G
(Form 1120)
(Rev. December 2011)
Department of the Treasury
Internal Revenue Service

Information on Certain Persons Owning the Corporation's Voting Stock

► Attach to Form 1120.
► See instructions.

OMB No. 1545-0123

Name

Entrepreneur, LLC

Employer identification number (EIN)

99-1234567

Part I **Certain Entities Owning the Corporation's Voting Stock.** (Form 1120, Schedule K, Question 4a).
Complete columns (i) through (v) below for any foreign or domestic corporation, partnership (including any entity treated as a partnership), trust, or tax-exempt organization that owns directly 20% or more, or owns, directly or indirectly, 50% or more of the total voting power of all classes of the corporation's stock entitled to vote (see instructions).

(i) Name of Entity	(ii) Employer Identification Number (if any)	(iii) Type of Entity	(iv) Country of Organization	(v) Percentage Owned in Voting Stock

Part II **Certain Individuals and Estates Owning the Corporation's Voting Stock.** (Form 1120, Schedule K, Question 4b).
Complete columns (i) through (iv) below for any individual or estate that owns directly 20% or more, or owns, directly or indirectly, 50% or more of the total voting power of all classes of the corporation's stock entitled to vote (see instructions).

(i) Name of Individual or Estate	(ii) Identifying Number (if any)	(iii) Country of Citizenship (see instructions)	(iv) Percentage Owned in Voting Stock
John Doe	111-22-3333	United States	100.00%

BAA For Paperwork Reduction Act Notice,
see the Instructions for Form 1120.

CPCA1901L 06/02/11

Schedule G (Form 1120) (Rev 12-2011)

2018	Federal Statements	Page 1
	Entrepreneur, LLC	99-1234567

Statement 1
Form 1120, Line 26
Other Deductions

Auto and Truck	$	5,400.
Dues and Subscriptions		1,650.
Insurance		7,400.
Legal and Professional		6,000.
Meals		700.
Office Expense		2,800.
Outside Services		10,000.
Supplies		2,000.
Telephone		1,500.
Travel		2,800.
Utilities		3,100.
	Total $	43,350.

Statement 2
Form 1120, Schedule M-1, Line 5
Book Expenses Not Deducted

Officer Life Insurance Premiums	$	600.
	Total $	600.

Form **1040** Department of the Treasury — Internal Revenue Service (99)
U.S. Individual Income Tax Return **2018** OMB No. 1545-0074 IRS Use Only — Do not write or staple in this space.

Filing status: ☒ Single ☐ Married filing jointly ☐ Married filing separately ☐ Head of household ☐ Qualifying widow(er)

Your first name and initial: John Doe
Last name:

Your social security number: **111-22-3333**

Your standard deduction: ☐ Someone can claim you as a dependent ☐ You were born before January 2, 1954 ☐ You are blind

If joint return, spouse's first name and initial:
Last name:

Spouse's social security number:

Spouse standard deduction: ☐ Someone can claim your spouse as a dependent ☐ Spouse was born before January 2, 1954
☐ Spouse is blind ☐ Spouse itemizes on a separate return or you were dual-status alien

☒ Full-year health care coverage or exempt (see inst.)

Home address (number and street). If you have a P.O. box, see instructions.: 123 Main Street   Apt. no.

Presidential Election Campaign (see inst.) ☐ You ☐ Spouse

City, town or post office, state, and ZIP code. If you have a foreign address, attach Schedule 6.: Saint Paul, MN 55101

If more than four dependents, see inst. and ✓ here ▶ ☐

Dependents (see instructions):

(1) First name Last name	(2) Social security number	(3) Relationship to you	(4) ✓ if qualifies for (see inst.): Child tax credit / Credit for other dependents

Sign Here
Joint return? See instructions.
Keep a copy for your records.

Under penalties of perjury, I declare that I have examined this return and accompanying schedules and statements, and to the best of my knowledge and belief, they are true, correct, and complete. Declaration of preparer (other than taxpayer) is based on all information of which preparer has any knowledge.

Your signature | Date | Your occupation: Entrepreneur | If the IRS sent you an Identity Protection PIN, enter it here (see inst.)

Spouse's signature. If a joint return, **both must sign.** | Date | Spouse's occupation | If the IRS sent you an Identity Protection PIN, enter it here (see inst.)

Paid Preparer Use Only
Preparer's name | Preparer's signature: Self-Prepared | PTIN | Firm's EIN | Check if: ☐ 3rd Party Designee ☐ Self-employed
Firm's name ▶
Firm's address ▶ | Phone no.

BAA For Disclosure, Privacy Act, and Paperwork Reduction Act Notice, see separate instructions. FDIA0112L 01/08/19 Form **1040** (2018)

Form 1040 (2018) Page 2

Attach Form(s) W-2. Also attach Form(s) W-2G and 1099-R if tax was withheld.	1 Wages, salaries, tips, etc. Attach Form(s) W-2	1	60,000.
	2a Tax-exempt interest 2a	b Taxable interest..... 2b	
	3a Qualified dividends ..... 3a 31,992.	b Ordinary dividends. 3b	31,992.
	4a IRAs, pensions, and annuities.. 4a	b Taxable amount..... 4b	
	5a Social security benefits..... 5a	b Taxable amount..... 5b	
	6 Total income. Add lines 1 through 5. Add any amount from Schedule 1, line 22	6	91,992.
Standard Deduction for — • Single or married filing separately, $12,000 • Married filing jointly or Qualifying widow(er), $24,000 • Head of household, $18,000 • If you checked any box under Standard deduction, see instructions	7 Adjusted gross income. If you have no adjustments to income, enter the amount from line 6; otherwise, subtract Schedule 1, line 36, from line 6	7	87,753.
	8 Standard deduction or itemized deductions (from Schedule A)	8	12,000.
	9 Qualified business income deduction (see instructions)	9	
	10 Taxable income. Subtract lines 8 and 9 from line 7. If zero or less, enter -0-	10	75,753.
	11 a Tax (see inst.) 10,369. (check if any from: 1 ☐ Form(s) 8814 2 ☐ Form 4972 3 ☐)		
	b Add any amount from Schedule 2 and check here ▶ ☐	11	10,369.
	12 a Child tax credit/credit for other dependents		
	b Add any amount from Schedule 3 and check here ▶ ☐	12	
	13 Subtract line 12 from line 11. If zero or less, enter -0-	13	10,369.
	14 Other taxes. Attach Schedule 4	14	8,478.
	15 Total tax. Add lines 13 and 14	15	18,847.
	16 Federal income tax withheld from Forms W-2 and 1099	16	
	17 Refundable credits: a EIC (see inst.) b Sch. 8812 c Form 8863 Add any amount from Schedule 5	17	
	18 Add lines 16 and 17. These are your total payments	18	0.
Refund Direct deposit? See instructions.	19 If line 18 is more than line 15, subtract line 15 from line 18. This is the amount you **overpaid**	19	
	20a Amount of line 19 you want **refunded to you.** If Form 8888 is attached, check here ▶ ☐	20a	
	▶ b Routing number .... ▶ c Type: ☐ Checking ☐ Savings		
	▶ d Account number		
	21 Amount of line 19 you want applied to your 2019 estimated tax ▶ 21		
Amount You Owe	22 Amount you owe. Subtract line 18 from line 15. For details on how to pay, see instructions	22	18,847.
	23 Estimated tax penalty (see instructions) ▶ 23		

Go to www.irs.gov/Form1040 for instructions and the latest information. Form **1040** (2018)

279

C.S. THOMAS, CPA

SCHEDULE 1
(Form 1040)

Department of the Treasury
Internal Revenue Service

Additional Income and Adjustments to Income

▶ Attach to Form 1040.
▶ Go to www.irs.gov/Form1040 for instructions and the latest information.

OMB No. 1545-0074

2018

Attachment
Sequence No. 01

Name(s) shown on Form 1040
John Doe

Your social security number
111-22-3333

Additional Income	1–9b	Reserved	1–9b	
	10	Taxable refunds, credits, or offsets of state and local income taxes	10	
	11	Alimony received	11	
	12	Business income or (loss). Attach Schedule C or C-EZ	12	
	13	Capital gain or (loss). Attach Schedule D if required. If not required, check here ▶ ☐	13	
	14	Other gains or (losses). Attach Form 4797	14	
	15a	Reserved	15b	
	16a	Reserved	16b	
	17	Rental real estate, royalties, partnerships, S corporations, trusts, etc. Attach Schedule E	17	
	18	Farm income or (loss). Attach Schedule F	18	
	19	Unemployment compensation	19	
	20a	Reserved	20b	
	21	Other income. List type and amount _____	21	
	22	Combine the amounts in the far right column. If you don't have any adjustments to income, enter here and include on Form 1040, line 6. Otherwise, go to line 23	22	0.
Adjustments to Income	23	Educator expenses	23	
	24	Certain business expenses of reservists, performing artists, and fee-basis government officials. Attach Form 2106	24	
	25	Health savings account deduction. Attach Form 8889	25	
	26	Moving expenses for members of the Armed Forces. Attach Form 3903	26	
	27	Deductible part of self-employment tax. Attach Schedule SE	27	4,239.
	28	Self-employed SEP, SIMPLE, and qualified plans	28	
	29	Self-employed health insurance deduction	29	
	30	Penalty on early withdrawal of savings	30	
	31a	Alimony paid b Recipient's SSN ▶	31a	
	32	IRA deduction	32	
	33	Student loan interest deduction	33	
	34	Reserved	34	
	35	Reserved	35	
	36	Add lines 23 through 35	36	4,239.

BAA For Paperwork Reduction Act Notice, see your tax return instructions.　Schedule 1 (Form 1040) 2018

SCHEDULE 4
(Form 1040)

Department of the Treasury
Internal Revenue Service

Other Taxes

▶ Attach to Form 1040.
▶ Go to www.irs.gov/Form1040 for instructions and the latest information.

OMB No. 1545-0074

2018

Attachment
Sequence No. 04

Name(s) shown on Form 1040
John Doe

Your social security number
111-22-3333

Other Taxes	57	Self-employment tax. Attach Schedule SE	57	8,478.
	58	Unreported social security and Medicare tax from: Form a ☐ 4137 b ☐ 8919	58	
	59	Additional tax on IRAs, other qualified retirement plans, and other tax-favored accounts. Attach Form 5329 if required	59	
	60a	Household employment taxes. Attach Schedule H	60a	
	b	Repayment of first-time homebuyer credit from Form 5405. Attach Form 5405 if required	60b	
	61	Health care: individual responsibility (see instructions)	61	
	62	Taxes from: a ☐ Form 8959 b ☐ Form 8960 c ☐ Instructions; enter code(s) _____	62	
	63	Section 965 net tax liability installment from Form 965-A.... 63		
	64	Add the amounts in the far right column. These are your total other taxes. Enter here and on Form 1040, line 14	64	8,478.

BAA For Paperwork Reduction Act Notice, see your tax return instructions.　Schedule 4 (Form 1040) 2018

SCHEDULE B
(Form 1040)

Department of the Treasury
Internal Revenue Service (99)

Interest and Ordinary Dividends

► Go to *www.irs.gov/ScheduleB* for instructions and the latest information.
► Attach to Form 1040.

OMB No. 1545-0074

2018

Attachment
Sequence No. **08**

Name(s) shown on return

John Doe

Your social security number

111-22-3333

Part I	1	List name of payer. If any interest is from a seller-financed mortgage and the buyer used the property as a personal residence, see the instructions and list this interest first. Also, show that buyer's social security number and address ►		Amount
Interest				
(See instructions and the instructions for Form 1040, line 2b.)			1	
Note: If you received a Form 1099-INT, Form 1099-OID, or substitute statement from a brokerage firm, list the firm's name as the payer and enter the total interest shown on that form.				
	2	Add the amounts on line 1	2	
	3	Excludable interest on series EE and U.S. savings bonds issued after 1989. Attach Form 8815	3	
	4	Subtract line 3 from line 2. Enter the result here and on Form 1040, line 2b ►	4	0.

Note: If line 4 is over $1,500, you must complete Part III.

Part II	5	List name of payer ►		Amount
Ordinary Dividends		Entrepreneur, LLC		31,992.
(See instructions and the instructions for Form 1040, line 3b.)			5	
Note: If you received a Form 1099-DIV or substitute statement from a brokerage firm, list the firm's name as the payer and enter the ordinary dividends shown on that form.				
	6	Add the amounts on line 5. Enter the total here and on Form 1040, line 3b ►	6	31,992.

Note: If line 6 is over $1,500, you must complete Part III.

Part III	You must complete this part if you (a) had over $1,500 of taxable interest or ordinary dividends; (b) had a foreign account; or (c) received a distribution from, or were a grantor of, or a transferor to, a foreign trust.		Yes	No
Foreign Accounts and Trusts	7a At any time during 2018, did you have a financial interest in or signature authority over a financial account (such as a bank account, securities account, or brokerage account) located in a foreign country? See instructions			X
(See instructions.)	If 'Yes,' are you required to file FinCEN Form 114, Report of Foreign Bank and Financial Accounts (FBAR), to report that financial interest or signature authority? See FinCEN Form 114 and its instructions for filing requirements and exceptions to those requirements			
	b If you are required to file FinCEN Form 114, enter the name of the foreign country where the financial account is located ►			
	8 During 2018, did you receive a distribution from, or were you the grantor of, or transferor to, a foreign trust? If 'Yes,' you may have to file Form 3520. See instructions			X

BAA For Paperwork Reduction Act Notice, see your tax return instructions.   FDIA0401L   07/26/18   Schedule B (Form 1040) 2018

2018	**Federal Worksheets**	Page 2
	John Doe	111-22-3333

Qualified Dividends and Capital Gain Tax Worksheet (Form 1040, Line 11)

1.	Enter the amount from Form 1040, line 10		75,753.
2.	Enter the amount from Form 1040, line 3a	31,992.	
3.	Are you filing Schedule D?		
	[ ] Yes. Enter the smaller of line 15 or 16 of Schedule D, but do not enter less than zero		
	[X] No. Enter the amount from Schedule 1, line 13	0.	
4.	Add lines 2 and 3		31,992.
5.	If you are claiming investment interest expense on Form 4952, enter the amount from line 4g of that form. Otherwise enter zero.		0.
6.	Subtract line 5 from line 4. If zero or less, enter zero.		31,992.
7.	Subtract line 6 from line 1. If zero or less, enter zero.		43,761.
8.	Enter: $38,600 if single or married filing separately, $77,200 if married filing jointly or qualifying widow(er), $51,700 if head of household		38,600.
9.	Enter the smaller of line 1 or line 8		38,600.
10.	Enter the smaller of line 7 or line 9		38,600.
11.	Subtract line 10 from line 9. This amount is taxed at 0%		0.
12.	Enter the smaller of line 1 or line 6		31,992.
13.	Enter the amount from line 11		0.
14.	Subtract line 13 from line 12		31,992.
15.	Enter: $425,800 if single, $239,500 if married filing separately, $479,000 if married filing jointly or qualifying widow(er), $452,400 if head of household.		425,800.
16.	Enter the smaller of line 1 or line 15		75,753.
17.	Add lines 7 and 11		43,761.
18.	Subtract line 17 from line 16. If zero or less, enter zero.		31,992.
19.	Enter the smaller of line 14 or line 18		31,992.
20.	Multiply line 19 by 15% (.15)		4,799.
21.	Add lines 11 and 19		31,992.
22.	Subtract line 21 from line 12		0.
23.	Multiply line 22 by 20% (.20)		0.
24.	Figure the tax on the amount on line 7. (Use the Tax Table or Tax Computation Worksheet)		5,570.
25.	Add lines 20, 23, and 24		10,369.
26.	Figure the tax on the amount on line 1. (Use the Tax Table or Tax Computation Worksheet)		12,610.
27.	Tax on all taxable income (including capital gain distributions). Enter the smaller of line 25 or line 26 here and on Form 1040, line 11		10,369.

ABOUT THE AUTHOR

Christopher S Thomas is a practicing CPA out of Saint Paul, MN. He started his firm many years ago after working in other CPA firms and following several years with the department of Revenue. His practice focuses on serving small businesses and the self-employed with accounting, tax and advisory services. Aside from solving accounting emergencies, he is a family man with a wife and four kids.

Made in the USA
Lexington, KY
24 March 2019